The American Crisis Series
Books on the Civil War Era

Steven E. Woodworth, Associate Professor of History,
Texas Christian University
<small>Series Editor</small>

∽ The Civil War was the crisis of the Republic's first century —the test, in Abraham Lincoln's words, of whether any free government could long endure. It touched with fire the hearts of a generation, and its story has fired the imaginations of every generation since. This series offers to students of the Civil War, either those continuing or those just beginning their exciting journey into the past, concise overviews of important persons, events, and themes in that remarkable period of America's history.

Volumes Published

James L. Abrahamson. *The Men of Secession and Civil War, 1859–1861* (2000). Cloth ISBN 0-8420-2818-8 Paper ISBN 0-8420-2819-6

Robert G. Tanner. *Retreat to Victory? Confederate Strategy Reconsidered* (2001). Cloth ISBN 0-8420-2881-1 Paper ISBN 0-8420-2882-X

Stephen Davis. *Atlanta Will Fall: Sherman, Joe Johnston, and the Yankee Heavy Battalions* (2001). Cloth ISBN 0-8420-2787-4 Paper ISBN 0-8420-2788-2

Paul Ashdown and Edward Caudill. *The Mosby Myth: A Confederate Hero in Life and Legend* (2002). Cloth ISBN 0-8420-2928-1 Paper ISBN 0-8420-2929-X

Spencer C. Tucker. *A Short History of the Civil War at Sea* (2002). Cloth ISBN 0-8420-2867-6 Paper ISBN 0-8420-2868-4

Richard Bruce Winders. *Crisis in the Southwest: The United States, Mexico, and the Struggle over Texas* (2002). Cloth ISBN 0-8420-2800-5 Paper ISBN 0-8420-2801-3

Ethan S. Rafuse. *A Single Grand Victory: The First Campaign and Battle of Manassas* (2002). Cloth ISBN 0-8420-2875-7 Paper ISBN 0-8420-2876-5

10668404

John G. Selby. *Virginians at War: The Civil War Experiences of Seven Young Confederates* (2002). Cloth ISBN 0-8420-5054-X Paper ISBN 0-8420-5055-8

Edward K. Spann. *Gotham at War: New York City, 1860–1865* (2002). Cloth ISBN 0-8420-5056-6   Paper ISBN 0-8420-5057-4

Anne J. Bailey. *War and Ruin: William T. Sherman and the Savannah Campaign* (2002). Cloth ISBN 0-8420-2850-1 Paper ISBN 0-8420-2851-X

Gary Dillard Joiner. *One Damn Blunder from Beginning to End: The Red River Campaign of 1864* (2003). Cloth ISBN 0-8420-2936-2   Paper ISBN 0-8420-2937-0

Steven E. Woodworth. *Beneath a Northern Sky: A Short History of the Gettysburg Campaign* (2003). Cloth ISBN 0-8420-2932-X Paper ISBN 0-8420-2933-8

John C. Waugh. *On the Brink of Civil War: The Compromise of 1850 and How It Changed the Course of American History* (2003). Cloth ISBN 0-8420-2944-3   Paper ISBN 0-8420-2945-1

Beneath a Northern Sky

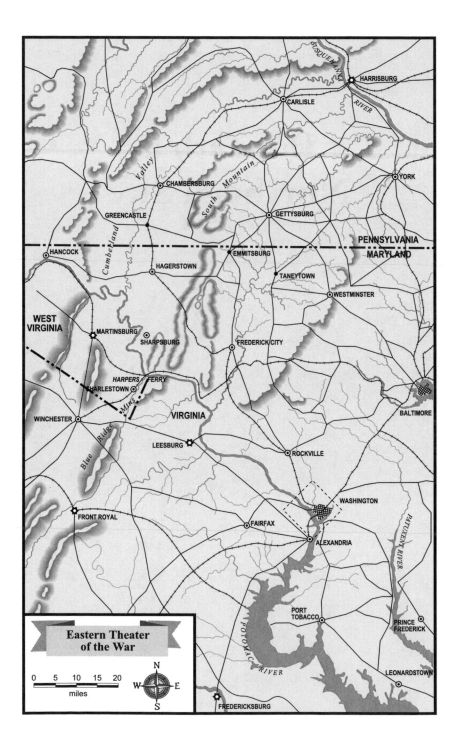

Eastern Theater of the War

0 5 10 15 20 miles

Beneath a
Northern Sky
A Short History of the
Gettysburg Campaign

The American Crisis Series
BOOKS ON THE CIVIL WAR ERA
NO. 12

Steven E. Woodworth

A Scholarly Resources Inc. Imprint
Wilmington, Delaware

First published 2003
Second printing 2003
Printed and bound in the United States of America

Scholarly Resources Inc.
104 Greenhill Avenue
Wilmington, DE 19805-1897
www.scholarly.com

Library of Congress Cataloging-in-Publication Data

Woodworth, Steven E.
Beneath a northern sky : a short history of the Gettysburg Cam-
    paign / Steven E. Woodworth
        p. cm. — (The American crisis series ; no. 12)
    Includes bibliographical references and index.
    ISBN 0-8420-2932-X (alk. paper) — ISBN 0-8420-2933-8 (pbk. :
alk. paper)
    1. Gettysburg Campaign, 1863. I. Title. II. Series.
E475.51 .W66 2003
973.7'349—dc21   2002015783

∞ The paper used in this publication meets the minimum requirements of the American National Standard for permanence of paper
for printed library materials, Z39.48, 1984.

For my son Daniel

To God Alone Be the Glory

ABOUT THE AUTHOR

Steven E. Woodworth received a B.A. in history from Southern Illinois University and a Ph.D. from Rice University. He is currently associate professor of history at Texas Christian University in Fort Worth. Woodworth is the author of numerous books on the Civil War, including *Jefferson Davis and His Generals: The Failure of Confederate Command in the West* (1990); *While God Is Marching On: The Religious World of Civil War Soldiers* (2001); and *A Scythe of Fire: The Civil War Story of the Eighth Georgia Regiment* (2002).

Upon the field of Gettysburg

The summer sun was high,

When Freedom met her haughty foes

Beneath a Northern sky.

—From "The Children of the Battlefield"
by James Gowdy Clark

CONTENTS

Preface   xiii

List of Maps   xv

CHAPTER ONE
THE CONFIDENCE OF CERTAIN VICTORY
– 1 –

CHAPTER TWO
AN INVADING ARMY AMONGST THEM
– 21 –

CHAPTER THREE
THEY WILL COME BOOMING
– 35 –

CHAPTER FOUR
I WILL FIGHT THEM INCH BY INCH
– 47 –

CHAPTER FIVE
LIKE GRASS BEFORE A SCYTHE
– 73 –

CHAPTER SIX
FORWARD AND TAKE THOSE HEIGHTS!
– 103 –

CHAPTER SEVEN
ONE MORE CHARGE AND THE DAY IS OURS
– 135 –

CHAPTER EIGHT
STAY AND FIGHT IT OUT
– 161 –

CHAPTER NINE
THE APPALLING GRANDEUR OF THE STORM
– 181 –

CHAPTER TEN
I HOPE I MAY LIVE TO SEE THE END OF THE WAR
– 209 –

Bibliographical Essay   221

Index   225

PREFACE

GETTYSBURG WAS ONE of the largest and, in some ways, the most dramatic battle of the Civil War. It pitted against each other the largest army of each side, and saw the first clear-cut defeat of the already legendary Robert E. Lee and his storied Army of Northern Virginia. It was the only major Civil War battle fought north of the Mason-Dixon Line. That and its proximity to Washington, DC, made it seem as if Gettysburg could possibly decide the course of the war, and the battle was such a near-run that different actions at any one of a dozen points by men of either side might, to all appearances, have changed the outcome of the battle.

The fact that Gettysburg proved only the near impossibility of decisive action in the eastern theater has not diminished its drama for generations of Americans. The courage and self-sacrifice of the soldiers have evoked the admiration of thousands, and the story of the battle, twisting and turning again and again on the momentous decisions of individual men, holds a fascination beyond questions of what it all might finally have decided.

Accordingly, Gettysburg has spawned a voluminous literature. Hundreds of books have been written about the battle, and whole books have been written merely cataloging and assessing the other ones. Why, therefore, was this book written? The last two decades of the twentieth century (and first year of the twenty-first) have seen a remarkable outpouring of rigorous, detailed research on the battle of Gettysburg. Thick studies, each several times the size of this one, have examined the action in one or another part of the battlefield or in a particular chronological segment of the battle, or they have chronicled the participation of units or individuals. In doing so, they have greatly increased our knowledge of the course of the battle and the actions of the participants. They have dispelled myths and brought to light little-known incidents that help us understand better why the battle went the way it did. The purpose of this book is to bring together and synthesize this large body of research into a single fast-paced, yet comprehensive, narrative that will be useful to those who are just embarking on their study of Gettysburg as well as to those more experienced students who desire a summary overview of the recent scholarship.

In writing this book, I have relied much more than usual on secondary sources—a few classics, but mostly works published within the last decade and, to a surprising degree, even within the past year. When the best scholars have disagreed about details of the fight, I have either structured my narrative so as to leave open the points of disagreement or else I have checked the sources, weighed the arguments, and given my own best judgment. Throughout the book I have tried to use enough primary sources—mostly the letters and diaries of the soldiers themselves—to keep the feel and flavor of the 1860s.

It is a pleasure to render thanks and acknowledge my debt of gratitude to those who have helped me with this project. Matthew Hershey and Brooks D. Simpson gave aid, encouragement, and good advice. Robert E. Schultz's work on the maps was invaluable. Bob Sexton was a great help in finding information on the interesting 44th New York Regiment. Richard Sommers, David Keogh, Pamela Cheney, and James Baughman assisted me in my research at the United States Army Military History Institute archives and always made my visits to the quiet confines of the reading room at Carlisle Barracks, Pennsylvania, both productive and pleasant. My wife, Leah, as always, was very supportive throughout the process.

List of Maps

Eastern Theater of the War	frontispiece
July 1, 11:00 A.M.	56
July 1, 2:30–3:30 P.M.	82
July 1, 3:30–4:00 P.M.	85
July 2, 4:00 P.M.	115
July 2, 4:00–7:00 P.M.	117
July 2, 7:30–11:00 P.M.	153
July 3, 3:30–4:00 P.M.	193
July 5 to July 12, 1863	213

CHAPTER ONE

THE CONFIDENCE OF CERTAIN VICTORY

AS SPRINGTIME GAVE WAY to the third summer of America's Civil War, events in the narrow eastern theater of operations were rapidly developing toward a great collision of armies. Confederate general Robert E. Lee, commanding the hitherto almost always victorious Army of Northern Virginia, hoped it would be a victorious climax. Across the way, in the ranks and among the leadership of the blue-clad Army of the Potomac, many feared in their hearts that Lee might achieve his purpose.

The conflict had started twenty-six months before. Southern states had reacted with outrage to the election of Republican president Abraham Lincoln. Like all Republicans, Lincoln was pledged not to disturb the institution of slavery in the states where it existed but not to allow its extension to new states in the West. Southerners refused to tolerate a national government that would thus place a moral taint on their beloved institution. In response to Lincoln's election, seven Deep South states declared themselves to be no longer part of the United States and organized themselves into the Confederate States. They chose Mississippi senator Jefferson Davis as their president and Montgomery, Alabama, for their capital. When Lincoln refused to evacuate U.S. troops posted in one of these states that claimed to have seceded—a garrison of a few-score lonely soldiers in Fort Sumter in the harbor of Charleston, South Carolina—the Confederates attacked it, thus triggering what would become America's bloodiest war.

When Lincoln reacted by calling on the states to provide troops to put down the rebellion—the regular U.S. Army was an almost laughably small 16,000 officers and men at the time—four more states of the Upper South chose to cast their lots with the Confederacy rather than fight against fellow slaveholders. Among those four Upper South states was Virginia. With a relatively large white population (by the standards of the sparsely settled South), valuable manufacturing capacity, and prestige as the home of Washington, Jefferson, and Madison, Virginia was a prized addition to the Confederacy. It was also directly adjacent to the U.S. capital at Washington, DC. Both these facts assured that it would be the scene of serious fighting in the war that was just starting. Because President Davis wanted to be as near as possible to that fighting, and in order to take advantage of Virginia's prestige, the Confederacy moved its capital to Richmond, less than one hundred miles from Washington. The proximity of the rival capitals only intensified the political vortex that would soon draw armies into lethal combat in the land that lay between and around them.

The swath of Virginia between the mountains and the sea, only a few hundred miles wide, was a narrow segment out of the wide expanse of the continent's settled territory. The nation's heartland, even then, lay farther west, and there other blue- and gray-clad armies would ultimately decide the war, while the geography of Virginia seemed to conspire against any conclusive result within its borders. Mountains hemmed in the zone of maneuver, and rivers barred the attacker's advance. Yet neither side could leave the eastern theater alone or even accord it less than top priority. Total victory—victory in a single day's showdown battle—beckoned like a Lorelei to the leaders of both sides, and even if such a crushing triumph might prove elusive in the end, a massive commitment of manpower would be needed to deny that victory to the enemy. In short, the geographical barriers of Virginia were not enough to make total victory impossible, but they were enough to allow each side— with a maximum effort—to stop the other from winning that kind of success. And then there was always the tantalizing prospect that the next big push might be the one that brought the final triumph.

Each side fielded its largest army in Virginia. Since in this war recruitment was a local matter and each government tended to funnel most regiments into the fighting fronts closest to their home states, the great armies that fought in Virginia were largely composed of men from the relatively heavily populated cities, towns, and farms of the East Coast. Those places also harbored some of the nation's largest newspapers, which naturally followed the hometown boys and their part of the war. The result was that the Virginia theater, while deciding only that it would decide nothing, nevertheless drew not only the largest armies but also the lion's share of attention, both at home and abroad. Many observers, then and since, almost came to believe that the conflict in Virginia was

General Robert E. Lee. Library of Congress, Prints and Photographs Division, LC-B8172-0001

the whole war, and that the destiny of the continent would be decided there sooner or later. Each side's morale, at least in large part, rose or fell with the fortunes of its Virginia army, and that in turn gave the massive operations there an importance beyond their true military weight. The eastern theater of the Civil War became the sideshow that eclipsed the center ring.

For two years that life-and-death sideshow had been a dismal one for the North. In July 1861 the first Union "on to Richmond" drive had suffered humiliating defeat at a little Virginia stream named Bull Run, initiating Union men in the East to gnawing questions about whether they were really as good as their Southern counterparts. In the wake of that debacle, Lincoln had tapped Major General George B. McClellan to take over the Union's Virginia war effort. McClellan had taken the collection of dispirited Bull Run survivors together with a swelling tide of new recruits and molded them into *his* army, the Army of the Potomac. He made the men feel like soldiers, and they loved him for it as they would never love any other commander. He made the officers feel like professionals, and they tried to make themselves in his image: skillful, brave, thorough, and cautious.

The problem for McClellan was using his magnificent army, for he lacked the nerve to send it into battle. After a long delay he put it in motion in the spring of 1862 in a campaign that was a model of creative strategy and hesitant execution. Having crept to the very outskirts of Richmond by skillful maneuvering against a Confederate general equally reluctant to fight, McClellan suffered a grave setback. One of his men shot the timid Rebel general, and Jefferson Davis replaced that general with his own military adviser, General Lee. A man of brilliant and inventive mind, rock-solid character, and sublime audacity, Lee gave McClellan the fight he never wanted, a week-long battle to see if either army could crush the other. Neither could, but McClellan's nerve failed him and he drew back from Lee's furious blows. For the first of many times the rank and file of the Army of the Potomac found themselves marching away from their foes after giving a good account of themselves on the field of battle, knowing in their hearts that they had not been beaten. They had fought splendidly, and some of their officers had already started to build reputations as crack fighting leaders: brigade commanders such as John F. Reynolds and George G. Meade had been solid performers, while McClellan called their fellow brigadier Winfield S. Hancock "superb."

The Confederates in this sector, now christened the Army of Northern Virginia, were jubilant at their victory and all the more certain that any one Southerner could whip ten Yankees with a cornstalk. They too had their heroes from the Seven Days' battles. There was cavalry commander J. E. B. "Jeb" Stuart, who had set up the campaign with his daring ride all the way around the Army of the

Lieutenant General James Longstreet. Library of Congress, Prints and Photographs Division, LC-B8172-2014

Potomac. In the reports of the hard fighting appeared soon-to-be legendary names such as that of tough, taciturn James Longstreet, hard-driving division commander Ambrose Powell Hill, and the sad-faced, tawny-bearded leader of Texas infantry named John Bell Hood. If any body of soldiers on Earth could halt the headlong onslaught of Hood and his fierce Texas Brigade, it had not yet appeared in this part of the continent.

Tiring of McClellan's halting operations and constant whining, Lincoln turned to the bold-talking Major General John Pope, but Lee humbled Pope in the second battle of Bull Run and then crossed the Potomac into Maryland in the late summer of 1862. Desperate, Lincoln turned to McClellan again, and that officer managed to corner Lee in the western part of Maryland, behind a creek called Antietam. Afterward, however, McClellan proceeded to fritter away his numerical advantage in piecemeal attacks during a day of appalling carnage and succeeded only in driving Lee back into Virginia when he ought to have annihilated the Army of Northern Virginia. McClellan pursued at a snail's pace, and Lincoln's considerable patience was exhausted at last. He sacked McClellan, this time for good.

Nevertheless, the proud general who had sometimes been called "the young Napoleon" left his stamp on the army he had made, especially its officer corps. Many were Democrats, like McClellan, and suspicious of Lincoln. Of more direct impact on operations, they were, by and large, brave and skillful fighters but, again like McClellan, they somehow lacked the driving aggressiveness and ruthless will to victory that characterized both their opponents as well as the more successful Union armies in the West. The rank and file never forgot that they were soldiers—McClellan had taught them that—and they bore themselves with soldierly fortitude through a dismal series of military mishaps. Often defeated despite sublime courage and appalling casualties, they exchanged their youthful enthusiasm for a tired cynicism about generals and their plans. Yet they retained a commitment to duty and country that kept them in the ranks despite the bungling of McClellan's successor, Ambrose Burnside, who got thousands of them slaughtered in obviously hopeless assaults at the December 1862 battle of Fredericksburg. Burnside's successor, the brash-talking Joseph Hooker, succeeded in raising morale during the early months of 1863 only to have it dashed again in May with another inexplicable defeat at an obscure Virginia hamlet named Chancellorsville. Not only had Hooker been sadly out-generaled by Lee, but the once-bold Union general had also begun to act disturbingly like McClellan.

Lee, for his part, was not satisfied with the discomfiture of one Union general after another. The South had begun the war with far less than the North's resources in men and material. Lee's victories had saved Richmond, prolonged the war, and raised Confederate morale, but those victories came at a high cost. The South could not go on taking the losses that Lee's army had sustained since he had taken command a year ago. Exhaustion—of men and horses and of the national spirit—would take its toll sooner or later. Meanwhile, the Confederacy was slowly losing the war for America's heartland. Even as Lee contemplated his victory at Chancellorsville during the first week of May, Ulysses S. Grant, leading a Union army whose confidence and striking power matched that of Lee's own, had penetrated deep into the vitals of the Confederacy and was maneuvering to trap a Rebel army at Vicksburg on the Mississippi River. The South could not win a grinding war of attrition with the larger and more populous North. Somehow the Confederacy must do something to crush the Northern spirit and break the Union's will to go on fighting before it was too late.

This attitude had been Lee's from the first, and it had been the impetus of his all-out, no-tomorrow style of fighting. Now, as he saw it, the need was more urgent than ever. Perhaps in another campaign the will-o'-the-wisp prospect of a complete victory—destroying the enemy army—would finally become a reality. If that or any victory occurred north of the Potomac, in the enemy's country, the effect on Union morale would be all the more powerful. Just the presence of the Confederate army, marching through Pennsylvania towns, ransacking Pennsylvania dry-goods shops, and eating Pennsylvania food, should be a body blow to Union spirits. It would be a massive risk, of course. Battle with a more numerous enemy always was. Incursion into enemy territory carried the added risk of being trapped and losing the war in an afternoon, but Lee was determined to try.

The first hurdle was convincing President Davis and his cabinet to approve the operation. Davis and Lee were alike in some ways. Both men shared a West Point education, combat experience in the Mexican War, a strong sense of duty, a deep commitment to the Confederacy, and a desire to hold as much of its territory as possible. Both Lee and Davis were fiercely combative at heart and longed to strike hard blows at their enemies.

Davis, however, was not by nature a man to take risks if he could achieve his ends by other means. Lee was a born gambler whose strong morals kept him from wagering anywhere but in war, where he believed it necessary. Davis considered Southern morale resilient, almost unbreakable. For that reason the South was bound to win the war, in Davis's view, so long as it did not suffer a catastrophic defeat. Lee, by contrast, saw the weaknesses of the smaller South in comparison to the larger North and believed that the Confederacy was doomed to be worn down and crushed unless it could discourage the North by winning one or more great victories. In short, while Davis liked the idea of a bold offensive, his instincts told him not to take dangerous risks to launch it. Lee knew the risks but believed the South dared not avoid them. These differences were muted by the two men's courtesy and mutual commitment to the cause. They esteemed each other highly, trusted each other deeply, worked well together, and never squabbled or bickered.

So it was that in the wake of the battle of Chancellorsville, the next campaign Lee mounted was one to persuade his own government not to weaken his army by detaching troops to reinforce the hard-pressed Confederates out in Mississippi. A number of influential Confederate generals and politicians, notably Secretary of War James A. Seddon, favored this strategy. Such a policy agreed both with Davis's natural concern for his own home country—his plantation was only a few miles from Vicksburg, the target of the Union campaign—and his tendency to avoid the chance of catastrophic defeat. However, Davis's deep regard and trust for Lee sufficed to overcome such tendencies. Lee argued that the hot climate of the lower Mississippi Valley would soon drive the Federals out of those environs and suggested that he could make a campaign himself that would effectively draw Union forces away from other threatened points around the Confederacy. On one of Lee's dispatches, Davis noted, "The answer of General Lee was such as I anticipated, and in which I concur."[1]

Lee wrote to suggest that Davis make one of his periodic visits to army headquarters, adding, "There are many things about which I would like to consult Your Excellency."[2] The president, however, was at that time confined to Richmond by one of his frequent illnesses and requested that Lee come down to the capital for discussions. Lee arrived in Richmond on May 14. Early talks with the president and secretary of war led to the decision to release three of the five brigades of Major General George E. Pickett's division that were being held in reserve near the Confederate capital. A War Department clerk watched as "the long column marched through the city northward" early on the morning of May 16.[3]

Subsequent discussions were more difficult, however, and involved the whole cabinet. The topic was whether Lee should be permitted to launch an offensive across the Potomac. Lee presented his plan in conservative terms. He played down his desire for a showdown, end-the-war battle and emphasized another real and important element of the plan: his desire to take the conflict out of ravaged Virginia and into the North, where his army could live off the enemy's country and make the enemy's people feel the scourge of war.[4] Postmaster General John Reagan of Texas objected. He wanted to see about one-third of Lee's army detached and sent west to try to save Vicksburg and the Confederacy's hold on the Mississippi River, and he contended that nothing Lee could do north of the Potomac would help the beleaguered Confederates out west. But, as Reagan later admitted, "This view was not favored by any other member of the cabinet, and I had to give it up." The decision was made, and Lee was given the go-ahead to take his army across the Potomac. Although he did not say so at the time, Reagan later claimed that he understood Lee's real thinking. "He favored such a campaign," the Texan wrote years later, "because he believed he commanded an invincible army, which had been victorious in so many great battles, and in all of them against greatly preponderating numbers and resources."[5]

Among the soldiers of the Army of Northern Virginia, some 75,000 strong, confidence in Lee and in themselves was absolute. Cavalry officer Fitzhugh Lee, nephew of the commanding general, wrote that "the heart of every Southern soldier beat with the lofty confidence of certain victory."[6] Private Sam Brewer of the Eighth Georgia, part of Hood's division, said much the same in more prosaic terms. To his wife he wrote that the men had total confidence in Lee and that everything he ordered "is done with alacrity, nothing doubting." As for his fellow soldiers, "We have evidently proven ourselves too much for the Yankees to do anything with us and I think they are beginning to feel it at home and this but drives our boys to new action, for I really believe our troops generally are more anxious to fight them now than they ever were."[7] David Holt of the Sixteenth Mississippi recalled, "We had the most serene confidence in Marse Bob."[8] Artillery officer Edward Porter Alexander summed it up years later. "I am sure there can never have been an army with more supreme confidence in its commander than that army had in Gen. Lee," Alexander wrote. "We looked forward to victory under him as confidently as to successive sunrises."[9]

Lee had equal confidence in his men. If "properly organized and officered," he wrote to Hood, the Army of Northern Virginia "would be invincible." Its soldiers would "go any where and do anything if properly led."[10] Others were also impressed. Colonel Arthur Fremantle, on leave from Her Majesty's Coldstream Guards to observe the war in America, was traveling with the Army of Northern Virginia. "At no period of the war," he noted of Lee's soldiers on this campaign, "have the men been so well equipped, so well clothed, so eager for a fight, or so confident of success."[11]

Before putting his army in motion, Lee dealt with some issues of command. The victory at Chancellorsville had cost the Confederacy the services of Stonewall Jackson, mortally wounded in one of history's most famous friendly fire incidents. Lee would therefore have to find a new commander for one of the army's two corps. He decided to do more than that. He had for some time thought the corps were too large for one commander to handle well. With the irreplaceable Jackson now gone, Lee opted not to replace him—at least not directly—but rather to reorganize the army. Lieutenant General James Longstreet would retain command of his First Corps, now reduced from four divisions to three. The stolid Longstreet handled his corps commander duties well and also exuded a confidence that steadied his fellow generals and greatly enhanced the fighting power of his troops.

Jackson's old Second Corps, also shorn of one of its four divisions, would go to newly promoted Lieutenant General Richard S. Ewell. The bald-headed, somewhat eccentric Virginian had been Stonewall Jackson's best division commander up until he was wounded at the battle of Groveton on August 28, 1863, in part of the Second Bull Run campaign. The wound had necessitated the amputation of a leg, and while recuperating, Ewell had married the object of his unrequited youthful love, Lizinka Brown, then a widow. Opinion was sharply divided within the Army of Northern Virginia as to whether the addition of a wife had compensated for the loss of a limb, but Ewell had a sterling combat record. As soon as he was fit for action again, Lee assigned him to command the Second Corps.

The largest change wrought by Lee's reorganization was the addition of a Third Corps under the command of another newly promoted lieutenant general, Ambrose Powell Hill. A diminutive Virginian, Hill was a West Point contemporary of George B. McClellan, who in the 1850s had left Hill far behind in the class standings and then had bested him in the contest for the hand of the lovely Ellen Marcy. It was hard to imagine McClellan beating

Hill in anything else, however, for the Virginian seemed to possess a double portion of all the combativeness that his Northern classmate lacked. If he showed any fault during 1862 it might have been overaggressiveness, but his hard marching and fierce fighting had saved Lee and Jackson on more than one occasion during that year's combat. Hill's command, the Third Corps, was composed of one division from the First Corps, one from the Second, and a third division cobbled together from spare brigades and green troops transferred to Virginia from quieter sectors.

With permission secured from Jefferson Davis and the reorganization of his army complete, Lee put his troops in motion and launched the most daring campaign of his audacious career. On Wednesday morning, June 3, the first of Lee's divisions marched out of their camps around Fredericksburg—where Lee's army had faced the Army of the Potomac across the Rappahannock River since the previous year—and tramped westward up the south bank of the Rappahannock.[12] Lee's plan was to swing his army wide to the left in order to get past the Army of the Potomac. He would move west and cross the Blue Ridge into the Shenandoah Valley. Once in the valley, sheltered by the mountain rampart of the Blue Ridge from the prying eyes of probing Yankee cavalry, his troops could march northeastward, down the valley toward the Potomac and the green fields and rich towns of the North.

By the time the first Confederate divisions cleared their camps around Fredericksburg, Hooker was aware that something was afoot. His scouts brought him word of abandoned Confederate camps, and he immediately surmised that Lee was trying another turning movement such as he had used the previous summer in the Second Bull Run and Antietam campaigns. On Friday, June 5, Hooker reacted by sending infantry of Major General John Sedgwick's Union Sixth Corps probing across pontoon bridges to the south bank of the Rappahannock near the mouth of Deep Run, above Fredericksburg, igniting a skirmish with troops of Hill's Confederate Third Corps, still holding the line there.[13]

Meanwhile, Hooker telegraphed Lincoln in Washington suggesting that if Lee's forces were strung out with rear guards around Fredericksburg and leading elements well to the west, the Army of the Potomac should try to cross the river and attack Lee's rear. The idea appalled Lincoln, who probably saw it as one more in a long series of proposals from his generals for winning the war without the inconvenience of fighting the enemy army head-on. He wired

Hooker to express his disapproval. In his typical homey way, he suggested that Hooker's army, in trying to fight its way across the Rappahannock with Lee threatening its rear on the north bank, would be like "an ox jumped half over a fence and liable to be torn by dogs front and rear, without a fair chance to gore one way or kick the other." Lincoln believed that if Lee crossed over to the north bank of the Rappahannock, Hooker should fight him there.[14]

Lee paused his movement briefly until he could see what Hooker meant by the incursion at Deep Run, but after watching the situation throughout the day on Saturday, June 6, Lee decided that it was only a reconnaissance and ordered his troops west again. That evening he had his own headquarters packed up and started westward.[15] Two days later, Lee arrived at Culpeper Court House, where by this time he had assembled the bulk of his army (Hill's Third Corps was still actively skirmishing with Sedgwick back at Deep Run).

In honor of Lee and the other high brass, Jeb Stuart, at his headquarters at nearby Brandy Station, held an impressive mass review of his cavalry corps, complete with booming cannon, flashing sabers, and galloping steeds. Stuart had put on the same show several days earlier for local dignitaries and large crowds of hoop-skirted admirers. With his ostrich-plume hat and his staff banjo player, Stuart looked anything but a grim-visaged modern warrior. Yet his panache was part of his effectiveness, helping to infuse his outnumbered troopers with the esprit that had enabled them literally to ride circles around the inept Union cavalry in Virginia. Lately, however, the blue-jacketed horsemen had been improving. Around a cadre of tough prewar regulars such as division commander John Buford, the Union cavalry was mastering its difficult trade and was threatening the seemingly effortless superiority of Stuart and the troopers whom he paraded for Lee and the other spectators on June 8.

That threat became a reality the next day when Union cavalry commander Alfred Pleasanton came calling with 7,000 horsemen and another 4,000 infantry and artillery behind them. Hooker, still uncertain about Lee's intentions, had come to suspect that the Confederates were preparing a mass cavalry raid, and he decided to disrupt their effort by striking first. Accordingly, on his orders, early on the morning of Tuesday, June 9, Pleasanton's 7,000 horses went splashing through the shallow waters of Beverly's and Kelly's Fords on the Rappahannock and straight into the biggest cavalry battle the continent had yet seen. Stuart was caught by surprise by the Federal strike on Brandy Station, but he quickly threw in his whole force, about 10,000 men. Massed sabers flashed this time in earnest as the two sides charged. Clouds of white smoke rolled across the battlefield from the far more lethal carbines. The battle lasted all day. Stuart, supported by Confederate infantry, finally succeeded in halting Pleasanton's thrust. The Union general took his men back to the north bank of the Rappahannock. The Union cavalry had not succeeded in disrupting Lee's movement and had added little to what Hooker already knew about Confederate dispositions. However, the cavalry had demonstrated in terms as sharp as a saber's edge and as direct as a carbine bullet's flight that they could stand up to the Confederate horsemen and give as good as they got.[16]

Hooker's reaction to the great cavalry fight at Brandy Station was a strange one. He concluded that the Rebels were indeed preparing to launch a major cavalry raid but were supporting it with a large column of infantry. That being the case, Hooker proposed to strike straight southward at whatever Confederates were left around Fredericksburg and then march on the Rebel capital, fifty miles away. "Will it not promote the true interest of the cause," he pleaded with Lincoln the next day, "for me to march to Richmond at once?"[17] The key factor seemed to be that Hooker wanted to go anyplace other than where Lee and his army were to be found. As the Army of the Potomac's provost general, Marsena Patrick, put it, "Hooker knows that Lee is his master & is afraid to meet him in fair battle."[18]

Lincoln thought this tactic was all wrong. Whatever cities or towns or other strategic points the Union might take, the war would not be won as long as Lee and his army remained intact. In a telegram in reply to Hooker the same day he pointed out, "If you had Richmond invested to-day, you would not be able to take it in twenty days: meanwhile your communications, and with them your army, would be ruined." Then, cutting to the heart of Union strategic needs in the eastern theater, he wrote, "I think Lee's army, and not Richmond, is your sure objective point." Lincoln's advice: "If he comes toward the Upper Potomac, follow on his flank and on his inside track, shortening your lines while he lengthens his. Fight him, too, when opportunity offers. If he stays where he is, fret him and fret him."[19]

Lee had no intention of staying where he was. The morning after Brandy Station, he put Ewell's corps in motion, leading the march westward toward the Blue Ridge, twenty-five miles away.[20] The Second Corps stepped out at a pace reminiscent of the days when it was known as Stonewall Jackson's "foot cavalry." Across the Blue Ridge at Chester Gap, down through the town of Front Royal, marched Ewell's gray-clad columns; they then waded the clear, cold waters of the Shenandoah River and pushed on to Cedarville by the night of June 12, having covered fifty miles in three days. Already, Ewell's advanced elements were skirmishing with Union forces stationed in the lower Shenandoah Valley. The next day, Ewell began moving in on the main body of those forces, some 6,900 men under the command of Major General Robert H. Milroy, who had foolishly remained at Winchester rather than falling back on Harpers Ferry.[21]

At his headquarters on the north bank of the Rappahannock near Fredericksburg, Hooker was beginning to grasp the magnitude of Lee's movement and the necessity of doing something about it. The Army of the Potomac could not afford to remain static opposite Fredericksburg while Lee made an end run to the west. That same June 13, as Ewell was moving in on Winchester, Hooker gave orders for his army to close out its supply line via Aquia Creek in eastern Virginia, pull back from the Rappahannock after nightfall, and begin marching northwest to counter Lee's broad turning maneuver. Gone were the once-bold Yankee general's ideas of seizing the initiative and striking a blow. He now thought only of placing his army in northern Virginia to cover Washington.[22]

Lee knew of Hooker's movement almost immediately. Hill noted the withdrawal of Union troops from the Deep Run sector, watched the Union columns march northward out of sight over the Stafford hills, and sent word to Lee the next morning. By the morning of June 15, Lee had ample scouting reports to indicate "a general movement of the enemy up the Rappahannock."[23] If Hooker was moving to counter him, then Lee would act all the faster. That same day he gave orders for Longstreet's corps to leave its camps around Culpeper and follow Ewell into the Shenandoah Valley. Stuart's cavalry would also move out and take up screening positions on the east side of the Blue Ridge, where it was soon skirmishing heavily with probing Union horsemen.[24]

Meanwhile, Ewell was dealing with Milroy. After reaching the west bank of the Shenandoah on June 12, Ewell detached Major General Robert E. Rodes's large division to advance to Martinsburg, on the Potomac, while with his other two divisions, those of Jubal A.

Early and Edward Johnson, he spent the 13th and 14th maneuvering into position to strike Milroy at Winchester. Despite orders from Washington to pull out of his dangerous position, Milroy underestimated the danger at Winchester and stayed put. On the evening of June 14, Ewell threatened his left and center and then crushed his right. In dire circumstances that night, Milroy decided to abandon his artillery and wagons and make a desperate retreat the next morning. During the night, however, Ewell moved Johnson's division to block the escape route, and on the morning of the 15th Milroy's force flailed vainly at the encircling Confederates. Thousands of bluecoats were captured, and the cavalry brigade attached to Ewell's command spent the day rounding up those who had fled into the woods and fields. In all, Ewell could boast of capturing 4,000 men, twenty-three fine pieces of artillery, and 300 wagons, plus horses and abundant supplies. Rodes bagged another 200 prisoners, five guns, and more supplies on his way to Martinsburg.[25] A dozen miles beyond that town ran the Potomac River, and not a single organized body of Union soldiers remained between it and Ewell's troops. The campaign was off to a spectacular start, and the spirit of Stonewall Jackson seemed to stalk the Shenandoah Valley again, even if the great commander had now been five weeks in his grave.

In Washington, Lincoln and his top military adviser, Major General Henry W. Halleck, fumed at the impunity with which Lee was marching around Hooker's western flank. Noting the reports from Winchester and Martinsburg in the lower Shenandoah Valley as well as Hooker's dispatches that Lee was still maintaining a presence along the Rappahannock east of Culpeper, Lincoln consistently emphasized the one theme that was foremost in his mind: destroying Lee's army. "If the head of Lee's army is at Martinsburg and the tail of it on the Plank road between Fredericksburg and Chancellorsville," Lincoln wired Hooker on the evening of Milroy's discomfiture, "the animal must be very slim somewhere. Could you not break him?"[26] Hooker's columns were on the march by this time, moving north to stay between Lee and Washington, but Hooker was not in a position—nor a frame of mind—to try to take advantage of Lee's far-flung deployments as Lincoln hoped. The Confederate general had a firm grasp on the initiative now, and Hooker showed no inclination to challenge him.

On the evening of June 15, Rodes's division, accompanied by Albert G. Jenkins's brigade of cavalry, splashed across the Potomac opposite the Maryland town of Williamsport. Rodes marched on another five miles or so to Hagerstown, which he held for the next few days, being joined by Johnson's division. Jenkins, on Rodes's orders, took his brigade galloping on across the Pennsylvania line and all the way to the town of Chambersburg, twenty-five miles north of the Potomac. Lee ordered Ewell to pause there, with two divisions in Maryland and one, Early's, at Shepherdstown on the Virginia side, threatening a Union force downstream at Harpers Ferry. Ewell had successfully accomplished his mission of clearing the Shenandoah Valley and securing the crossings of the Potomac, and now he had to wait while the Army of Northern Virginia's other two corps closed up, marching through several days of heavy rain.[27]

While Ewell waited and two-thirds of the army's infantry marched to catch up, the cavalry brigades attached to the army's advance began the work of destruction north of the Potomac. Brigadier General John D. Imboden's cavalry brigade wreaked a whole catalog of destruction on the economically important Baltimore & Ohio Railroad, which Lee happily communicated in a dispatch to Jefferson Davis—a half-dozen bridges, including "Fink's patent iron bridge," a three-span affair some 400 feet long, had been put out of commission. "All the depots, water-tanks, and engines between the Little Cacapon and Cumberland are also destroyed," added Lee. Railroads were not the only targets. Confederates cut embankments on the Chesapeake & Ohio Canal in at least two places, letting the canal's waters rush out and rendering it unusable.[28]

As Union forces had pulled away from their positions threatening the Rappahannock line and moved north, Lee had given A. P. Hill orders to put his Third Corps on the march, west to the Blue Ridge, through the gaps, and northward down the Shenandoah Valley toward the Potomac. The trek began on June 14. On the 20th, with Hill's troops nearing the river, Lee set the rest of his army in motion. Ewell would have the lead again, proceeding up the Cumberland Valley, an extension of the Shenandoah that arched northeastward and increasingly east. The Second Corps was to press on through this pleasant valley all the way to the Susquehanna River, on the far bank of which stood Harrisburg, Pennsylvania's capital. Hill's Third Corps would follow behind Ewell, and this time Longstreet and the First Corps would bring up the rear. Lee himself crossed the river along with Pickett's division of Longstreet's corps on a bleak and rainy June 25, but he was nevertheless greeted on the far shore by a collection of secessionist Maryland ladies who clustered under their umbrellas and waved their handkerchiefs in welcome. Pickett's troops, Virginians to a man, marched through the river "in good order as if on review, cheering at every step."[29] The last of Longstreet's troops crossed the Potomac on June 26 and by the following day had reached Chambersburg.[30]

In Washington, Lincoln felt increasing frustration with Hooker. The general had not been quick to react to the disappearance of most of the Rebel force from his front. Even at the very time that Ewell was whipping Milroy out of Winchester, Hooker was still speculating about where the missing Confederates might be and begging Washington to tell him what to do. Despite making such pleas, Hooker shrugged off Lincoln's suggestions for aggressive action and contented himself with concentrating most of his army around Centerville, Virginia, about thirty miles west of Washington.[31]

That in itself represented hard marching for many of the soldiers of the Army of the Potomac, whose stamina was now called upon to compensate for the uncertainty of their commander. Pennsylvania soldier Roswell L. Root recalled that his regiment, part of Major General John F. Reynolds's First Corps of the Army of the Potomac, marched on half an hour's notice at 5:00 A.M., June 12, and made twenty-five miles that day. The 13th was another day of marching, and the 14th brought orders that the corps must reach Manassas Junction, near Centerville, by the next morning. By evening, Root and his comrades had covered thirty miles but were still far short of Manassas, and they trudged on through the night. "It was hard," Root wrote ten weeks later, "but we had to do it." The next morning they reached the junction, having gone forty-eight miles in twenty-four hours. After four hours' rest they were on the road again. When that march ended, later that day, Root had to report himself sick for the first time since he joined the army.[32]

In the midst of this crisis, Hooker found time to take up once more a long-standing feud with General Halleck. The two men's problems went back to their days as officers in the old prewar U.S. Army and had to do at least in part with Halleck's disgust with Hooker's debauched personal habits. Their animosity carried over into their official relations and was not beneficial to the war effort, but this was hardly the time to pursue the matter. "You have long been aware, Mr. President," wrote Hooker while Ewell's troops were crossing the Potomac, "that I have not enjoyed the confidence of the major-general commanding the army [Halleck], and I can assure you so long as this continues we may look in vain for success."[33]

This was a sort of power play. With Lee moving north, Union success against him was vital. That success would not be had, Hooker hinted, unless the bothersome Halleck was reined in or, better still, removed.

Lincoln had tried to cultivate a good personal relationship with Hooker, communicating with him directly instead of through Halleck. Now he reacted immediately, though not quite the way Hooker had anticipated. "To remove all misunderstanding," Lincoln wired Hooker that same day, "I now place you in the strict military relation to General Halleck of a commander of one of the armies to the general-in-chief of all the armies. I have not intended differently, but as it seems to be differently understood, I shall direct him to give you orders and you to obey them."[34]

Thus chastened, Hooker set to work at the task of countering whatever it was that Lee was trying to do. The biggest difficulty seemed for several days to be finding out just what that was. Was Lee crossing the Potomac? Or was that only a feint? Was he merely trying to distract Union attention while he detached troops for service in the West? Was he about to attack the Union garrison at Harpers Ferry? Or was he actually about to lunge straight east across the Blue Ridge to catch Hooker's army unprepared and strung out marching northward? Dispatches full of speculation and fragmentary information flew back and forth between Hooker's headquarters near Fairfax, Virginia, and the authorities in Washington: Lincoln, Halleck, and Secretary of War Edwin M. Stanton.

At the heart of the problem was the successful job Jeb Stuart was doing of screening Lee's movements. Stuart's cavalry spread out across the Virginia piedmont east of the Blue Ridge and stubbornly turned back the probing cavalry of the Army of the Potomac. Skirmishing was heavy and constant, but information was less than Hooker wished. On Halleck's advice he kept the Army of the Potomac moving northward. Its lead corps, the Twelfth under Major General Henry W. Slocum, reached Leesburg on the Potomac about midway between Washington and Harpers Ferry on June 19, with the other six corps extended over about thirty miles to the south of it.[35] That meant that although Hooker did not fully realize it, his advance guard was only forty crow's-flight miles southeast of Lee's leading infantry in Hagerstown. For the next six days Hooker kept his army where it was, waiting to see what Lee would do.

NOTES

1. U.S. War Department, *The War of the Rebellion: Official Records of the Union and Confederate Armies*, 128 vols. (Washington, DC: Government Printing Office, 1881–1901), vol. 25, pt. 1, p. 790 (hereafter cited as *OR*; except as otherwise noted, all references are to Series 1).

2. *OR*, vol. 25, pt. 1, pp. 782–83.

3. John B. Jones, *A Rebel War Clerk's Diary*, ed. Earl Schenck Miers (New York: Sagamore, 1958), 210.

4. Charles P. Roland, "Lee's Invasion Strategy," *North & South* 1, no. 6 (June 1998): 34–38.

5. Scott Bowden and Bill Ward, *Last Chance for Victory: Robert E. Lee and the Gettysburg Campaign* (Cambridge, MA: Da Capo Press, 2001), 2, 29–36; John H. Reagan, *Memoirs*, ed. Walter F. McCaleb (New York: Neale, 1906), 121–22, 150–51.

6. Quoted in Bowden and Ward, *Last Chance for Victory*, 99.

7. Samuel J. G. Brewer, *My Dear Wife from Your Devoted Husband: Letters from a Rebel Soldier to His Wife* (Warrington, FL: privately printed, 1968), 129–30.

8. David Holt, *A Mississippi Rebel in the Army of Northern Virginia*, ed. Thomas D. Cockrell and Michael B. Ballard (Baton Rouge: Louisiana State University Press, 1995), 192.

9. Edward Porter Alexander, *Fighting for the Confederacy: The Personal Recollections of General Edward Porter Alexander*, ed. Gary W. Gallagher (Chapel Hill: University of North Carolina Press, 1989), 222.

10. Clifford Dowdey and Louis H. Manarin, eds., *The Wartime Papers of R. E. Lee* (New York: Bramhall House, 1961), 490.

11. Arthur Fremantle, *The Freemantle Diary*, ed. Walter Lord (Boston: Little, Brown, 1954), 176.

12. *OR*, vol. 27, pt. 2, p. 293.

13. *OR*, vol. 27, pt. 1, pp. 32–33; pt. 2, p. 293.

14. *OR*, vol. 27, pt. 1, p. 31.

15. *OR*, vol. 27, pt. 2, p. 293.

16. *OR*, vol. 27, pt. 1, p. 36; Edwin B. Coddington, *The Gettysburg Campaign: A Study in Command* (New York: Simon & Schuster, 1968), 56–66; Bowden and Ward, *Last Chance for Victory*, 93–95.

17. *OR*, vol. 27, pt. 1, p. 34.

18. Quoted in Bowden and Ward, *Last Chance for Victory*, 139.

19. *OR*, vol. 27, pt. 1, p. 35.

20. *OR*, vol. 27, pt. 2, p. 293.

21. *OR*, vol. 27, pt. 2, pp. 440, 459.

22. Coddington, *The Gettysburg Campaign*, 73–84; *OR*, vol. 27, pt. 2, p. 293.

23. *OR*, vol. 27, pt. 2, p. 295.

24. *OR*, vol. 27, pt. 2, p. 357.

25. *OR*, vol. 27, pt. 2, pp. 440–41.

26. *OR*, vol. 27, pt. 1, p. 39.

27. *OR*, vol. 27, pt. 2, p. 442; Robert T. Coles, *From Huntsville to Appomattox: R. T. Coles's History of the 4th Regiment, Alabama Volunteer*

Infantry, C.S.A., Army of Northern Virginia, ed. Jeffrey D. Stocker (Knoxville: University of Tennessee Press, 1996), 100.

28. *OR*, vol. 27, pt. 2, p. 297.

29. Charles Minor Blackford and Susan Leigh Blackford, *Letters from Lee's Army: Memoirs of Life in and out of the Army in Virginia during the War between the States* (New York: A. S. Barnes, 1947), 182; Francis W. Dawson, *Reminiscences of Confederate Service, 1861–1865*, ed. Bell I. Wiley (Baton Rouge: Louisiana State University Press, 1980), 90–91.

30, *OR*, vol. 27, pt. 2, pp. 296, 357–58, 443, 613.

31. *OR*, vol. 27, pt. 1, pp. 40–44.

32. Roswell L. Root to "Dear Grand Father," August 23, 1863, Roswell L. Root Papers, Civil War Miscellaneous Collection, United States Army Military History Institute, Carlisle, Pennsylvania (hereafter USAMHI).

33. *OR*, vol. 27, pt. 1, p. 45.

34. *OR*, vol. 27, pt. 1, p. 47.

35. *OR*, vol. 27, pt. 1, pp. 47–53.

CHAPTER TWO

AN INVADING ARMY AMONGST THEM

WHILE HOOKER WAITED, Lee marched. Ewell's corps led the way up the Cumberland Valley. Rodes's and Johnson's divisions kept to the main road, through Greencastle and Chambersburg to Carlisle, arriving there on June 27. Early's division paralleled the other two on roads lying farther east, on the very edge of the valley. Ewell's troops found this a very satisfying march, especially those of Rodes's division, which had the lead. Ewell officially reported that at Chambersburg, Shippensburg, and Carlisle he had demanded supplies from the overawed townspeople. "The shops were searched," Ewell added with satisfaction, and "many valuable stores [were] secured." The Confederates seized some 5,000 barrels of flour in one place. By the time it reached Chambersburg, Ewell's corps had collected such a surplus that a special wagon train was started back toward the south bearing the plunder. So too was a herd of 3,000 head of cattle. From Greencastle, Ewell dispatched a brigade on a detour thirty miles west to McConnellsburg to round up even more cattle and horses, while his main column continued to sweep up the wealth of the Cumberland Valley.[1]

Rodes and his men seized some especially interesting booty in Carlisle—a large quantity of Pennsylvania whiskey. Celebrating the success of their campaign thus far, both officers and men imbibed freely. A soldier in the ranks noted that "mint juleps in tin cans were plentiful," while an aide to the division commander wrote, "I never saw Rodes intoxicated before or since." When the entire division formed up for a parade on the grounds of Carlisle Barracks (a U.S. Army installation), a young lieutenant was so drunk that he attempted to address the assembly in an impromptu speech and had to be hauled off.[2]

Leading the way for Ewell's march—out in front even of Rodes's infantry—Albert Jenkins's cavalry brigade introduced Pennsylvanians to the concept of a hostile army in their midst. Their dramatic entrances into the various towns of the Cumberland Valley immediately cowed the quiet civilians. Shippensburg resident John

Stumbaugh wrote to his son of Confederate horsemen charging through the streets "with the awful yells you ever herd." Then followed the infantry, swinging along with a jaunty stride, then the artillery, and finally the wagons, in a column that Stumbaugh guessed must have been five miles long. Stumbaugh was an apothecary, and he soon had numerous Confederates in his shop taking "such drugs as would suit them," to a value that he guessed was somewhere between $100 and $1,000. The loss throughout the town of Shippensburg he reckoned at "20 or 25 thousand dollars worth."[3]

Elsewhere, the Southerners "plundered everything such as Horses, Stores, Mills and ware Houses & so forth." Ewell's men were not only taking, they were also destroying. In Chambersburg they tore down the depot and all the railroad shops. Mills and workshops went up in flames all along the way. As word of the Rebels' approach spread up the valley, refugees thronged the roads moving northeastward toward Harrisburg and what they hoped would be safety beyond the Susquehanna—"men women & children" and "thousands and thousands of Horses" as thrifty farmers strove to keep their means of livelihood away from the invaders. The refugees with the most real and urgent reasons to flee were thousands of free black citizens of the Cumberland Valley. For them, whether former slaves or born to freedom in the North, falling into the hands of the invaders would mean being carried off to bondage in the South.[4]

The men of Ewell's corps, in the lead, had the best opportunities, but their comrades coming along behind were just as industrious. Private W. C. Ward of the Fourth Alabama, in Hood's division of Longstreet's corps, near the tail end of Lee's invading army, noted that when his regiment made camp for its first night in Pennsylvania, near Greencastle, "many of the men went into the country foraging, returning, some, with chickens; some, with honey; some with butter and whatever else that was edible on which their hands could be laid."[5]

As Hood's division marched through Greencastle the next morning, its bands played "The Bonnie Blue Flag," and the soldiers were in high spirits. A hatless soldier of the Fourth Alabama spied a man and two ladies standing at a fence that enclosed a cottage, watching the passing Confederate column. As he proceeded past the trio, the soldier snatched the hat from the civilian's head and kept on marching. A few yards farther on, another Alabamian played the same trick on an elderly Pennsylvanian, grabbing the man's "beautiful new felt hat, and at the same time carelessly dropping his own well-worn Confederate wool covering." As the Alabamians strode on, they could hear the old man saying, "I really believe that soldier has taken my hat."[6]

At other times the plundering took on a more serious tone. As the Sixteenth Mississippi was halted in one of the streets of Chambersburg, Private Bill Phipps saw a large man, about his size, standing in front of his comfortable-looking house. Phipps thought the civilian did not look sufficiently abashed at having an invading army in the street in front of his house, and so he abruptly demanded, "Come out of that hat. And don't say you ain't in there, for I see your legs sticking out from under it."

"I'll come out of it when you are man enough to make me," the civilian bristled.

Phipps was not inclined to measure physical prowess with the Pennsylvanian, so he loaded his rifle, cocked it, and aimed it at the unarmed civilian's chest. "Will you once? Will you twice? Will you three . . . ?"

The man hastily threw the hat to the ground. "There, take it," he spat. "The Lord knows you need it, and a lot more clothes besides, you ragged Rebel."

Phipps kept his gun pointed at the now hatless civilian's midsection and demanded, "Come out of that coat."

"I won't pull off my coat for any man except to fight him."

"You can take your choice of pulling it off alive," replied Phipps coolly, "or have me pull it off of you when you are dead." The civilian gave in and tossed his coat on the ground next to his hat, as the whole Sixteenth Mississippi, seated or lying in the street, looked on with amusement. Phipps was not finished. "Come out of them breeches," he snarled.

"I demand the protection of an officer!" exclaimed the civilian. "I appeal to the captain, or commanding officer of this company to save me from the disgrace of disrobing on the street." There were plenty of officers on the scene, but they all pretended not to hear.

"I don't care a pickled damn about your being naked in the street," said Phipps. "I want them breeches." Finally the civilian and the gray-clad highwayman worked out a compromise. They both went into the man's house, and Phipps emerged dressed in a complete suit of stolen clothes.[7]

Statistically, at least, civilians were unlikely to suffer bodily injury from the invading Rebels. A Southern newspaper boasted some months later that the campaign had occasioned only one rape and two murders perpetrated by Confederate soldiers and suggested that the guilty parties would be severely punished.[8] This record was comparable to the one Union armies would compile during the war when they marched through various parts of the South.

Staying home to greet the invaders could be frightening. However, as was the case when Union armies marched through the South at various times during the war, civilians who fled at the approach of the hostile army were more likely to suffer loss or damage to the houses and personal effects they left behind. One Rebel soldier congratulated himself for not "going into a man's garden & lots and pressing vegetables and shooting down his stock without remunerating him"—in worthless Confederate money. Even this soldier admitted that "after a house had been abandoned by the family and pillaged by our troops, if I saw any thing thrown about liable to be lost, I would be willing to take it."[9] Lieutenant Thomas F. Boatright of the Forty-fourth Virginia wrote to his wife regarding civilians who fled at the approach of the Confederate army and swelled the tide of refugees heading for the east bank of the Susquehanna: "All such the soldiers took every thing from them even striped [sic] their houses."[10]

Foodstuffs were the chief items stolen. "It was at a season of the year when the trees drooped with ripening cherries," recalled the Fourth Alabama's Robert Coles, "and in every direction you could see these trees filled with Confederate soldiers helping themselves to that most luscious fruit." Coles also remembered the milk and the Chester White pigs yielding "boiled hog's head and spareribs." On another occasion during the march, Coles noted that he and his fellow soldiers had "materially reduced the supply of apple butter and light bread of our Pennsylvania Dutch hosts."[11] Lieutenant Boatright wrote that in every town they visited, the Confederates "pressed every thing such as flour corn molasses whiskey clothes cattle horses and every thing else that would be useful to the army."[12] Theoretically such "pressing" was to be restricted to duly authorized commissary officers. "What is needed for our comfort," Boatright explained to his wife, "will be taken by proper authorities."[13]

Johnny Reb, however, was not about to pass up his opportunities. "Our boys have been foraging all over the neighboring country," wrote Alabama soldier Turner Vaughan. "No one has committed any outrage upon the people that I have heard of, though they have perhaps taken from them more than they should have done of chickens, turkeys, ducks, etc." Vaughan admitted that there were "stringent orders" against such behavior.[14]

Those orders had come from Lee himself. As his army prepared to cross the Potomac, Lee had issued General Orders Number 72, admonishing his troops not to plunder Northern civilians as he and other Confederates believed that Union soldiers had done in the South. This order had a definite purpose, to make the Confederacy appear more virtuous than the Union. At the same time, however, Lee had always stated to the Confederate high command that a major part of his purpose in crossing the Potomac was to feed his army at the enemy's expense. The dual need to subsist the army while seeming more virtuous than an enemy who had occasionally met the same need in the same way led to a number of expedients. Storekeepers were not plundered; they were merely compelled at gunpoint to sell their entire stock for Confederate money. These paper notes were well nigh worthless south of the Potomac and entirely so north of it. The effect was the same. As one Confederate officer described the situation in a letter to his wife, "There is to be no pillaging except by systematic process under the control of the quartermaster and commissary. All supplies to be taken that way are to be paid for in Confederate money."[15]

Nevertheless, the forced "purchases" were not confined to official commissaries nor to items of military use. From Chambersburg on June 27, Thomas Boatright wrote his wife, "Our money is not good here though they are forced to take it." He went on to explain that this practice was only done "in som places" and only for certain items, "that is, those we buy." Most things, he noted, they simply took without any pretense of payment. Boatright added, "I have purchased two dresses for you and a pair of shoes." Whether bought with worthless money or not, Boatright also mentioned that he and his men were enjoying a steady supply of such military necessities as "coffee, tea, sugar, whisky, and candy, sigars, nuts of different kinds."[16]

Another ploy was to issue receipts for plundered property, promising payment at some vague future date after a treaty of peace was signed recognizing Confederate independence. On Sunday, June 28, Lieutenant John Hampden Chamberlayne led a detachment of men seeking horses for his battery of artillery. He came upon a church building where a service was in progress. The yard outside was filled with buggies and wagons in which the worshipers had come, and hitched to those buggies and wagons were horses. Revolver drawn, Chamberlayne strode boldly into the church, and while he held the congregation at bay, his men unhitched the horses. Then Chamberlayne distributed receipts for the animals and rode off.[17]

In other cases, soldiers carried on their own private foraging while their officers remained—or appeared to remain—completely oblivious. Tally Simpson of the Third South Carolina wrote his sister, "The officers in command issued some very stringent orders with reference to the destruction of private property, but the soldiers paid no more attention to them than they would to the cries of a screech owl. Every thing in the shape of vegetables, from a cow pea up to a cabbage head, was 'pressed' without the least ceremony, and all animal flesh from a featherless fowl to full grown sheep and hogs were killed and devoured without the least compunction or conscience." Significantly, Simpson added, "The brigadiers and colonels made no attempt to enforce Lee's general orders."[18]

The willingness to look the other way, or even to give open approval, went beyond brigadiers and colonels. Many Confederates, including some high-ranking officers, were eager to take revenge on the Yankees for the destruction that war had wrought in Virginia during the past two years. Major General William Dorsey Pender, commanding a division in Hill's Third Corps, was one of them. "Our people have suffered from the depredations of the Yankees," he wrote to his wife, "but if we ever get into their country they will find out what it is to have an invading army amongst them. Our officers—not Gen. Lee—have made up their minds not to protect them and some of our chaplains are telling the men they must spoil and kill." Another Confederate of more humble rank expressed similar thoughts: "I don't think we would do wrong to take horses, burn houses, and commit every depredation possible upon the men of the North."[19]

Pender was not the only division commander who thought as he did. During his division's march through Pennsylvania, Major General John B. Hood sat outside his headquarters on a commandeered chair, apparently intent on studying a map, while his soldiers raided a nearby poultry yard. One soldier even chased a chicken under Hood's chair, caught it there, and triumphantly carried off the fluttering fowl while the general's eyes never strayed from his map.[20]

Lee himself was riding along the marching column of his army one day when he came on a similar scene, with thirty or forty Confederate soldiers staging a bold assault on the feathered population of a roadside farm. It was a noisy affair, with ducks, geese, turkeys, and chickens squawking, soldiers whooping with delight, and the old lady of the place screaming for them to stop. Catching sight of Lee, the frantic woman recognized him—perhaps from published pictures—and began shouting, "General Lee, General Lee, I wish to speak to you, sir!" The courtly Lee, keeping his eyes straight ahead, touched the brim of his hat and said, "Good morning, madam," and rode on. "It caused a great deal of amusement," recorded a South Carolina soldier, "as the old lady, panting with anger, was compelled to witness the departure of her last favorite pullet and the old family gobbler."[21]

In most respects, the Confederate army that marched through Pennsylvania was no better or worse than the Union armies that marched through various parts of the South at different times during the war. It was in the nature of an army to use up the countryside through which it passed, and doubly so if that countryside belonged to the enemy. As the *Richmond Sentinel* complained after taking Lee's General Orders Number 72 at face value, "You cannot possibly introduce an army for one hour into an enemy's country without damaging private property, and in a way often in which compensation cannot be made."[22] The citizens of south-central Pennsylvania could have vouched for the truth of that statement, and Lee knew it. His order was a matter of propaganda, and considering the myth of Confederate restraint in Pennsylvania that lives on to this day, it may well have been the most effective order he gave during the operation.

In one respect, however, the Confederate army in Pennsylvania was a scourge far worse than any troops who ever marched behind William Tecumseh Sherman, and that was in kidnapping free citizens and carrying them off into slavery. Precise numbers are hard to come by, but indications are that Confederate troops bound and dragged off perhaps as many as several hundred Pennsylvanians of African descent, many of them free-born. This was plundering with an ideological bent and a reminder of why the two sides were fighting and what the real issue was between them.

The practice was not limited to private soldiers on the sly nor was it condemned by any echelon of the Confederate high command. Longstreet himself instructed one of his division commanders, George Pickett, to make sure to bring along the captured blacks.[23]

The abductions started as soon as Lee's soldiers reached free soil. Albert Jenkins's cavalry, leading the way, searched Chambersburg for blacks, most of whom had been born free and had spent all their lives there. A Union soldier's wife, Rachel Cormany, a white resident of the town, wrote of seeing the local blacks "driven by just like we would drive cattle." She noted that most of those caught were women and children. "One woman was pleading wonderfully with her driver for her children—but all the sympathy she received from him was a rough 'March along.' " Mrs. Cormany wondered what the Rebels "want with those little babies." When another white Chambersburg woman, Mrs. Jemima Cree, remonstrated with a Confederate officer whose men had kidnapped her free-born black employee, he replied that he could do nothing. Orders were orders. According to Mrs. Cree, the Rebels were taking "all they could find, even little children, whom they had to carry on horseback before them." Many blacks hid in the woods or in the houses of their employers, but the Confederates succeeded in rounding up and sending into bondage some 250 Chambersburg citizens of African descent. The story was much the same in other towns.[24]

The Cumberland Valley felt the brunt of Confederate depredations during this first week of the invasion. The Southern soldiers were impressed with the broad and fertile swath of country. "I never have seen finer crops of wheat in my life," wrote Thomas Boatright. He had yet to see a field that looked other than excellent. The farms were small, by Virginia standards, but "have good and convenient buildings, more convenience about them than any one could have thought of but a yankee."[25] Staff officer Charles Minor Blackford found the fields entirely too small and the barns too large for his tastes. "The land is rich and highly cultivated," he observed in a letter to his wife, "much more highly than the men who own it."[26]

South Carolinian Tally Simpson had exactly the same assessment of the state's agriculture, adding, "Pennsylvania is one of the prettiest countries through which I have ever passed. The scenery is beautiful, and the soil is exceedingly fertile." Like the other gray-clad visitors, Simpson thought the food was fine, "every thing that one's appetite could crave." His only complaint was the absence of hot biscuits. The Pennsylvanians "say they can't stand bread with grease in it because it is heavy." Simpson perceived a dearth of blacks, noting that the white people did all their own labor. Still, they seemed to prosper. Simpson averred that he had not seen "a single pretty woman" in his whole trek, but he had to admit that the Pennsylvania women were "always neat and clean and very industrious" and that the houses were "kept as neat and clean as possible."[27] Blackford sneered, "Never in my life have I seen so many ugly women." He thought the men looked "Dutch" and bore a striking similarity to their large draft horses. Both men and women spoke with a terrible accent, "a yankee twang that grates against my nerves and ear-drums most terribly."[28] Simpson was somewhat more generous. "It is certainly a delightful country to live in," he concluded, but its inhabitants did not believe in slavery, so Simpson was sure this was not the country for him.[29]

Simpson revealed his commitment to the cause of slavery in describing his regiment's march through Chambersburg. "All the ladies had pinned to their dresses the Union flag," he observed. With more irritation, he noted that many of these ladies were stopping the black body servants whom some Confederate officers still kept with them and were urging those slaves to make their escape. The infuriated Simpson wrote that if he had heard one of them speaking to his personal slave, "I would have felt like jerking the very hide off of her back with a Confederate cow skin, woman or not."[30] Blackford, a Virginian, also felt disgust for Northern society. "I see no signs of social refinement," he wrote disdainfully to his wife. The problem was the lack of an aristocracy. "All seems to be on a dead level," Blackford complained, "like a lot of fat cattle in a clover field."[31]

The Pennsylvanians looked with curiosity and a mixture of both admiration and disdain on the ragged legions of the famous Army of Northern Virginia. The Pennsylvania women often made a point of displaying as many small U.S. flags as possible when Lee's troops marched through their towns. A Virginian reported that when Pickett's division went through Chambersburg, "the windows and porches were filled with women who were covered with flags, and each one had a flag, waving it over our troops as they passed along the street."[32] Lee's vast reputation led civilians to hope for a glimpse of him and lent a certain aura to even the private soldiers of his command. Some Pennsylvanians, however, were unimpressed. In one village an elderly woman called out to the passing Confederates, "You are marching mighty proudly now, but you will come back faster than you went."

"Why so, old lady?" asked a Southern officer.

"Because you put your trust in General Lee and not in the Lord Almighty."[33]

While the bulk of the Army of Northern Virginia lived high on the good things of the hardworking residents of the Cumberland Valley, others looked eastward, across South Mountain. Just as the Blue Ridge forms the eastern wall of the Shenandoah Valley down in Virginia, so north of the Potomac, the long ridge of South Mountain stands as an eastern rampart to the Cumberland Valley. Jubal Early's division, part of Ewell's Second Corps, was the first major Confederate formation to cross that rampart. The division first marched along the western base of South Mountain, on the fringe of the Cumberland Valley, until it reached the crossroads town of Greenwood, where its route crossed the turnpike leading from Chambersburg southeastward to Gettysburg. Near there, Early's men came to the Caledonia Ironworks, which belonged to Congressman Thaddeus Stevens, an abolitionist. The Confederates were eager to strike a blow against one of their political archenemies, and Early turned his men loose on the premises and Stevens's adjoining lands. "Our men took pleasure," wrote a Louisianan, "in helping themselves most bountifully to the products of his broad and fertile acres." After "luxuriating in old Thad's provider and good things generally" for two days, the division prepared to take up its march again. On Early's orders they burned "two large iron mills of Stevens, together with the adjoining storehouses" before leaving. For good measure, they broke the windows of the houses where lived the families of Stevens's 200 employees.[34]

After consulting with Ewell at Chambersburg, Early changed the direction of his march, taking the pike heading southeast, over South Mountain, and then down the eastern slope to enjoy the equally great bounty of Adams and York counties. His orders were to proceed through Gettysburg and York all the way to the Susquehanna at Wrightsville. A bridge there, if taken intact, would give him access to Lancaster County, across the river, and allow him to give its rich fields and bulging barns the Confederate treatment that its western neighbors were getting. That enjoyable task finished, Early was to rejoin Ewell somewhere near Harrisburg, where the latter was expected by that time.[35]

Early's division struck out eastward over South Mountain on the morning of a rainy June 26. By late afternoon they were approaching the crossroads town of Gettysburg, where the Twenty-sixth Pennsylvania Militia briefly attempted to bar their progress. The inexperienced militiamen fled, however, at the first sign of real fighting, and in his memoirs Early sneered that it was just as well. If they had stayed to fight, some of them might have gotten hurt. Early's men marched into the town unhindered, and their commander demanded that the authorities of Gettysburg furnish supplies to his troops, plenty of food, 1,000 pairs of shoes, and 500 hats. Alternatively, he was prepared to accept $10,000 in cash. The town fathers professed their inability to comply, and a quick search by Early's men turned up food enough for 2,000 rations, which the Rebels seized. They also burned a train of ten or twelve cars along with a small railroad bridge. Then regretting that time did not permit him to turn little Gettysburg inside out and find out what sort of supplies it might really afford, Early marched on the next morning, June 27, toward York. Members of Early's Louisiana brigade, however, had found in Gettysburg liquid plunder highly congenial to them, and a number of them marched off roaring drunk, causing headaches for their officers for much of the day.[36]

The division marched into York unopposed on the morning of June 28, and, as was the practice of Confederate officers this summer when first entering a Pennsylvania town, Early presented the city fathers with his shopping list. He demanded 2,000 pairs of shoes, 1,000 hats, 1,000 pairs of socks, $100,000 in cash, and food enough to feed his whole force for three days. If the loot was not delivered up promptly, the townspeople of York could expect to bear the consequences. In the end, what Early got was shoes, hats, and socks for about 1,500 men, with food enough to feed the same number for a single day. The York city government could come up with only a paltry $28,600. Early took the money and generously agreed not to burn the town.[37]

Early's soldiers found York County as lovely as their comrades were finding the Cumberland Valley. "I never enjoyed myself more than I did on that march," wrote William D. Lyon three weeks later. "We passed through the most beautiful and highly cultivated country that I ever saw. It was literally a land of plenty."[38] "Immense fields of golden grain flashed in the sunlight—dotted here and there with neat little cottages," recalled another Confederate. He noted the size and fine construction of the Pennsylvania barns that were "literally bursting with wheat, oats & corn." As in the Cumberland Valley, the Confederates took special interest in the Pennsylvanians' horseflesh and laughed over the thrifty farmers' efforts to save their property. On one occasion a quartermaster called on a prosperous Pennsylvanian who was rumored to have a very good horse. This the farmer stoutly denied, but at that unfortunate moment the Confederate officer heard a neigh coming from the next room. There he discovered a fine horse in a fine front parlor next to a fine rosewood piano. "Horses were found in bedrooms, parlours, lofts of barns and other out of the way places," wrote a Southerner, and the Rebels took them all.[39]

Continuing eastward on the evening of June 28, Early's men were too late to prevent the Pennsylvania militia from burning Columbia Bridge, which spanned the Susquehanna River at Wrightsville. Early "regretted very much the failure to secure this bridge . . . as the river was otherwise impassable, being very wide and deep at this point." The rich fields and barns of Lancaster County were thus out of his reach. Disappointed, Early turned his division back to York, where he made sure to destroy all the railroad cars and tore up the tracks in the vicinity. Then he proceeded northward, west of the Susquehanna, toward a planned junction with the rest of Ewell's corps somewhere in the vicinity of Harrisburg.[40]

That same day, June 29, Ewell was at Carlisle, into which his men had marched, lustily singing "Dixie," two days before. His march had been much like Early's, with plenty of looting, plundering, and a thorough destruction of every bit of railroad track his men could lay their hands on, including a 600-foot-long trestle belonging to the Cumberland Valley Railroad. Ewell was preparing to continue his eastward march toward Harrisburg when he received a message from Lee: Ewell, including Early's division, was to reverse his direction in order to join the rest of the Army of Northern Virginia in assembling at Cashtown, on the eastern slope of South Mountain between Chambersburg and Gettysburg. Lee had discovered the whereabouts of the Army of the Potomac. It was north of its namesake river and coming north hard. The Army of Northern Virginia must now prepare to meet it somewhere between South Mountain and the Susquehanna.[41]

NOTES

1. *OR*, vol. 27, pt. 2, pp. 442–43.

2. Gregory W. Baxter, "Death's Mission: Baxter and Iverson at Gettysburg," *Civil War* 69 (August 1998): 50.

3. John Stumbaugh to "My Dear Son," July 9, 1863, John Stumbaugh Papers, Civil War Miscellaneous Collection, USAMHI.

4. Ibid.; Coddington, *The Gettysburg Campaign*, 150.

5. Coles, *From Huntsville to Appomattox*, 203.

6. Ibid., 203–4.

7. Holt, *Mississippi Rebel*, 191–93.

8. Rome [Georgia] *Courier*, September 5, 1863.

9. Guy R. Everson and Edward H. Simpson Jr., eds., *"Far, Far from Home": The Wartime Letters of Dick and Tally Simpson, Third South Carolina Volunteers* (New York: Oxford University Press, 1994), 262–63.

10. Thomas F. Boatright to "My Darling Wife," July 9, 1863, Boatright Papers, Southern Historical Collection, University of North Carolina, Chapel Hill (hereafter SHC).

11. Coles, *From Huntsville to Appomattox*, 102–3, 205.

12. Thomas F. Boatright to "My Darling Wife," July 9, 1863, Boatright Papers, SHC.

13. Thomas F. Boatright to "My Darling Wife," June 27, 1863, Boatright Papers, SHC.

14. Coles, *From Huntsville to Appomattox*, 270 n. 7.

15. Blackford and Blackford, *Letters from Lee's Army*, 180–81.

16. Thomas F. Boatright to "My Darling Wife," June 27, 1863, Boatright Papers, SHC.

17. John Hampden Chamberlayne, *Ham Chamberlayne, Virginian: Letters and Papers of an Artillery Officer in the War for Southern Independence, 1861–1865* (Richmond: Dietz, 1932; reprint, Wilmington, NC: Broadfoot, 1992), 191.

18. Everson and Simpson, *"Far, Far from Home,"* 261–62.

19. Both quoted in Reid Mitchell, *Civil War Soldiers* (New York: Viking, 1988), 154–55.

20. Coles, *From Huntsville to Appomattox*, 102.

21. Everson and Simpson, *"Far, Far from Home,"* 262.

22. Quoted in Coddington, *The Gettysburg Campaign*, 156.

23. Coddington, *The Gettysburg Campaign*, 161.

24. Ted Alexander, " 'A Regular Slave Hunt': The Army of Northern Virginia and Black Civilians in the Gettysburg Campaign," *North & South* 4, no. 7 (September 2001): 83–88.

25. Thomas F. Boatright to "My Darling Wife," July 9, 1863, Boatright Papers, SHC.

26. Blackford and Blackford, *Letters from Lee's Army*, 184–85.

27. Everson and Simpson, *"Far, Far from Home,"* 261–63.

28. Blackford and Blackford, *Letters from Lee's Army*, 186.

29. Everson and Simpson, *"Far, Far from Home,"* 261–63.

30. Ibid., 263–64.

31. Blackford and Blackford, *Letters from Lee's Army*, 184–85.

32. Ibid., 185.

33. Dawson, *Reminiscences of Confederate Service*, 93.

34. William J. Seymour, *The Civil War Memoirs of Captain William J. Seymour: Reminiscences of a Louisiana Tiger*, ed. Terry L. Jones (Baton Rouge: Louisiana State University Press, 1991), 64–65; Coddington, *The Gettysburg Campaign*, 166.

35. *OR*, vol. 27, pt. 2, pp. 464–65.

36. Seymour, *Civil War Memoirs*, 65–66; Coddington, *The Gettysburg Campaign*, 167.

37. *OR*, vol. 27, pt. 2, pp. 465–66.

38. William D. Lyon to his brother George, July 18, 1863, William D. Lyon Papers, Pearce Civil War Collection, Navarro College, Corsicana, Texas.

39. Seymour, *Civil War Memoirs*, 66.

40. *OR*, vol. 27, pt. 2, pp. 466–67; Seymour, *Civil War Memoirs*, 69.

41. *OR*, vol. 27, pt. 2, pp. 442–43; Coddington, *The Gettysburg Campaign*, 171–72.

CHAPTER THREE

THEY WILL COME BOOMING

UNION SIGNAL OFFICERS watched from towering Maryland Heights, above Harpers Ferry, as far to the northwest Hill's and Longstreet's troops splashed across the Potomac on the 23rd, 24th, and 25th of June. For a week prior to that, Hooker's army had done little. The Army of the Potomac's infantry lay in northern Virginia, in positions extending south from Leesburg on the Potomac, facing west, covering Washington, and waiting to see what would turn up, while the cavalry skirmished briskly in the no-man's-land that stretched westward to the Blue Ridge. Hooker was slow to grasp the import of Lee's movements, and even as the main strength of the Army of Northern Virginia streamed into Maryland and Pennsylvania, the Union commander dithered indecisively with one scheme and then another. Finally, on June 25, Hooker realized that Lee's whole army was going north and that the Army of the Potomac would have to follow.[1]

By that time, however, Lee had a two-day head start, and the tired legs of the long-suffering Yankee foot soldiers once again would have to make good by fast marches the slow perception of their commander. Twelfth Corps commander Henry W. Slocum, directing the army's right flank at Leesburg, had alertly placed a pontoon bridge over the river there in readiness for a quick northward movement. That helped, but soldiers still remembered the next few days of marching as the worst of the campaign, with many units covering more than twenty miles on June 25. In the ranks of the Forty-fourth New York, part of the Fifth Corps, Frasier Rosenkranz noticed a pattern to the days of hard marching. The soldiers rose to the sound of the drums at about 3:00 A.M. each morning, brewed and drank their coffee, and gathered up their gear. By 4:00 A.M. they took the road, and the rest of the day fell into a predictable rhythm: two miles of marching, then a fifteen-minute rest. By 5:00 P.M. they had usually covered their twenty miles.[2]

To lead the northward drive, screening the rest of the army against any possible eastward lunge by Lee, Hooker detailed three of his seven corps—the First, Third, and Eleventh, all under the command of the First Corps's Major General John F. Reynolds.[3] A native of Lancaster County, Pennsylvania, Reynolds was an 1841 West Point graduate. He had served in the artillery and won two brevets in the Mexican War. Later he was commandant of cadets at West Point. In the Civil War he had risen rapidly in rank, commanding first a brigade of the famed Pennsylvania Reserves and then the whole division. Captured and exchanged, Reynolds had commanded the First Corps since September 29, 1862, and he was one of the most admired and respected generals in the Army of the Potomac.

After Chancellorsville, Reynolds had heard a rumor that he was to replace Hooker. Hurrying to Washington, Reynolds met with the president and insisted that he would not accept command of the army unless he were to be given a completely free hand, without regard for the political needs of a government whose capital lay in the army's immediate rear. Since this demand was tantamount to a request to have Virginia transported to some other part of the world, Lincoln could not comply. Hooker kept his job, and Reynolds kept his, which, as of June 25, included supervising the three corps that would be ranging closest to Lee's fast-moving columns out beyond South Mountain. As expected, Reynolds acted competently and energetically in moving his new command forward.[4]

By June 27, Hooker had his entire army on the north bank of the Potomac and his own headquarters at Frederick, Maryland. However, he still seemed to have little idea of what to do about Lee and, more ominously, a continued reluctance to meet in battle the man who had humiliated him at Chancellorsville. Hooker concocted a questionable scheme for pulling the garrison out of Harpers Ferry, uniting it with Slocum's Twelfth Corps, and sending the new force to cut the supply line that Hooker thought Lee must have—somewhere. The plan would have been far-fetched even if Lee had actually possessed the supply line Hooker imagined, but in any case Hooker's idea had for him one sovereign virtue: it might make Lee go away without the need to meet him in battle—a battle Hooker knew in his heart he would lose.[5]

The problem was that the Harpers Ferry garrison was part of a separate department, one that Hooker did not command, and getting those troops out of that strategic place would require an appeal to Halleck. What Hooker made was not so much an appeal as it was a peremptory demand, without explanation, and Halleck refused it. The general in Washington had been generous in releasing troops to Hooker from neighboring departments, sending him the best units from the Washington garrison. That was not good enough for Hooker, and he decided it was time to try another power play on Halleck. Renewing his demand for the Harpers Ferry garrison, Hooker added that if those troops were not released to him, he wanted to be relieved as commander of the Army of the Potomac. In the midst of a major military crisis, Hooker reasoned, with a Rebel army marching through Pennsylvania, Lincoln would not dare to permit a change of commanders in the republic's largest army and would have to make Halleck back down. But Lincoln did dare, and in the pre-dawn hours of the next morning orders came from Washington relieving Hooker and turning over the Army of the Potomac to Fifth Corps commander Major General George G. Meade.

Born in Spain to American parents forty-seven years before, Meade had become a Pennsylvanian, graduated from West Point in 1835, and served a career in the regular U.S. Army, winning a brevet in the Mexican War. Like Reynolds, he had risen rapidly in the Civil War volunteer army, and also like Reynolds, he had done so in the Pennsylvania Reserves division. Indeed, at Fredericksburg, where Meade had led the division with distinction, Reynolds had been his corps commander. The fact that Reynolds and Slocum outranked Meade was a problem, but both men had previously expressed their willingness to serve under Meade. The new commander was ungainly in appearance and had a notorious temper. Nonetheless, Meade was solidly competent, cautious, thorough, and well respected by his fellow officers. News of the change spread through the ranks later that morning. The common soldiers knew little of Meade and cared less. The men of the Army of the Potomac had seen generals come and go. Since George McClellan had left nine months earlier, they no longer fought for generals but for the cause, for their comrades, and, in this campaign unlike all others, for their home country.[6]

With the new assignment, Halleck gave Meade orders to maneuver the Army of the Potomac so as first to cover Washington and Baltimore and then to defeat Lee's army. Pursuant to those orders, Meade's first problem was the fact that Confederate troops were threatening to cross the Susquehanna well north of him at Wrightsville and Harrisburg, the state capital. To put a stop to this dangerous enemy movement, Meade decided to keep his own tired

Major General George G. Meade. Library of Congress, Prints and Photographs Division, LC-B8172-2171

troops going north hard, with the seven corps spread out on a broad front and taking up positions just south of the Pennsylvania line on the evening of June 29.

Wearily, the veteran troops faced another day of forced marches. This time, however, there was a difference from the long tramps with which the campaign had begun down in Virginia. Maryland was a slave state, but most of its slaveholders lived in the eastern part of the state, and here west of Washington, DC, the majority of the population was staunchly loyal. So was Pennsylvania. The enthusiastic reception was something new for the Army of the Potomac's soldiers, who had campaigned for two years among the sullen stares of the rebellious Virginians. "It is refreshing to get out of the barren desert of Virginia into this land of thrift and plenty," wrote Lieutenant Colonel Rufus Dawes of the Sixth Wisconsin. "Everybody, great and small, is overjoyed at the coming of our banners."[7] Daniel Crotty of the Third Michigan also remarked on the lovely countryside as well as the groups of young ladies who stood beside the road here and there singing "The Star Spangled Banner" and "Rally 'Round the Flag." In the villages and towns the Stars and Stripes seemed to hang from every building. The Union flag was draped above the streets as bunting and was waved in smaller versions by the cheering citizens who lined the roadsides, while the troops marched with colors unfurled, drums beating, and fifes playing. The "lovely village" of Taneytown was especially memorable, for there Crotty remembered the womenfolk not only waving their handkerchiefs but also showering the marching column with flowers. In other towns along the routes of the various corps the citizens lining the streets offered buckets of cold spring water to the sweating, dusty troops, while others handed out choice eatables. Spirits rose in the ranks, and the men felt confident of chastising "the arrogant rebel army."[8]

The Rebel army was in high spirits too. The men of Ewell's Second Corps, now on the march back to the southwest, knew what their change of direction meant. "It was evident to the dullest comprehension that a battle was imminent," wrote Louisiana soldier William Seymour in the ranks of Early's division, "and it was inspiring to see the spirits of our men rise at the prospect of a fight." Ewell's corps's wagon train along with Major General Edward Johnson's division marched back the way the corps had come, along the southwestward-curving Cumberland Valley to join the bulk of the army around Chambersburg, while Rodes's and Early's men moved along the abundant road network of south-central Pennsylvania, cutting across the arc on a more direct route to Cashtown.

The troops around Chambersburg, Longstreet's First Corps and Hill's Third, had less data with which to predict an imminent battle, but they too were supremely confident. They now enjoyed a couple of days' rest in their camps near Chambersburg, completing the process of trampling into the muddy soil what had days before promised to be a bumper wheat crop. The only vexation for them was that Ewell's men had swept the neighborhood almost clean of victuals and booty, but Longstreet's and Hill's men were nothing if not diligent in devouring the last morsels of the hapless Pennsylvania farmers and storekeepers in the neighborhood.[9]

Their commander was confident too, if somewhat less carefree. Lee's order for the army to concentrate at Cashtown was prompted by the report of a Mississippi scout named Henry T. Harrison, who had come into camp on Sunday, June 28, with word that the entire Army of the Potomac was by then north of its namesake river and that Hooker had been replaced by Meade. Such information was not supposed to come from that source, at least not primarily, and therein lay a difficulty for Lee as he faced the prospect of impending battle somewhere in south-central Pennsylvania.[10]

For the year that Lee had now commanded the Army of Northern Virginia, his main reliance for intelligence had been on his cavalry chief, Major General Jeb Stuart, a master of cavalry scouting. Stuart, however, was having a bad month. Surprised at Brandy Station on the 9th, he now had made highly questionable use of the discretion Lee had given him and had taken himself and half his cavalry corps—including the best troops and commanders—on an attempt to ride completely around the Army of the Potomac, as he had done twice before at earlier stages of the war. While Lee was moving northward on the west side of the Army of the Potomac, Stuart would stay east of it, get well north of it, and then cross in front of it to join Lee to the west of the enemy, presumably bringing lots of good information about just where every Federal unit was located.

Unfortunately for Stuart, about the time he launched this effort, Hooker had put the Union army into rapid northward movement, and subsequently Meade had continued that march to the north. Taking the long outside arc and trying to move past the hard-marching blue-coat foot soldiers, Stuart certainly had his information about where the enemy's main body lay. It was right between his own command and the rest of Lee's army, but he could not share that discovery with Lee. Stuart's gray-clad cavaliers had to ride a great deal farther than he had planned to get around the Army of the Potomac, and they were out of contact with Lee at a time when they were supposed to be doing the army's scouting. Although Stuart had left Lee with half the army's cavalry, the brigade commanders he had left behind were not particularly enterprising, and in any case it was Stuart on whom Lee depended to conduct reconnaissance.[11]

The absence of Stuart was a problem but not necessarily a fatal development. Lee had gotten the information he needed, though not from the source he would have preferred. As for the Army of the Potomac, Lee was surprised to hear that it was that close, assuming that Stuart would have informed him as soon as it crossed the river. Nonetheless, it was natural for the Yankees to be where they were. Lee had promised Jefferson Davis that his own northward move would pull the Federals after him, bringing them out of Virginia, and that is what had happened. The silence from Stuart had led Lee to believe that the showdown battle he had come north to seek might be delayed longer than he had initially thought. Harrison's report told him that it was at hand after all. Lee respected Meade, but no general could be expected to have his army fully in hand and responding efficiently to his orders within the space of a few days. That suited Lee well, for he intended to meet the Army of the Potomac, still adjusting to its new commander, just as soon as he could get his own army concentrated. Until that time, perhaps another four or five days hence, he would wait.

Waiting had never come easy to Confederate Third Corps commander Lieutenant General Ambrose Powell Hill. An 1847 West Point graduate and veteran of the Old Army, Hill had during the past year won a reputation as an impetuous and hard-hitting infantry division commander, and in the recent reorganization of the Army of Northern Virginia he had moved up to command the newly created Third Corps, which now lay in its camps in the Cashtown area.

Among Hill's subordinates was the Army of Northern Virginia's newest division commander, Major General Henry Heth. Son of a Virginia planter, Heth had ranked last in the West Point class of 1847, where he had excelled only in accumulating demerits. A regular army officer before the war, he had gone with his native state, and rapid wartime promotion had by this time made him a major general. Heth was at loose ends these last days of June, looking for plundering opportunities that had hitherto been relatively scarce for a division near the middle of the army's far-flung column. Now that he was in Cashtown, at the eastern foot of South Mountain, the lush fields and prosperous villages of Adams County beckoned to him. Somewhere he had heard that there were large quantities

of shoes to be had in Gettysburg, eight miles to the southeast, so on
June 30 he dispatched one of his brigades under Brigadier General
James J. Pettigrew to march over there and see about it. Footwear
was much in demand given the rate at which tens of thousands of
men had been expending shoe leather on the roads of Maryland
and Pennsylvania in recent weeks, but sending an infantry brigade
on a sixteen-mile round trip into unscouted territory was perhaps
not the wisest way to search for it, particularly in a town that had
already received at least a cursory scouring by Early's men. At any
rate, go they did, but around midmorning, on the outskirts of
Gettysburg, they spotted blue-clad soldiers, militia perhaps, but
some of the Confederate officers thought they acted more like veteran troops. Pettigrew decided not to risk a fight and fell back to
Cashtown.

Hill, Heth, and their officers discussed the incident that evening.
Heth felt certain the blue-clad figures spotted that day near
Gettysburg had to be a small and unsupported cavalry force or else
some home guards, probably the latter. Pettigrew, a college professor in civilian life, was not so sure. Those horsemen had looked
like veterans. Hill sided with Heth. He had just talked to Lee, and
the latest intelligence at army headquarters placed the Army of the
Potomac's main strength much farther south, across the state line
in Maryland. Besides, if the Army of the Potomac was indeed near
Gettysburg, that was fine with Hill, who was eager for a fight.
Would Hill have any objection, Heth wanted to know, to his taking
his whole division out to Gettysburg the next day, chasing off those
few horsemen, and giving the town a proper cleaning out?

"None in the world," Hill replied, and so Heth made his plans.
Hill cleared the operation with Lee, who really did not want to
start a battle the next day—not until his whole army was concentrated. However, he had no objection to Heth making a reconnaissance toward Gettysburg, with strict orders that if he encountered
veteran infantry—not militia—he was to halt and report the fact to
headquarters, and, above all, he was not to bring on a major engagement. Hill faithfully repeated his commander's orders to Heth,
who remained unconcerned. Hill also decided to send Major General William Dorsey Pender's division along the road behind Heth,
just in case. In the camps of Heth's division, Pettigrew sought out
his fellow brigade commander, James J. Archer, whose Tennessee
Brigade was slated, in the normal rotation, to have the lead in the
next day's march. Pettigrew wanted Archer to understand that a

solid force of Yankees was out there somewhere to the southeast, and they stood a good chance of running into it around Gettysburg. He also briefed his fellow brigade commander thoroughly on the terrain he would encounter, but Archer remained skeptical.[12]

The troops that Pettigrew's men had spotted near Gettysburg on June 30 belonged to Brigadier General John Buford's cavalry division, scouting ahead of Reynolds's advanced wing of the Army of the Potomac. They rode into Gettysburg that afternoon, 4,000 strong, and the citizens, who had seen Pettigrew's Rebels turn back just outside of town, gave their deliverers an even more emphatic version of the welcome that Pennsylvania and Maryland towns had been showing the troops of the Army of the Potomac in the past few days. Crowds lined the street, cheering, waving flags, and singing patriotic songs. Riding into town from the south, on the Emmitsburg Road, the head of the column reached the town's central square—whence a bewildering multiplicity of roads branched out to the north, east, and west—and paused there while Buford directed his two brigades to the positions he wanted them to take, north and west of town. While the dusty cavalrymen sat their horses in the main street, a little girl dashed out from the cheering crowd on the sidewalk, ran up to a trooper of the Eighth Illinois Cavalry, and tried to reach up and pin a small bouquet of flowers to his jacket. Seeing she could not reach him, he swung down from the saddle, and the child succeeded in pinning her token to his chest. Then she handed him a purple ribbon. "Soldier," she said, "I want you to wear this ribbon in the next fight you're in, the one you're going to have now."

"Thank you, my little lady," replied the cavalryman, "and I will, if there is a fight, but I don't think we will have one."

"Oh, yes, you will, soldier," countered the little girl with a very serious face. "There's thousands of Rebels here, and you will surely have a fight."[13]

Buford would have agreed. As savvy a cavalryman as either side could boast, he smelled trouble. Born in Kentucky, Buford had grown up around Rock Island, Illinois. In 1848, just a year behind Hill and Heth, he graduated from West Point and then went on to serve in the dragoons and become a seasoned veteran of the Old Army's skirmishes with the Sioux. At Blue Water Creek in Nebraska Territory back in 1855 he had won mention for "conspicuous gallantry." He had done well in this war too, gaining a reputation as one of the Army of the Potomac's best cavalry officers, a tough commander

Brigadier General John Buford. Library of Congress, Prints and Photographs Division, LC-B8172-1702

who was "not to be trifled with." In this war, cavalry rarely stood up to infantry for very long, but last summer when Longstreet's corps needed crucial Thoroughfare Gap in Virginia's Bull Run Mountains, Buford and his troopers had held the gap against them for six long hours, waiting for the Federal infantry to come up and relieve them. But the infantry never came. Buford had to give up the gap, and Longstreet went through it and played a key role in the subsequent Confederate victory at Second Bull Run.[14]

Buford at once grasped the importance of Gettysburg. Though a town of only about 2,400 inhabitants, it sat at a hub of the local road network. Like the spokes of a wheel, ten roads radiated out from Gettysburg in all directions. With both armies maneuvering in the area, this was a natural place for them to collide. Buford's patrols had already told him that the main body of the Confederate army lay to the northwest of him, around Cashtown and just beyond it toward Chambersburg. A fine macadamized road, the Chambersburg Pike, ran straight there from Gettysburg. Other patrols, ranging northward in the direction of Carlisle and Heidlersburg, had found substantial numbers of Rebels there too, and Buford even had to worry about some unconfirmed reports of Rebels to the east, on the York Road. He sent full reports to Reynolds, who was encamped with the First Corps about six miles back on the Emmitsburg Road at Moritz's Tavern, and he posted numerous pickets on every possible line of enemy approach. The commander of the Union cavalry corps, Major General Alfred Pleasonton, had given him orders to secure Gettysburg, and he meant to do it. When one of his own subordinates, brigade commander Colonel Thomas C. Devin, remarked that he expected no major Confederate forces and could easily handle anything that might come his way on the morrow, Buford disagreed. "No, you won't," he warned. "They will attack you in the morning and they will come booming—skirmishers three deep. You will have to fight like the devil to hold your own until supports arrive."[15]

Most of Buford's men would have agreed with Devin, expecting no heavy fighting the next day as they cooked their suppers or, in many cases, ate the good food carried out to them by the grateful citizens of Gettysburg. Equally confident of a quiet July 1 were the Rebels, whose campfires Buford's men could dimly see twinkling in the darkness, several miles to the northwest.

NOTES

1. Coddington, *The Gettysburg Campaign*, 111–22.
2. Frasier Rosenkranz to "Dear Cousin," July 20, 1863, Frasier Rosenkranz Papers, Civil War Miscellaneous Collection, USAMHI.
3. Coddington, *The Gettysburg Campaign*, 119–22; OR, vol. 27, pt. 1, pp. 530, 723.
4. Edward J. Nichols, *Toward Gettysburg: A Biography of John F. Reynolds* (University Park: Pennsylvania State University Press, 1958), 3–196; Coddington, *The Gettysburg Campaign*, 122–23.

5. *OR*, vol. 27, pt. 1, p. 144; Coddington, *The Gettysburg Campaign*, 126–31.

6. Freeman Cleaves, *Meade of Gettysburg* (Norman: University of Oklahoma Press, 1960), 3–126; Coddington, *The Gettysburg Campaign*, 209–11; Daniel G. Crotty, *Four Years Campaigning in the Army of the Potomac* (Kearny, NJ: Belle Grove, 1995), 89. On soldier motivation see James M. McPherson, *For Cause and Comrades: Why Men Fought in the Civil War* (New York: Oxford University Press, 1997).

7. Rufus R. Dawes, *A Full Blown Yankee of the Iron Brigade: Service with the Sixth Wisconsin Volunteers* (Madison: State Historical Society of Wisconsin, 1962; reprint, Lincoln: University of Nebraska Press, 1999), 158.

8. Crotty, *Four Years Campaigning*, 88–89.

9. Seymour, *Civil War Memoirs*, 70.

10. Harry W. Pfanz, *Gettysburg—The First Day* (Chapel Hill: University of North Carolina Press, 2001), 21; Bowden and Ward, *Last Chance for Victory*, 142–43.

11. Bowden and Ward, *Last Chance for Victory*, 105–23.

12. Coddington, *The Gettysburg Campaign*, 264; Richard S. Shue, *Morning at Willoughby Run: July 1, 1863* (Gettysburg, PA: Thomas Publications, 1995), 45, 48; David G. Martin, *Gettysburg, July 1* (Conshohocken, PA: Combined Books, 1995), 28–31.

13. Shue, *Morning at Willoughby Run*, 36–37.

14. Pfanz, *Gettysburg—The First Day*, 36; Shue, *Morning at Willoughby Run*, 29.

15. Shue, *Morning at Willoughby Run*, 47; Martin, *Gettysburg, July 1*, 49.

CHAPTER FOUR

I WILL FIGHT THEM INCH BY INCH

DAWN BROKE shortly after 4:30 A.M. on Wednesday morning, July 1, 1863, and about half an hour later Heth's division was on the march for Gettysburg. A light, misty rain had fallen during the night, but the sun rose to partly cloudy skies and the promise of a bright but humid day. In the early hours, before the muggy heat settled down, Heth's marching soldiers enjoyed the fresh, mild breezes and morning smells of field and forest. Their division commander, sporting a new felt hat removed from the dry goods shop of an unhappy Pennsylvanian, rode along with casual unconcern, so oblivious to any possibility of enemy action that he let the corps artillery battalion, under the command of the youthful William J. Pegram, lead the march, while the infantry tramped along behind the guns and caissons.[1]

Meanwhile, six miles south of Gettysburg, Reynolds was reading Meade's marching orders for the day. Meade had been proceeding cautiously, probing forward with his seven small corps but at the same time preparing a contingency plan to fall back and fight along a line his engineers had surveyed near Pipe Creek, in Maryland—provided, of course, that Lee could be induced to such folly as to attack him there. That Meade was still very new to army command was sometimes painfully obvious. Headquarters staff work was not always what it should have been. Also, Meade was showing a bad habit of setting up subordinate commands, such as Reynolds's wing command over the First, Third, and Eleventh Corps, but then ignoring those arrangements and sending orders directly to the corps commanders. This policy had produced bad results on June 30, when Third Corps commander Major General Daniel E. Sickles had received conflicting orders from Meade and Reynolds.[2]

The confusion that followed would not have been so bad if Sickles had possessed one shred of competence for corps command. It was hard to say which aspects of Dan Sickles's career were most notorious. As a corrupt New York politician he was arrogant, flamboyant, and spent money far beyond his visible—that is, legal—means of support. His private life was an ongoing public scandal. His patronage of women of ill repute became difficult to ignore when he escorted one of them into the state legislative chambers. Having married a wife half his age, much to the horror of the young lady's parents, Sickles graduated from fornication to adultery, which he practiced with the same reckless abandon and sordid shamelessness as ever. His story took a new twist when he gunned down Philip Barton Key, son of the author of "The Star Spangled Banner," on the streets of New York for an alleged dalliance with Sickles's wife—with whom the errant husband promptly reconciled. Sickles's successful legal defense on the grounds of "temporary insanity" may have been the nation's first of that sort. Naturally this man without private morals had no public ones either, and as a politician he became an important cog in New York's corrupt Tammany Hall political machine.

When the Civil War broke out, Sickles raised a whole brigade of New York troops, five regiments, and with no other qualifications got himself appointed brigadier general to command them. From that early jump to high rank he had climbed slowly higher until under Hooker's regime he had risen to command the Third Corps. Hooker could empathize with a man who had no morals, and the two became cronies. That closeness helped when Sickles turned in a very questionable performance at Chancellorsville; Hooker let it pass.[3] Thus, on June 30, with conflicting orders from Meade and Reynolds, Sickles took long enough in straightening out the mess that the Third Corps fell well behind the other units of Reynolds's left wing. Its march that day was short and did not start until after midday. If any trouble developed around Gettysburg on July 1, the First and Eleventh Corps would have to get along without the Third.[4]

Meade's marching orders for the first day of July gave destinations for each of the seven corps. The First was to march to Gettysburg, and the Eleventh was to follow and stay in supporting distance, with the Third trailing along behind and just making Emmitsburg. Slocum's Twelfth Corps, part of another wing of the army, would also end its day's march within supporting distance, setting up camp at Two Taverns, four miles southeast of Gettysburg on the Baltimore Pike. The other three corps would be farther off: the Second at Taneytown, the Fifth at Hanover, and the Sixth well to the east at Manchester. Meade directed his generals to dispose

Major General Daniel E. Sickles. Library of Congress, Prints and Photographs Division, LC-8172-1702

of unnecessary impedimenta and to travel light. He also warned that the enemy's "movements indicate a disposition to advance from Chambersburg to Gettysburg," and he called for the distribution to the troops of three days' rations and sixty rounds of ammunition per man, sure signs that a battle was in the offing. Still, Meade was not sure when and where he wanted to meet the enemy. Pipe Creek was appealing, but he was open to Reynolds's advice about whether to fight at Gettysburg.[5]

After receiving Meade's orders, Reynolds put his troops on the march promptly. He did not expect a collision with the Rebels at Gettysburg but rather intended to establish his corps there in support of Buford, who would then probe even farther toward South Mountain and the heart of the Rebel concentration. In the ranks, however, veteran soldiers sensed that battle was not far off, if not this day then not many days thence. With that thought in mind, the men of the Twenty-fourth Michigan, part of the renowned Iron Brigade, assembled for a special prayer service with their chaplain that morning before drawing their hardtack and ammunition in preparation for the day's march. By 8 A.M. the Twenty-fourth, along with the other regiments of the Iron Brigade and the division to which they belonged, Brigadier General James Wadsworth's, was pressing up the road toward Gettysburg, with Reynolds riding at the head of the column. Before leaving he directed Major General Abner Doubleday, the First Corps's senior division commander, to bring up the corps's other two divisions.[6]

It was just as well that Reynolds moved as promptly as he did, for by the time Wadsworth's men took the road, Heth's division had already arrived in the vicinity of Gettysburg. During the march toward Gettysburg, Heth had received another order from Lee, directing him, as he later recalled, "to get the shoes even if I encountered some resistance." This warning may have sobered Heth somewhat and moved him to place some infantry in front of the artillery at the head of his column. Apparently others quickly found out about the order, although in garbled form. A staff officer told Colonel John Brockenbrough, commanding Heth's trailing brigade, that "Gen. Heth is ordered to move on Gettysburg and fight or not as he wishes," leading that officer to comment, "We must fight then; no division general will turn back with such orders."[7]

The first contact between Heth's men and Buford's came about 7:30 A.M., three miles west of Gettysburg on the Chambersburg Pike. Heth's advance guard exchanged shots with the cavalry pickets of the Eighth Illinois Cavalry, and soon each side had deployed a line of skirmishers who were popping away at each other while a couple of Pegram's guns went into battery and started lobbing shells at the Yankees. The cavalry skirmish line grew to include about 300 men. Heth deployed about twice that many in his skirmish line but kept the rest of his 7,000 men in column. A few cavalry pickets were not a problem that would require shaking out a major battle line. Slowly but steadily the Confederate foot soldiers worked their way forward, methodically firing their muzzle-loading rifles—weapons typical of what all the infantry of both armies carried. Stubbornly the dismounted cavalrymen tried to slow them down, firing back with their single-shot, breech-loading carbines—Sharps and other makes. The cavalrymen's weapons had a faster rate of fire, but the infantry rifles held the edge in range.

Man-for-man firepower might have been comparable, but the Confederates had a great many more men, and that enabled them to keep on shoving the blue-jacketed skirmishers farther and farther back. For the cavalrymen, it was a hard fight; for the infantry, a routine skirmish exercise. An hour and a half went by, as did a mile and a half of Pennsylvania countryside, green and still draped here and there with morning mist. About 9:00 A.M., Heth's skirmishers topped out on a ridge, one of the gentle slopes with which this rolling country abounded. Beside the road near the crest stood a tavern owned by a man named Herr, whose name stuck to the landform as well. A long, shallow valley opened out in front of them, bisected by the brush- and briar-choked course of a small stream called Willoughby Run. On the far side of the valley, the better part of a mile away, rose a similar swell of ground called McPherson's Ridge, and on that ridge Buford had drawn up his main battle line, supported by a battery of six guns—all he had.

Immediately the intensity of the fight began to increase. Buford heavily reinforced his skirmish line, down in the brush along Willoughby Run, and Heth reciprocated by adding manpower to his skirmish line as it worked its way down the forward slope of Herr Ridge. Firing picked up, and so did the casualty rates. The Union artillery, Lieutenant John H. Calef's Battery B, Second U.S., opened up, and Pegram responded with seventeen guns of his own. Soon a more or less continuous thunder of artillery was mingling with the crackle of small-arms fire.

Heth now faced the fact that no skirmish line was going to move these stubborn cavalrymen out of his way. He would have to deploy a regular line of battle, and that would take time. He had Pegram cover his front with an artillery bombardment while he deployed Archer's Tennesseeans south of the road and the Mississippians of Brigadier General Joseph Davis's brigade on the north. Davis was a good example of how a young man could advance if he had the right connections. Having Uncle Jefferson in the Confederate White House had done wonders for the career of this young Mississippi lawyer, who could boast no other qualifications for leading a large body of troops in battle. Now he was about to get his first chance to do just that. It would also be the first serious combat for many of his men, since several of his regiments had previously been assigned to garrison duty.

By half past nine, Heth was finally ready to press ahead once more—Archer's and Davis's brigades in line of battle, Pettigrew's and Brockenbrough's well closed up in support, resting in column on the reverse slope of the ridge just behind Herr's tavern. Meanwhile, Heth's artillery and skirmishers had been giving Buford's overmatched cavalry and horse artillery a hot half-hour along Willoughby Run and over on McPherson's Ridge. The battle line swung down from the ridge, and Pegram's guns fell silent as the infantry blocked their field of fire. Calef's Union guns, on the ridge across the way, were anything but silent as they hammered harder than ever at the advancing Confederates. So gradual was the slope of Herr Ridge that the Confederate guns could not open fire again until the infantry line had gone nearly half a mile and was approaching Willoughby Run. Then the ever-combative Willie Pegram had his guns firing again the moment they had a clear shot. In the gray-clad line out front, infantryman W. H. Moon of the Thirteenth Alabama, part of the Tennessee Brigade, felt the universal foot soldier's sentiment about outgoing artillery fire. Recalling the shells "whizzing just above our heads," he thought it "the sweetest music I have ever heard."[8]

Archer's and Davis's men were soon hotly engaging Buford's thin line of dismounted troopers. The Confederates once again had a hefty advantage in numbers, and they overlapped both of Buford's flanks. As the Rebels began to crowd the line closely, Calef's guns became threatened. On the lieutenant's orders the crews limbered up and headed for the rear, subtracting desperately needed firepower. The cavalrymen began to give ground, and it was clear that their line could not hold very long. Buford knew it all too well, but he still had hope that help would arrive in time to save the town of Gettysburg and its important road junctions. About halfway between Buford's line and the town of Gettysburg stood the Lutheran Theological Seminary, and from the cupola of its building some of Buford's signal officers had spotted the head of the First Corps column marching up the Emmitsburg Road. Buford fired off a dispatch to Reynolds, and shortly thereafter the wing commander arrived in person along with several staff officers, having galloped ahead of the marching column. Buford was in the cupola when

Reynolds rode up and dismounted outside the seminary. Clatter-
ing down the stairway, Buford met Reynolds on the way up. "What's
the matter, John?" asked Reynolds.

"The devil's to pay," answered a grim Buford.

Reynolds assured the cavalryman that he would hurry his
whole corps forward to support him. Could Buford hold that
long?

"I reckon I can," came the horse soldier's reply. The two generals then rode out to look over Buford's position and the situation
on his front. What Reynolds saw there was enough to convince him:
he would fight here, but he would have to hurry if he were to get
his First Corps up in time to save Gettysburg and the cavalry. He
sent a series of dispatches—to Wadsworth to get his division closed
up and hurry it onto the battlefield, leaving the Emmitsburg Road
south of town and cutting across the open fields to get to the scene
of the fighting on the west side; to Doubleday to press the march of
the rest of the First Corps; to Oliver O. Howard to speed the march
of the Eleventh Corps; and finally to Meade. To the army commander, fourteen miles away at Taneytown, Maryland, Reynolds
warned, "The enemy are advancing in strong force." But he promised, "I will fight them inch by inch, and if driven into the town, I
will barricade the streets and hold them back as long as possible."
Reynolds told the staff officer carrying that message not to spare
his horse, and apparently he did not. Less than an hour and a half
later, Meade received the message. "Good!" the army commander
exclaimed on hearing it. "That is just like Reynolds; he will hold on
to the bitter end!"[9] By this, however, Meade apparently meant that
Reynolds would hold on and fight inch by inch in a bitter delaying
action as he fell back toward the Pipe Creek line—not that Reynolds
would stay in Gettysburg until the bitter end, for Meade still did
not want to fight his battle there.[10]

Meanwhile, back on the ridges outside Gettysburg, it looked
as if the end was going to be very bitter indeed and soon, too, if
Reynolds could not get his troops up in time. Having given his
dispatches he galloped off with his staff to meet Wadsworth's column and hurry it on. Wadsworth's men were thus far remarkably
oblivious to the crisis toward which they were marching. The same
hazy, moist air that had intensified the pleasant smell of new-mown
hay during the first miles of their march and drenched them with
sweat as the miles wore on seemed also to be smothering the roar
of battle just a few miles away. Several soldiers mentioned hearing

the distant rumble of artillery, but it seemed far off. As the head of the column came within a couple of miles of Gettysburg, soldiers in the lead brigade, Brigadier General Lyman Cutler's, began to meet distraught civilians going the other way, refugees fleeing a Gettysburg that was already feeling the shocking effects of war in its own dooryard; a steady stream of wounded men; and the still more disturbing whine, buzz, or whistle of stray bullets and shells. A soldier of the Seventy-sixth New York in Cutler's brigade remembered seeing "gray-haired old men tottering along; women carrying their children, and children leading each other, while on the faces of all were depicted the indices of the terror and despair which had taken possession of them."[11]

A dawning awareness of the situation gradually spread backward through the column. At the rear of Wadsworth's division marched the Iron Brigade. The Army of the Potomac's only all-western brigade, the Iron Brigade included the Second, Sixth, and Seventh Wisconsin, the Nineteenth Indiana, and the Twenty-fourth Michigan. One of their early brigade commanders back in the spring of 1862 had been John Gibbon, an outstanding officer who both trained them well and also insisted on their unique appearance. While the rest of the army was adopting the less dressy uniform of sack coats and kepi headgear, Gibbon had insisted that his men wear the longer regulation dress frock coat and the regulation Hardee hat, a broad-brimmed, high-crowned black hat worn with one side of the brim pinned up. The uniforms became a badge of honor and the source of one of the unit's nicknames: "the Black Hat Brigade." The "Iron" in their other name had come from a comment by former Army of the Potomac commander George B. McClellan and had been inspired by their remarkable fighting qualities.[12] Gibbon had since been promoted to other duties, and Brigadier General Solomon "Long Sol" Meredith now commanded the Iron Brigade. An Indiana politician before the war, Meredith was short on military knowledge, but at six feet, seven inches in height, he looked imposing.[13]

Bringing up the rear of the Iron Brigade this morning was the Sixth Wisconsin. Its men had been in high spirits, with the regiment's German company, F, belting out one of their stirring marching songs. When the performance concluded, Company K responded with a less majestic but equally spirited rendition of "On the distant prairie where the heifer wild, Stole into the cabbage in the midnight mild." Both were received with hearty cheers by the rest of the regiment. With the town of Gettysburg only another mile or so ahead, the Sixth's commander, Lieutenant Colonel Rufus Dawes, anticipating a joyous greeting from the local citizens and wanting "to make a show in the streets of Gettysburg," had the color bearer unfurl the banner and the regimental fifes and drums strike up "The Campbells Are Coming." The men marched along with a more lively step, apparently still not close enough to Gettysburg to encounter the refugees who were beginning to meet Cutler's men up ahead. Soon the Wisconsin boys heard the rumble of distant cannon, but like the others, Dawes thought it sounded dull and far away and "did not attract our attention as indicating any serious engagement." The sound continued to grow, however, and the final assurance of impending battle came to Dawes when he saw Cutler's brigade, at the head of the column, turn off the road and angle across the open fields to the left, heading straight for the sound of the firing. They were about one mile south of Gettysburg. Dawes, a prosaic soul when combat loomed, told the musicians to stop playing. It seemed that serious business was at hand. Soon both brigades were trotting forward at the double-quick.[14]

In the valley of Willoughby Run, the situation seemed to be developing satisfactorily for Henry Heth and his men. The last of those pesky cavalry skirmishers had finally been cleaned out of the Willoughby Run thickets and driven in on their main line. Now that line looked like it was giving way. Davis's brigade was bending back the north end of the Union line, and Archer's had reached the banks of Willoughby Run. Heth was ready to send it charging across and up the slope beyond to crush the Yankee cavalry for good and all. Archer had his doubts. He was quite a distance now from the support of the rest of the division, and the fighting advance, some of it through woods and brush, had partially disorganized his brigade. The brush along Willoughby Run would increase the disorganization, as would a patch of woods that started on the other side of it, the woodlot of a farmer named Herbst. Heth would have none of it and repeated the order to advance.[15]

Archer's men plunged into the brush and woods, splashed through the creek, and started up the slope beyond, still moving through Herbst's Woods. Carbine fire rattled faster than ever in front of them. Men went down. No matter; Archer's Tennessee and Alabama boys knew they could drive the cavalry. The horse soldiers knew it too, and immediately in front of Archer's men, the Eighth New York Cavalry began to waver.

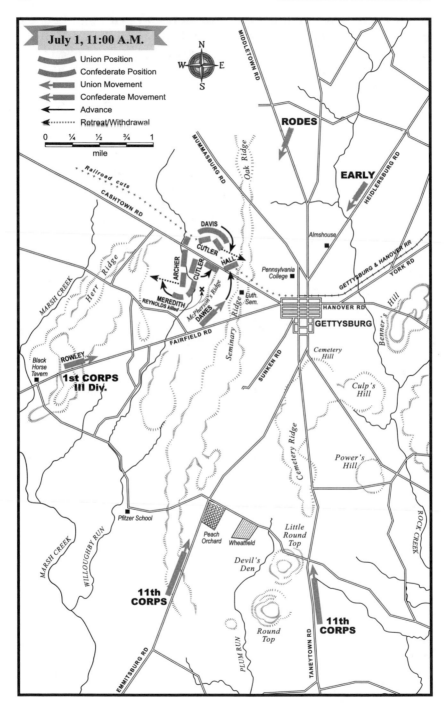

July 1, 11:00 A.M.

Union Position
Confederate Position
Union Movement
Confederate Movement
Advance
Retreat/Withdrawal

0   ¼   ½   ¾   1
mile

On the backside of the ridge, Reynolds and his staff officers galloped this way and that, directing the approaching units of the First Corps. Reynolds sent Captain James A. Hall's newly arrived Battery B, Maine Light Artillery, out the Chambersburg Pike and into battery in a perilously exposed position on the forward edge of McPherson's Ridge. Reynolds told Hall he needed his battery to keep the enemy artillery off the infantry while the men were deploying; then he would pull Hall back to a safer position. He ordered Wadsworth to hustle some infantry in position to support Hall, and Wadsworth passed the order to Cutler, whose five regiments were double-timing past the seminary and across the shallow valley separating Seminary and McPherson's Ridges: support Hall's guns and relieve the crumbling cavalry line north of the pike.

South of the pike the situation was even more desperate. The Eighth New York Cavalry could not keep its grip on Herbst's Woods much longer. Reynolds galloped back to meet the lead regiment of the Iron Brigade, the Second Wisconsin, near the seminary. He led them up the back slope of McPherson's Ridge, loading and fixing bayonets on the run. The other Black Hat regiments double-timed after them, also loading as they went. "You have not a second to lose," a staff officer shouted to the colonel of the Nineteenth Indiana. "The enemy are upon you."[16]

Up ahead, the Second Wisconsin neared Herbst's Woods—no time to wait for the rest of the brigade to catch up, no time for any of the Wisconsin men who had not yet finished loading. Reynolds sent them straight into the woods and followed, urging them on. Just as they reached the edge of the woods a devastating volley erupted almost in their faces. The Fourteenth Tennessee had cut loose at a range of forty or fifty yards. Dozens of Wisconsin boys went down—30 percent of the regiment. The rest returned the fire. Reynolds was right there, spurring his horse up close behind the line. "Forward, men!" shouted Reynolds. "Forward, for God's sake, and drive those fellows out of the woods!" The Second did press forward, fighting their way another fifty yards through the increasingly bullet-torn and smoke-shrouded woodland and driving the Tennesseeans back before them. The colonel and lieutenant colonel of the Second went down.[17]

Reynolds reined his horse around toward the edge of the woods to see if the other regiments of the Iron Brigade were coming up in support. Then, without a word, he slumped and toppled forward to the ground. Startled staff members and orderlies hurried over to him, but he never spoke again. A bullet had struck him in the back of the neck. Aides placed his body on a blanket and carried him off the field, while others dashed off to inform Abner Doubleday, who had just arrived on the field ahead of his troops, that the battle was all his now.[18]

An 1842 West Point graduate, Doubleday was a career army officer who later would be best remembered for something he never did: inventing baseball. His truest moment of fame hitherto had come when the Rebels had started the war by firing on Fort Sumter back in April 1861. It had been Captain Abner Doubleday of the First U.S. Artillery who fired the first answering shot for the Union. Since then he had risen to command a division in the First Corps and had fought in many of the Army of the Potomac's great battles. His tendency to be slow about army maneuvers had gained him a nickname that was a play on his surname, "Old Forty-eight Hours." As it was, about half an hour passed after Reynolds's death before Doubleday even learned of the event. The responsibility fell heavily on Doubleday, for he had not been privy to Reynolds's plans. To a staff officer he commented grimly that "all he could do was fight until he got sufficient information to form his own plans."[19]

The battle surged on. The Second Wisconsin continued to fight Archer's troops in the smoky confines of Herbst's Woods. One by one the other regiments of the Iron Brigade came surging down off Seminary Ridge, deploying and loading their rifles on the run as they crossed the valley to McPherson's Ridge, and then plowed in on the left of the Second. With the impact of each new regiment, the situation of Archer's men became more and more desperate. Legend has it that one of the Tennessee soldiers cursed when he saw the Iron Brigade, taking the appearance of "those Black Hatted fellows again" as proof that this was the Army of the Potomac rather than local militia. At any rate, Archer and his men had good reason to know that they were in serious trouble. With the brigade's left gradually being driven back by the Second Wisconsin, the center and right were not only driven but flanked, enveloped, and all but swallowed up by the rest of the Iron Brigade. Resistance collapsed, and the fight turned into a foot race, with the Tennesseeans and Alabamians thrashing their way frantically back across the broken ground over which they had confidently advanced an hour before and the Black Hat boys in hot pursuit. Several hundred of the Rebels were taken prisoner, including a panting and disheveled Brigadier General James J. Archer, wrestled down by Private

Patrick Maloney of Company G, Second Wisconsin, near Willoughby Run. The Iron Brigade pursued the fleeing remnants all the way to the slopes of Herr Ridge before pulling back to McPherson's Ridge in obedience to orders from Doubleday.[20]

Simultaneous with the fight in Herbst's Woods and the pursuit across Willoughby Run, a much different battle was raging north of the Chambersburg Pike. As ordered, Hall's guns swung into battery on the crest of McPherson's Ridge next to the pike and opened fire on the Confederate guns on Herr Ridge. Cutler's brigade moved up to support Hall, two regiments to his left (south of the pike but north of Herbst's Woods) and three regiments north of the pike. Those three regiments were in for a rude shock. Joseph Davis's Mississippi brigade had drifted north during its advance just as Archer's Tennesseeans had drifted south. That put the two Confederate brigades out of position to support each other, but it also put Davis's brigade on the right flank of the Union troops going into position to support Hall's guns. Worse, Davis outnumbered the three rather small Union regiments by a comfortable margin. The two forces collided, and a short, sharp, and bloody combat flared up. Wadsworth saw that his men were getting the worse of the exchange and ordered the three regiments to pull back. The Seventy-sixth New York and the Fifty-sixth Pennsylvania did so— at high speed and without bothering about formalities of order and formation.[21]

In the 147th New York, however, the message arrived just seconds before the commanding officer was shot. No one else knew of the order to withdraw, and so the men of the 147th, nicknamed "the Ploughboys," stood where they were, on the forward crest of McPherson's Ridge just north of the Chambersburg Pike, and fought on until most of them were down and the rest were all but surrounded. To the 147th's Captain James Coey the sound of a Confederate volley passing over his head "could almost be felt—not the zip of bullets, but a rushing, forcing sound."[22]

Next door, the fight finally got too hot for Hall. At his order the battery limbered to the rear and galloped off, leaving one abandoned gun. Still the 147th stood and fought. Ploughboys might be their nickname, but none could deny they were soldiers this day. Finally, Wadsworth saw what was happening and sent a message to the beleaguered regiment. By that time, getting out of the trap meant a desperate hand-to-hand melee and a mad dash for safety. Some of the New Yorkers stampeded into a railroad cut that paralleled the pike on its north side where it passed over the crest of the ridge. The Rebels trapped scores of them there, blocking the outlet, lining the top of the 15-foot cut, and calling on the fleeing Yankees to throw down their arms. The Federals had no choice but to do so.[23] Less than a quarter of the men of the 147th made it back to where the Fifty-sixth Pennsylvania and the Seventy-sixth New York were regrouping on Seminary Ridge, but the regiment's courageous stand had covered those two regiments' retreat and bought time for Hall to get five of his six guns away and for Union forces south of the pike to react.

Cutler's two regiments south of the pike were the Ninety-fifth and Eighty-fourth New York. The latter preferred to be called by its militia designation, the Fourteenth Brooklyn, or, even better, its nickname, "the Red-legged Devils," derived from the baggy red pants of its French-style chasseur uniforms. When things went to pieces north of the pike, the Red-legged Devils and their fellow New Yorkers of the Ninety-fifth started taking fire from that direction. In response, their commanding officers pivoted them to the right so that their line faced north instead of west, as it had before. They could get away with this because Archer, having drifted away to the south during his advance, was currently getting his brigade roundly thrashed down in Herbst's Woods, a couple of hundred yards farther south. Thus, the Ninety-fifth New York and the Fourteenth Brooklyn could concentrate on Davis's threat from the north side of the pike.

Whether they would have succeeded in stopping Davis by themselves is anybody's guess. Just then the Sixth Wisconsin came trotting up to join the fight. The Sixth was the last regiment in the Iron Brigade's march column, and Doubleday had hastily decided to detach it as a divisional reserve. So instead of joining their fellow Black Hats in rounding up Tennesseeans and Alabamians along Willoughby Run, the Sixth veered off and then almost immediately got orders from Doubleday to move north fast and try to retrieve the situation there. As Rufus Dawes brought his regiment up on the right of the two New York regiments, he saw the opposing Confederate line, which had been advancing toward him just across the pike, suddenly vanish, as though they had dropped into a fissure of the Earth.[24] In a manner of speaking, that is just what had happened to Davis's Mississippians—they had found the railroad cut and jumped into it as a ready-made trench. As a trench, however, the railroad cut had distinct drawbacks. It worked all right at its eastern and western extremities, but in the middle it was so deep that the men could not scramble up the side to use their rifles.

The two lines now exchanged a series of volleys at murderously close range, the Federals south of the pike and the Confederates a few yards north of it in the cut. Bullets flew so thickly around the combatants that a soldier of the Fourteenth Brooklyn thought "the whirring noise they made sounded like the steady rhythm of machinery." Dead and wounded were dropping on all sides. To avoid the intense fire, more of the Confederates crowded into the railroad cut, so that the useless middle section was soon packed from one rocky wall to the other.[25]

Dawes decided to charge. As the Sixth started forward, Dawes saw Major Edward Pye of the Ninety-fifth New York approaching and shouted, "Let's go for them, Major!" Pye turned at once to his troops and shouted, "Forward guide right." Seeing the Black Hats and the Ninety-fifth go forward, the Red-legged Devils joined the movement. Confederate defensive fire was deadly and strewed the pike and the field beyond with blue-clad bodies. The flag of the Sixth Wisconsin fell again and again, till the whole color guard was down, but the Stars and Stripes rose once more, with Dawes carrying it this time and shouting, "Align on the colors! Close up on that color! Close up on that color!" An eager enlisted volunteer took the flag from Dawes as the advance continued.[26]

The last Rebel volley crashed out when the Black Hats were only fifteen feet from the edge of the cut, toppling scores of Wisconsin soldiers. Then Dawes and his men reached the lip of the cut, and the tables were turned as the Union soldiers stood poised to fire down into the packed Confederates. The Sixth's adjutant, Lieutenant E. P. Brooks, lined up a detachment across the mouth of the cut and started firing down its length. With that, the Rebels found themselves in the same trap that had snared the fleeing 147th New York. "Throw down your muskets! Down with your muskets!" shouted the Black Hats, and hundreds of Confederates complied. Lieutenant Colonel Dawes found himself in the embarrassing situation of having his arms filled with no less than seven surrendered swords until the ever-efficient Adjutant Brooks hurried up to relieve him.[27]

Elsewhere along the line, fierce hand-to-hand fighting raged around the Confederate regimental flags. Corporal Eggleston of the Sixth spotted the flag of the Second Mississippi and lunged for it. A Rebel shot him at point-blank range, and he fell mortally wounded.

His comrade, a private whom everyone called "Rocky Mountain" Anderson, brought the butt of his gun crashing down on the head of the Confederate who had shot Eggleston. Lieutenant William Remington went for the flag next, and he, too, was shot. The melee at this particular point ended with Corporal Francis Waller seizing the Rebel flag and keeping it.[28]

Around other knots of resistance, gunshots, bayonet thrusts, and the heavy blows of rifle butts piled the dead and wounded on top of each other, but the Black Hats would not be denied. The New Yorkers soon came up and joined them. Together they took several flags, a few hundred prisoners, Hall's abandoned cannon, and complete control of McPherson's Ridge. The remnants of Davis's brigade fled westward toward Herr Ridge. It was about 11:15 A.M., and for a time the battle subsided into a lull, as if both sides were stunned with the intensity of their collision.[29]

Davis's and Archer's brigades, numbering about 3,800 rifles all told, were wrecked and would take more than twenty-four hours to reconstitute themselves into even minimally effective fighting forces. The Union infantry they had met, two brigades numbering roughly 3,400 men, had suffered heavy casualties but were in much better shape for continued fighting. Cutler's brigade was still useable, and the Iron Brigade, though it had lost many killed and wounded, was as ferocious as ever and ready to take on all comers. When Doubleday rode by their position and exhorted them to hold Herbst's Woods to the last, the Black Hats called back, "If we can't hold it, where will you find men who can?"[30]

On the other side of the valley of Willoughby Run, spirits were not quite so high. The whereabouts of the Army of the Potomac, or a good-sized chunk of it at any rate, seemed to be fairly well established. Archer's and Davis's brigades had set out to drive off some pesky dismounted cavalry, and instead they had charged right into the maw of one of the Army of the Potomac's crack infantry formations and been chewed up and spat out by it. This was not at all the kind of meeting that Rebel soldiers had been telling themselves they would have with the Union army they so often had defeated.

Hill, however, was not finished. If the purpose of the morning's movement had been reconnaissance, as Hill had told Lee the day before, then that purpose would now have been fulfilled. If, on the other hand, the chief object of the movement were shoes, the project was by now obviously uneconomical. Most of the shoes in and around Gettysburg that day already had Union soldiers' feet in them. Confederates could surely find an easier way to supply their army. Hill may have simply been looking for a fight at Gettysburg on July 1. It would have been like him. At any rate, he arrived on the scene in late morning and gave orders to prepare to renew the attack. Earlier that morning he had ordered Pender's division of his corps to follow Heth on the road from Cashtown to Gettysburg. That powerful formation would be coming up to join the two remaining brigades of Heth's division for the next big push.

Despite his apparent eagerness for battle, Hill was a sick man this day and not performing at his usual level. Back in the mid-1840s, while a West Point cadet on leave in New York City, Hill had enjoyed the pleasures of sin for a season and contracted gonorrhea. Now, the better part of two decades later, his sin had found him out, as the disease had become complicated with prostatitis and grown more acute. It had chosen this day to make a grand flare-up and to render Hill more or less ineffective.[31]

Perhaps that was the reason why Hill did not notify his commanding officer that he was in the process of starting a major battle. Perhaps there were other reasons. At any rate, Lee's first notice of the fighting at Gettysburg that morning was the sound of distant artillery that he heard while riding eastward over South Mountain from Fayetteville to Cashtown, to which he had been planning to shift his headquarters. It made Lee nervous, and he fretted about Stuart and why he had heard nothing from his hitherto reliable and informative chief of cavalry. For the moment, however, the general could do nothing but quicken his horse's pace.[32]

Earlier that morning, however, Hill had sent word of his planned march on Gettysburg to Richard Ewell, who had been moving toward Cashtown from the northeast with two divisions. Ewell got the word about 8:00 A.M. Lee's orders had allowed Ewell the discretion to move toward either Cashtown or Gettysburg as circumstances might dictate. Ewell now used that discretion to turn his corps southward, toward the latter place. Rodes made his turn at Middletown and marched south on the Carlisle Road. Early marched toward Gettysburg from Heidlersburg, traveling on the Harrisburg Road. Thus, Early would approach the town from the northeast and Rodes from due north. During the midday hours, while the stillness west of Gettysburg was punctuated by occasional spatters of skirmish fire, three more of the Army of Northern Virginia's large infantry divisions marched steadily toward the once-peaceful crossroads town.

Union reinforcements were also on the way and beginning to arrive. Before his death, Reynolds had sent orders to speed the approach of the remaining two divisions of the First Corps as well as Howard's Eleventh Corps. In Doubleday's division, Simon Hubler, first sergeant of Company C, 143d Pennsylvania, went out foraging during a pause in what had been up to that time a relatively leisurely march, despite the distant rumble of cannon somewhere to the north. When he returned to the resting place, however, he was in for a shock. "The regiment, and in fact, the entire brigade had disappeared," Hubler later wrote. "I found my gun and blanket where I had placed them, and immediately picked them up and hurried on in the direction which the brigade had taken." While he had been scrounging food, a courier had arrived with what Hubler called " 'hurry' orders." Hubler indeed hurried himself and caught up with the 143d a good deal closer to Gettysburg.[33]

As they drew near the fighting, the men witnessed scenes they were to recall for the rest of their lives. Another soldier in the 143d Pennsylvania, Private Avery Harris, saw men, women, and children fleeing in the opposite direction with large numbers of horses, mules, and cattle. He especially remembered a small boy and girl riding a horse together and sobbing. Farther up the road, soldiers of the Ninetieth Pennsylvania passed an elderly gentleman standing in front of his house. Beside him stood his granddaughter, a "blooming lass of 14 or 15 years." As the troops marched past, the old man called out to them in "beseeching, tremulous tones, 'whip 'em, boys, this time. If you don't whip 'em now, you'll never whip 'em.' " The soldiers cheered enthusiastically.[34]

The Eleventh Corps got "hurry" orders too, late that morning several miles from Gettysburg, and the officers put their men to the double-quick to get to town as soon as possible. "The weather was sultry," explained division commander Major General Carl Schurz in his report, "and the troops, who had marched several hours without halting a single time, [were] much out of breath" when they reached Gettysburg early that afternoon.[35]

In the ranks of Howard's panting, sweating men was Sergeant Amos Humiston. In many ways, the thirty-three-year-old Humiston was typical of the older soldiers who had joined the Union army in the second year of the war. He had thought of enlisting when the first call for troops went out in 1861, but he was a family man, with a wife and three children, and it seemed his duty to stay home and take care of them. Union setbacks in the summer of 1862 prompted

Lincoln to issue a call for 300,000 more troops, an initiative that was met with one final patriotic outpouring of enlistment, including many men who, like Humiston, had hesitated at the first call because of family responsibilities. In the evenings, across the North, husbands and wives held hushed and earnest conversations after the children were in bed and concluded that if their country needed men that much, then maybe the man of the house had better go. The surge of enlistments was celebrated by James Sloan Gibbons's song, "We Are Coming, Father Abra'am, Three Hundred Thousand More."[36]

"We've left our plows and workshops," Gibbons had his poetic recruits say, "our wives and children too." Humiston left his harnessmaker's shop in Portsville, New York, in the western part of the state; his wife, Philinda; and his children. Frank had turned eight years old that spring, Alice was six, and Fred was four. Amos carried a photograph of the three in his pocket this day as he jogged along in the ranks of the 154th New York. It was his prized possession, that photo: the three cherubic children, Alice's dress fabric matching that of Frank's shirt, and the two sitting close by either side of little brother Fred. Philinda had sent the photo to Amos less than two months before. "It pleased me more than eney thing that you could have sent me," he had written in reply, "how I want to see them and their mother." But for this first day of July, Amos's prospect, and that of his comrades in the Eleventh Corps, was only for seeing more fighting at Gettysburg.[37]

Howard and his staff galloped ahead of the jogging columns of troops and reached Gettysburg about midday. As senior officer on the field, Howard now superseded Doubleday in command. At thirty-two, Howard was a few months younger than Amos Humiston—an age that was rather mature for a recruit but young for a corps commander. Howard was a military professional, and his intelligence, diligence, and courage had propelled him rapidly upward through the ranks. He had finished fourth out of forty-six in the West Point class of 1854 and served as an instructor at the academy before the war. In an 1862 battle he had lost his right arm. Returning to duty, he had continued to perform well and by the spring of 1863 had risen to command the Eleventh Corps. His first outing as a corps commander, Chancellorsville, had not been a success. Inexperienced at that level of command, he had taken at face value assertions from Hooker's headquarters that the enemy was in retreat and so had been victimized by the surprise flank attack that was Stonewall Jackson's last military accomplishment. It had not been a confidence builder for Howard or for the men of the Eleventh Corps. About half of them were ethnically German and had previously served under Franz Sigel, the dismal Union major general who had made a habit of being victimized by almost every general in the Rebel army before Lincoln mercifully sacked him. The Eleventh Corps would be fighting under the direct command of Carl Schurz today, while Howard assumed overall command of the field.

The first question facing the new Union commander was whether to maintain the position on McPherson's Ridge or to fall back to some other line. He seems not to have lingered long over this choice. Gettysburg was an important road junction, and, after all, Union forces under Reynolds's direction had set out to hold it. Why, then, should Howard not continue to do so? Howard did, however, post one of the three divisions of the Eleventh Corps, when it arrived, on a commanding hill just on the south edge of Gettysburg. That height, because it was the town's burying ground, was known as Cemetery Hill. There the division commanded by Brigadier General Adolph von Steinwehr, including Amos Humiston and the 154th New York, would be a useful reserve if things did not go well in the fields west and north of town.[38]

Conferring with Doubleday, Howard quickly learned that the First Corps commander had no fears for the security of his left flank, south of Herbst's Woods near the Fairfield Road, which he had just reinforced with the newly arrived First Corps division of Brigadier General John C. Robinson, while he held Rowley's division in reserve near the seminary. His right, however, was another story. Buford's patrols had brought continuous updates all morning regarding the approach of Ewell's corps from the north, and it was on that end of the field that Doubleday wanted support. He had already decided to angle his line backward at the railroad cut, so that his troops north of that point would face northwest. The terrain there became rather more complicated. McPherson's and Seminary Ridges gradually converged as they ran northward, and at the place of their convergence stood a somewhat higher eminence known as Oak Hill. The hill also lent its name to the northernmost stretch of Seminary Ridge, which went more commonly by the alternate name of Oak Ridge. As the ridges grew closer together near Oak Hill, the valley between them became little more than a shallow swale, scarcely lower than the level of the ridge tops. Thus, it

Major General Oliver O. Howard. Library of Congress, Prints and Photographs Division, LC-8172-3719

was practical for Doubleday to think in terms of angling his line back from McPherson's to Seminary (or Oak) Ridge.

To meet the threat to Doubleday's northern flank, Howard decided to deploy the two remaining divisions of the Eleventh Corps at right angles to the First Corps, facing north on a line that ran across a broad, open, and almost perfectly level valley north of town. That deployment might have had much to recommend it if Schurz's two divisions had been anywhere near large enough to cover the ground involved. As it was, their line was appallingly thin—in many places little more than a heavy skirmish line—and it did not connect with the north end of Doubleday's line, leaving a gap of several hundred yards. Still, if the Federals were going to hold Gettysburg that day, they had little choice but to form a line somewhere on the north side of town.

While Howard dealt with the immediate threats to the Union position at Gettysburg, he also fired off messages to Meade and to fellow corps commanders Sickles of the Third and Slocum of the Twelfth. Sickles was near Emmitsburg, and Slocum was about that time arriving with his corps at Two Taverns, about four miles southeast of Gettysburg on the Baltimore Pike. Howard, who had in the past twenty-four hours held thorough discussions with Reynolds and imbibed some of that general's aggressive spirit, hoped that both Sickles and Slocum would press their troops toward Gettysburg as he had done. Indeed, he seemed to assume that a mere statement that the First and Eleventh Corps were confronting the enemy there would suffice to bring the other two corps at the double-quick. Not all of the Army of the Potomac's generals, however, would necessarily react the same way to the same operational situation. This was especially true now because Meade, partly to stay flexible and partly because he was still not quite sure of himself in command of the army, had not enunciated a clear program of operations spelling out what the army was trying to do next. In fact, such direction as he had given thus far tended to discourage Slocum and Sickles from rushing to Gettysburg. That morning, Meade had set forth his Pipe Creek plan in a circular order to all of his corps commanders, but it was too late to reach Reynolds and Howard. The others, however, had evidence in black and white that what their commanding general wanted was a fighting withdrawal to the Pipe Creek line, not a hasty advance.

Indeed, along with the copy of the circular that went to Slocum, Meade included a note informing the Twelfth Corps commander that "the enemy are advancing in force on Gettysburg" and implying that Reynolds would make a slow fighting retreat before them. On notification from Reynolds that he had uncovered Slocum's assigned position at Two Taverns, Slocum was to implement the circular immediately, falling back to the Pipe Creek line. In the meantime, Meade ordered Slocum to halt the Twelfth Corps wherever he was when the order reached him (probably at Two Taverns) and to order Fifth Corps commander Major General George Sykes, now operating under Slocum's authority, to halt his corps at

Hanover, thirteen miles east of Gettysburg, and await develop-
ments. Strict and faithful obedience to orders was at the very core
of Slocum's character as a soldier. If Meade ordered him to stay
put at Two Taverns, notwithstanding whatever fighting might be
going on four miles up the road at Gettysburg, then that is exactly
what Henry W. Slocum would do.[39]

Meade was still inclined to withdraw to Pipe Creek. He worried that Confederate possession of the road junction at Gettysburg
and the high ground south and east of town might allow Lee to
block the consolidation of the Army of the Potomac on the Pipe
Creek line or even allow the Rebel commander to insert his own
army between the two severed and vulnerable halves of Meade's
force. Yet Meade remained uncertain as to whether Gettysburg
would be a good place to fight—more uncertain when he learned
about midday that Reynolds was dead. Rather than ride to
Gettysburg himself, as Lee was even then doing, Meade decided to
send another trusted subordinate. Second Corps commander Major General Winfield S. Hancock was one of the Army of the
Potomac's most junior corps commanders. Although thirty-nine
years old, he was outranked by Sickles, Howard, Slocum, Sixth
Corps commander Major General John Sedgwick, and (before his
death that very morning) Reynolds. Still, he was confident, force-
ful, and well liked by Meade, who ordered him early in the afternoon to ride to Gettysburg, take command of the forces in the
area—including his seniors Howard and Sickles—and decide what
to do.[40]

At about that same time, a little after midday, Slocum at Two
Taverns on the Baltimore Pike was receiving his own message from
Howard regarding the morning's events. It vouchsafed that the First
Corps had encountered the enemy at Gettysburg and that the Eleventh Corps was there. It did not mention that Reynolds was dead.
Slocum and his command had arrived at Two Taverns shortly before noon, and since no heavy fighting was occurring at that time,
they could hear only the rumble of moderate artillery fire. Slocum
assumed there was no reason for him to push his troops the additional four miles to join Howard in what was apparently an inconsequential skirmish. Indeed, the fighting apparently taking place
at Gettysburg was exactly what Meade had predicted in that
morning's dispatch, the same that had ordered Slocum to stop and
prepare to fall back on Pipe Creek.

Major General Winfield S. Hancock. Library of Congress, Prints and Photographs Division, LC-8172-1877

It is hard to fault Slocum for obeying orders, but his decision contrasts poorly with Ewell's prompt determination to march on Gettysburg in support of Hill. The difference between that spirit of aggressive cooperation and the stolid cross-purposes of the Army of the Potomac's generals goes far toward explaining why the Army of Northern Virginia was in the habit of beating its more numerous opponent.[41] For the next few hours, Howard would be on his own at Gettysburg with the First and Eleventh Corps.

NOTES

1. Pfanz, *Gettysburg—The First Day*, 51–68.
2. Martin, *Gettysburg, July 1*, 50–51.
3. William Glen Robertson, "The Peach Orchard Revisited: Daniel E. Sickles and the Third Corps on July 2, 1863," in *The Second Day at Gettysburg*, ed. Gary W. Gallagher (Kent, OH: Kent State University Press, 1993), 33–41.
4. Martin, *Gettysburg, July 1*, 50–51; *OR*, vol. 27, pt. 1, p. 530.
5. *OR*, vol. 27, pt. 3, p. 416; Martin, *Gettysburg, July 1*, 55.
6. *OR*, vol. 27, pt. 1, p. 244; Pfanz, *Gettysburg—The First Day*, 71.
7. Shue, *Morning at Willoughby Run*, 50, 58.
8. Martin, *Gettysburg, July 1*, 81–83.
9. Ibid., 97–98; Shue, *Morning at Willoughby Run*, 93–94.
10. *OR*, vol. 27, pt. 3, p. 462.
11. Shue, *Morning at Willoughby Run*, 90.
12. William Thomas Venner, *The 19th Indiana Infantry at Gettysburg: Hoosiers' Courage* (Shippensburg, PA: Burd Street Press, 1998), 18–19, 29.
13. Ibid., 9–11.
14. Dawes, *A Full Blown Yankee of the Iron Brigade*, 164; Pfanz, *Gettysburg—The First Day*, 72; Martin, *Gettysburg, July 1*, 101–2.
15. Martin, *Gettysburg, July 1*, 85.
16. Robert B. V. Bird to "Frend Rosey," August 21, 1863, Bird Family Papers, State Historical Society of Wisconsin, Madison; Roswell L. Root to "Dear Grand Father," August 23, 1863, Roswell L. Root Papers; quote from Venner, *The 19th Indiana*, 52.
17. *OR*, vol. 27, pt. 1, p. 273; Pfanz, *Gettysburg—The First Day*, 93.
18. Martin, *Gettysburg, July 1*, 140–45; Shue, *Morning at Willoughby Run*, 110; *OR*, vol. 27, pt. 1, p. 244.
19. Stewart Sifakis, *Who Was Who in the Civil War* (New York: Facts on File, 1988), 87–88; *OR*, vol. 27, pt. 1, p. 244; Jacob F. Slagle to "Dear Brother," September 13, 1863, Jacob F. Slagle Papers, USAMHI.
20. *OR*, vol. 27, pt. 1, pp. 245, 267–68, 274; Venner, *The 19th Indiana*, 54–58.
21. *OR*, vol. 27, pt. 1, pp. 266, 281–82.
22. Pfanz, *Gettysburg—The First Day*, 87.
23. *OR*, vol. 27, pt. 1, p. 245; Pfanz, *Gettysburg—The First Day*, 83–88.
24. Dawes, *A Full Blown Yankee of the Iron Brigade*, 164–66; *OR*, vol. 27, pt. 1, pp. 275–76.
25. Pfanz, *Gettysburg—The First Day*, 106–7.
26. Dawes, *A Full Blown Yankee of the Iron Brigade*, 166–68; Pfanz, *Gettysburg—The First Day*, 109.
27. *OR*, vol. 27, pt. 1, pp. 245–46, 275–76, 286–87; Dawes, *A Full Blown Yankee of the Iron Brigade*, 168–69.
28. Dawes, *A Full Blown Yankee of the Iron Brigade*, 168–69.
29. *OR*, vol. 27, pt. 1, pp. 245–46, 275–76, 286–87.
30. Coddington, *The Gettysburg Campaign*, 274–75; *OR*, vol. 27, pt. 1, p. 244.
31. James I. Robertson Jr., *General A. P. Hill: The Story of a Confederate Warrior* (New York: Random House, 1987), 11–12, 206–9.

32. Coddington, *The Gettysburg Campaign*, 280.

33. Simon Hubler Narrative, Simon Hubler Papers, Civil War Miscellaneous Collection, USAMHI.

34. Pfanz, *Gettysburg—The First Day*, 126, 129.

35. *OR*, vol. 27, pt. 1, p. 727.

36. Mark H. Dunkelman, *Gettysburg's Unknown Soldier: The Life, Death, and Celebrity of Amos Humiston* (Westport, CT: Praeger, 1999), 48–56.

37. Ibid., 104.

38. *OR*, vol. 27, pt. 1, p. 702.

39. *OR*, vol. 27, pt. 3, p. 462.

40. Coddington, *The Gettysburg Campaign*, 283–85.

41. Harry W. Pfanz, *Richard S. Ewell: A Biography* (Chapel Hill: University of North Carolina Press, 1998), 302–14; Brian C. Melton, "Henry W. Slocum" (Master's thesis, Texas Christian University, 2001).

CHAPTER FIVE

LIKE GRASS BEFORE A SCYTHE

FOUR MILES NORTH of Gettysburg, Major General Robert E. Rodes was startled to hear the sounds of heavy gunfire coming from the south about midmorning of that day. A former professor at the Virginia Military Institute, the thirty-four-year-old Rodes was one of the Army of Northern Virginia's most aggressive and successful officers, but he did not have the advantage of having under his command a cavalryman as tough and effective as John Buford. Whereas Buford kept his superiors constantly informed about the approach of Rodes's division, Rodes himself could get no information at all about what was going on at Gettysburg—except what the sound of the cannon told him when he was within four miles of town. That was his first hint that a major battle was in progress, but being the sort of commander he was—and the Army of Northern Virginia being the sort of army it was—he had no hesitation about what to do next.

Rodes's division was the largest in either army. With five brigades totaling 8,000 men, it was about the size of some of the smaller Union corps. It was also a crack unit—tough, experienced, and battle-proven. Rodes moved it rapidly toward the sound of the guns. On reaching the battlefield, he discovered that the Carlisle Road, approaching Gettysburg from the north, ran parallel and quite close to a northern extension of Oak Ridge, north of Oak Hill. Deploying off the road and onto the wooded ridge, Rodes realized that he could not only strike the Federals in flank and with an advantage of terrain but also take them by surprise. After advancing about a mile along the ridge, Rodes arrived on the summit of Oak Hill and surveyed the scene with intense satisfaction. Before him he could see the whole Union force that had stopped Henry Heth that morning. The Federal flank was about half a mile away, and Rodes could see not a single blue-coat foot soldier who was facing toward him. It was a glorious sight for an aggressive commander with a big, fresh division. Apparently he had succeeded in catching the Yankees by surprise, and now he would make them pay.[1]

His attached battalion of artillery opened fire on the bluecoats while Rodes lined up his division for the attack. The Confederate cannoneers on Oak Hill had an ideal position: high ground on the Federal flank that let them rake the whole length of the Union line. Union batteries near the Chambersburg Pike were soon returning the fire. Before Rodes could actually launch the attack, his excitement was abated somewhat by seeing the Eleventh Corps coming out of the north side of Gettysburg and deploying facing toward him in the open ground north of town, to his left front. Also, Lyman Cutler's brigade of the First Corps pulled back from its position near the railroad cut to a woodlot on the crest of Seminary Ridge, with about half the brigade facing north toward Rodes. Clearly, the Yankees were catching on. Still, the Eleventh Corps's line did not tie into that of the First Corps on Seminary Ridge. Very well, then. Rodes would stiff-arm the Eleventh Corps with one of his brigades, thus covering his left flank, and hope Jubal Early would show up soon to deal with those Federals properly. Meanwhile, Rodes would hold one brigade in reserve and use the remaining three to sweep the Yankees off of Oak, Seminary, and McPherson's Ridges and thus end the day's fighting with the customary glorious Confederate victory. At 2:30 P.M. all was finally ready, and Rodes's division launched its mighty juggernaut advance that he felt sure would sweep the length and breadth of the western ridges.[2]

The assault ran into trouble almost before Rodes's troops came down from Oak Hill. That was partly Doubleday's fault. He had not been taken by surprise, as Rodes had imagined. Thanks to Buford, he had had ample warning of the Confederates' approach. Aside from urging Howard to deploy the Eleventh Corps north of town—a movement that Rodes noticed—Doubleday had also responded to the threat to his flank by sending one brigade of his reserve division to strengthen and extend the north end of his line. That movement was noticed neither by Rodes nor by any of his officers. The new brigade, commanded by Brigadier General Henry Baxter, had marched north along the east side of Oak Ridge. The woods on the crest of the ridge, which Rodes had thought would conceal his own approach, turned out to work just as well for hiding Yankees as they might have done for hiding Rebels. Besides, the ridge itself helped keep Baxter's men from the eyes of Rodes's division. Baxter reached the Mummasburg Road, which angled northwest to southeast across Oak Ridge at the very foot of Oak

Hill on its way to Gettysburg. There, Baxter arranged his brigade with two regiments facing west and sheltering behind a low stone wall at the crest of the ridge while the other four regiments formed a line angling back very sharply (about 135 degrees) along the Mummasburg Road, facing northeast. Baxter then waited, ready for business on either front.

Not all of Rodes's problems, however, were of Doubleday's making. The two brigades that led off the assault were composed of good troops but had questionable commanders. One brigade was to advance on either side of the crest of Oak Ridge. Colonel Edward A. O'Neal, who was to take the east side with his Alabama brigade, went wrong from the start. Instead of leading his troops forward, as brigade commanders were expected to do, O'Neal sent them forward while he himself remained in relative safety in the rear. Compounding that error, he became confused, advanced only three of his five regiments, and sent them off on the wrong heading. That made Baxter's job easy. His men, steadying their rifles on the rails of the fence on the south side of the Mummasburg Road, mowed down O'Neal's Alabamians, breaking up the attack and sending three regiments of brave veteran troops fleeing to the rear in what was probably the quickest defeat they had ever suffered.

That left Baxter's four regiments along the Mummasburg Road with time on their hands and nothing to do. Behind them, their comrades of the two regiments along the stone wall quickly informed them of impending action there, as the other leading brigade of Rodes's advance was moving southward along the gentle west slope of Oak Ridge. Baxter and his officers deftly swung three of the four regiments from the Mummasburg Road up to the stone wall, so that five-sixths of the brigade's firepower was massed there. The Yankees crouched behind the wall and waited while the Confederate formation drew closer. Its splendid parade-ground lines were not marching toward Baxter's position but moving as if to pass directly across its front from north to south. Gradually the neat gray lines seemed to alter their course slightly to their left (eastward), still not marching toward Baxter's position along the stone wall, but now on a course to pass even more closely across its front. Perhaps the Confederates began making toward Cutler's brigade's position in a point of woods several hundred yards farther south. The fact was that Brigadier General Alfred Iverson had chosen to remain in the rear while his brigade of North Carolinians

marched forward without anyone actually commanding or control-
ling the course of the advance. The brigade was apparently drifting like a boat with no one at the tiller.

When the flank of Iverson's brigade, still seemingly completely
oblivious to Baxter's presence, reached almost point-blank range
directly in front of the stone wall, Baxter's line rose up and raked
the whole length of the Confederate formation with a devastating
volley that cut down whole ranks of North Carolinians. By one account, 500 fell killed or wounded in the first volley. Iverson's men
never had a chance. Their dead lay in the same neat rows in which
the brigade had been marching the moment before disaster struck.
Lieutenant George B. Bullock of the Twenty-third North Carolina
recalled that it was the only occasion in his wartime experience
"where the blood ran like a branch." The survivors tried to take
shelter by lying flat in the shallow swale in front of Oak Ridge, but
Baxter's men, now steadying their rifles on the top of the stone
fence, "done some wicked firing into the mass of Confederate soldiers lying down in the field within short musket range," as one of
the Union soldiers recalled.[3]

Iverson's men soon found that further attempts at resistance
would serve no purpose beyond getting the rest of them killed as
well. They began to wave handkerchiefs tied on the ends of ram-
rods in token of surrender. Baxter's troops dashed forward and
gathered in a massive haul of prisoners and several flags before
Rodes's artillery on Oak Hill forced them to scamper back to cover
in the original position. Iverson, who had been watching from a
safe distance, became hysterical and told Rodes that "one of his
regiments had raised the white flag and gone over to the enemy."
If he had been leading his troops as was his duty, he would have
known otherwise. "Deep and long," wrote one of the survivors,
"must the desolate homes and orphan children of North Carolina
rue the rashness of that hour."[4]

The third brigade in Rodes's assault had little choice but to
withdraw after the debacles of O'Neal and Iverson. With that, the
glorious opportunity Rodes thought he had perceived as he approached Gettysburg from the north had flickered out. Nothing had
been accomplished beyond the wrecking of two more Confederate
brigades. Things were not supposed to happen this way in the Army
of Northern Virginia, but Rodes immediately began preparing to
renew the attack with his remaining brigades.

Lee had arrived at Heth's position on the Chambersburg Pike at about 2:00 P.M. When Heth saw Rodes's division going into action on Oak Ridge, he asked Lee for permission to add the weight of his own division to the attack. Lee at first refused, still wanting to avoid a general engagement until Longstreet's corps came up. Heth persisted, however, pointing out that the Federals were shifting troops northward from his front to combat Rodes. Finally, Lee relented. Heth lined up his two as yet unused brigades, Pettigrew's and Brockenbrough's, for another go at Doubleday's position along McPherson's Ridge. His renewed push along the Chambersburg Pike coincided with Rodes's second effort against Oak Ridge.

James Johnston Pettigrew was a colorful character. He had graduated from the University of North Carolina at age fourteen and gone on to learn six languages, study in Europe, teach at the U.S. Naval Observatory, and then practice law. He had recently returned to duty after recovering from a wound received at Seven Pines. Pettigrew's brigade was large, containing as it did the oversized Twenty-sixth North Carolina. The war had been relatively kind, thus far, to the Twenty-sixth. It had spent much time in garrison duty on the North Carolina coast, and though it had seen such major battles as Seven Pines and Malvern Hill, it had escaped the kind of catastrophic casualties that by this stage of the conflict had reduced most regiments to less than half their original strength. The Twenty-sixth still boasted 800 men, three times the size of many regiments at Gettysburg. The regiment's colonel, twenty-one-year-old Henry K. Burgwyn, was almost as remarkable as Pettigrew. Young, handsome, and brilliant, Burgwyn was the idol of his regiment. As a Virginia Military Institute cadet, Burgwyn four years earlier had attended the hanging of old John Brown, the violent abolitionist crusader. In 1861, when Burgwyn graduated and the South chose secession and war, the young North Carolinian's military training had been at a premium, and he had risen rapidly to the command of the Twenty-sixth, which now formed the strong center of Heth's attacking line.[5] Brockenbrough's brigade, unlike Pettigrew's, was distinctly under strength. The two together numbered more than 3,500 men, and they formed a line that spanned the First Corps front on McPherson's Ridge and extended beyond it several hundred yards to the south.

Holding that Union line south of the Chambersburg Pike were three brigades. Colonel Roy Stone's brigade was composed of three

Pennsylvania regiments, the 143d, 149th, and 150th. They had been enlisted as expert marksmen and affected the title of "Bucktails" in imitation of the original Bucktails of the Thirteenth Pennsylvania Reserves Regiment, of which Stone had been major earlier in the war. Recruited in the late summer of 1862, the 143d, 149th, and 150th had been with the army for a number of months and had seen great battles. This, however, would be their first time to serve at the vortex of such a conflict. The brigade deployed around the buildings of the McPherson farm, just south of the Chambersburg Pike. It had two of its three regiments facing north to counter the pressure from Rodes's division.[6]

The constant skirmish firing and steady shelling made life tenuous in the exposed position near the McPherson farm. While the 143d Pennsylvania was standing in reserve prior to taking its position in line north of the Chambersburg Pike, a bullet from Confederate skirmishers several hundred yards out in front struck Jacob Yale above the eye, and he became the first fatality of the war from Company I of that regiment. Standing next in line to the fallen Yale, Sergeant Simon Hubler heard his company's first sergeant order the men to close up the gap in the line and noted, "This the men did with serious faces."[7]

Just south of Stone's brigade was the Iron Brigade still holding Herbst's Woods. During the noon lull, the Black Hat soldiers had received an unusual reinforcement. Gettysburg citizen John L. Burns, age seventy, was tall and rangy. Dressed in an ancient blue swallowtail coat and a high-crowned, broad-brimmed black hat of similar vintage, he looked to one soldier like an image of Uncle Sam sprung to life. In his hands, Burns carried a rifle, and his pockets bulged with ammunition. A veteran of the War of 1812, he had served for many years as Gettysburg's town constable. To one of the amused soldiers he explained that the Rebels had taken his cows and he intended to get even with them. "I will show you that there is one man in Gettysburg who is not afraid," the grim-faced Burns proclaimed. The soldiers chuckled at first but gained a new respect for him when they saw him down on the skirmish line along Willoughby Run, picking off unwary Rebels across the valley.[8]

Also joining the ranks of the Iron Brigade during the noon lull was the Nineteenth Indiana's color bearer, Sergeant Burl Cunningham. Wounded in the morning's fight with Archer's brigade, Cunningham had gone to the rear, been treated, and returned to his regiment. Now, his side swathed in bandages, he was once again carrying the Nineteenth's U.S. flag.[9]

To the left of the Iron Brigade, Colonel Chapman Biddle's brigade extended the line southward to the Fairfield Road. The position offered little cover, and Biddle's men were too few to defend it effectively. Beyond them, only the Eighth Illinois Cavalry, one of Buford's regiments, screened their southern flank. The First Corps had no reserve behind it now, since Doubleday had been compelled to dispatch his last brigade of reserves to reinforce Baxter's position up on the north end of the First Corps line.

John L. Burns with his flintlock after the battle. Library of Congress, Prints and Photographs Division, LC-B8171-2402

At 2:30 P.M., Heth's Confederates advanced and ran head-on into the Yankee line. What followed was one of the most ferocious hours of fighting in American history. Stone's Bucktails clung tenaciously to the McPherson farm despite their difficult position at the point where the Union line hinged back toward Oak Ridge, which exposed them to attack both from Heth's men, to the west, and Rodes's, advancing from the north. Ordered to commence firing, Sergeant Hubler could see no enemies closer than those on distant Herr Ridge. He had just taken a long-range shot in that direction when he saw the Rebels charging out of the railroad cut toward him and his comrades of the 143d Pennsylvania. "We fired into their ranks and drove them back," Hubler recalled.[10]

Colonel Stone skillfully maneuvered his brigade to meet the various threats and at one point used the railroad cut as a covered approach to launch the 149th Pennsylvania on a successful temporary counterattack. The tide of battle ebbed and flowed, with first one side and then the other charging and driving the foe back, only to give way in turn. Presently, Stone went down, and one of his colonels took over. Then he, too, was shot, and the command passed to another. Still, the Bucktails held their ground.[11]

To the south of Stone's brigade, in Herbst's Woods, the oversized Twenty-sixth North Carolina, of Pettigrew's brigade, ran up against the much smaller Twenty-fourth Michigan and Nineteenth Indiana of the Iron Brigade. A bit farther down the line, the Eleventh North Carolina bore down on the left half of the Nineteenth Indiana's line. Colonel Henry A. Morrow of the Twenty-fourth told his men to hold their fire for point-blank range, and when the Rebels came close the Michigan men blasted a devastating volley into their faces. The Hoosiers of the Nineteenth did the same, felling scores of Southerners. Nevertheless, the North Carolinians "came on with rapid strides," Colonel Morrow reported, "yelling like demons." At murderously close range the two lines traded rifle fire as fast as their soldiers could ram down new loads and squeeze their triggers. Swarms of bullets shredded the thick underbrush and whittled away at the trunks of trees. One of the first Confederate volleys cut down the bandaged Sergeant Cunningham bearing the national flag of the Nineteenth Indiana. The Stars and Stripes were soon up again, this time in the hands of Corporal Abe Buckles of the color guard. Moments later he went down, and another Hoosier took up the flag.[12]

While the Black Hat boys held their ground in Herbst's Woods and Stone's Bucktails clung to the McPherson farm like grim death, the brigade on the far left of the Union line was in serious trouble. Colonel Biddle's three small regiments had little cover in their position and now found themselves badly outflanked. They fought hard, but after more than a third of their number had been shot down, their line crumbled and went streaming back toward Seminary Ridge.[13]

Union dead near the McPherson farm. Library of Congress, Prints and Photographs Division, LC-B8171-0234

The defeat of Biddle exposed the left flank of the Iron Brigade, and Pettigrew's determined North Carolinians slowly and painfully began to pry loose its grip on Herbst's Woods. Half of the Eleventh North Carolina swept around the end of the brigade's line and slammed down on the single company of the Nineteenth Indiana covering that flank. The Hoosiers stood their ground with bayonets and rifle butts against ten times their number of Rebels, but the North Carolinians surged over them. Fighting furiously, the Eleventh rolled up the Nineteenth's line before its other companies, hard-pressed in front, could turn to face the new threat. The Nineteenth's left wing was slaughtered, and what was left of the regiment scrambled for safety.[14]

Next in line, the Twenty-fourth Michigan tried desperately to hang on. Colonel Morrow drew his line back a few feet to a position where his men could rally. The remnant of the Nineteenth Indiana took up position on their left flank again, now facing south. Twenty-year-old Sergeant Major Asa Blanchard rallied the Hoosiers, waving the now-tattered Stars and Stripes above his head. Together

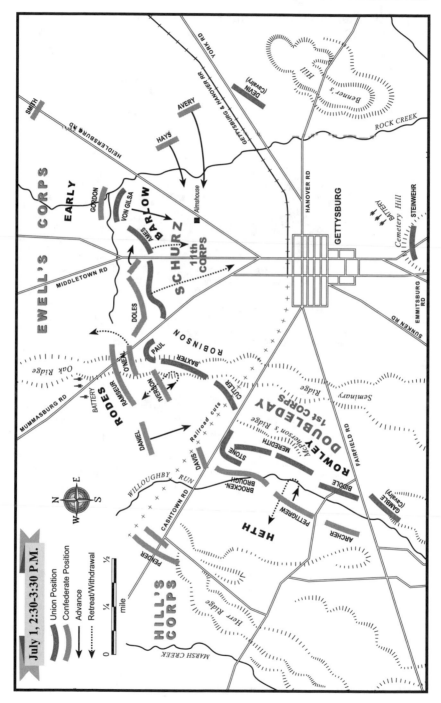

the Michigan and Indiana boys held on for a time there, but again the pressure became too great. Blanchard went down with a mortal wound. In the Twenty-fourth Michigan, on its way to an 80 percent casualty rate, little more than one in four remained of the 496 men the regiment had carried into battle that morning. When the regiment's fourth color bearer of the day went down, Morrow himself picked up the fallen flag, but Private William Kelly of Company E took it from him, saying, "The colonel of the Twenty-fourth shall never carry the flag while I am alive." The words were hardly out of his mouth when he fell to the ground, shot dead. By this time the regiment was being forced steadily back, grudgingly but inexorably, across the shallow valley toward Seminary Ridge. Still urging his men to hold fast, Morrow grabbed the colors from the soldier who had taken them from the dying Kelly and called on his men to rally. Not long afterward, he, too, went down, badly wounded, and the Twenty-fourth continued its fighting retreat to Seminary Ridge.[15]

For the Iron Brigade's foes of the Twenty-sixth North Carolina, the fight was equally intense. In its midst an aide-de-camp of General Pettigrew had ridden to Colonel Burgwyn with a message. "Tell him," Pettigrew had said, "his regiment has covered itself with glory today." By that time nine men had fallen carrying the regiment's colors. As the last member of the color guard fell, the Confederate flag remained lying on the ground. The two nearest companies, E and F, had been all but wiped out. Brigade staff officer Captain Westwood McCreery snatched up the fallen staff and waved the colors above his head as he stepped out to lead the regiment forward. Almost instantly a bullet slammed into his chest, and he toppled forward. Lieutenant George Wilcox pulled the blood-stained banner from under the fallen McCreery but had gone only a few steps when he, too, was hit, then hit a second time, and he collapsed. Young Colonel Burgwyn found the flag lying beside the fallen Wilcox. Seizing it, he flourished his sword in one hand, the flag in the other. "Dress on the colors," he shouted, and the dwindling survivors tried to close up their line and press forward behind the colonel. Burgwyn had just handed the flag to Private Frank Honeycutt when another searing volley flashed out from the lines of the Twenty-fourth Michigan. Honeycutt fell dead, Burgwyn dying.[16]

By the time the North Carolinians reached the crest of McPherson's Ridge, Lieutenant Colonel John R. Lane was leading them, carrying the colors. Watching from afar, Pettigrew thought Lane's was "the bravest act I ever saw." As the Twenty-fourth Michigan fell back toward Seminary Ridge, one of its soldiers put a bullet through Lane's jaw, and the colors of the Twenty-sixth North Carolina fell for the fourteenth and final time that day. The entire oversized Tarheel regiment, more than 800 strong, had by this time suffered a casualty rate of 73 percent. That evening there would be only 216 members of the Twenty-sixth North Carolina left unscathed by Union fire. In Company E, which started the attack with ninety-one men, only one man remained standing when the regiment's fight was over.[17]

Meanwhile, on the right of the Iron Brigade, the Second and Seventh Wisconsin fought hard and also suffered heavy casualties, but they, too, had to give way to the overwhelming pressure of numbers, front and flank. As the Black Hats grudgingly fell back and Pettigrew's survivors followed at a respectful distance, Stone's Pennsylvanians found themselves holding the hinge of a line that no longer existed in either direction. No friendly forces remained on their left, where only the dead and wounded of the Iron Brigade remained in Herbst's Woods. Still more alarming, Union forces no longer held the ground on Stone's right, the line slanting back to Oak Ridge. Under two-sided pressure that was becoming unbearable, Stone's men began their own fighting retreat. Crossfire swept the ground over which they had to flee. A piece of shrapnel struck the 149th Pennsylvania's Private George W. Soult in the left arm; moments later, a bullet struck his left leg. Neither missile hit bone, so after lying still in the tall grass for a minute or two Soult got up and hobbled into the railroad cut, hoping to use it as an escape route. It was no good. By this time the Rebels had sealed off the cut, and Soult became a prisoner of war.[18]

The unwounded members of Stone's brigade remained formidable in retreat. When a Confederate bullet felled the color bearer of the 143d Pennsylvania, Lieutenant Colonel John D. Musser ordered the regiment to face about and "charge back to meet the Rebels, who were charging for the colors," as Simon Hubler described it. They recovered the flag and, after several volleys, continued their retreat.[19]

Simultaneous with the unraveling of the First Corps line south of the Chambersburg Pike, the Union position north and west of Gettysburg had begun to come apart in at least two other places, and the process of collapse proceeded with remarkable speed. Even

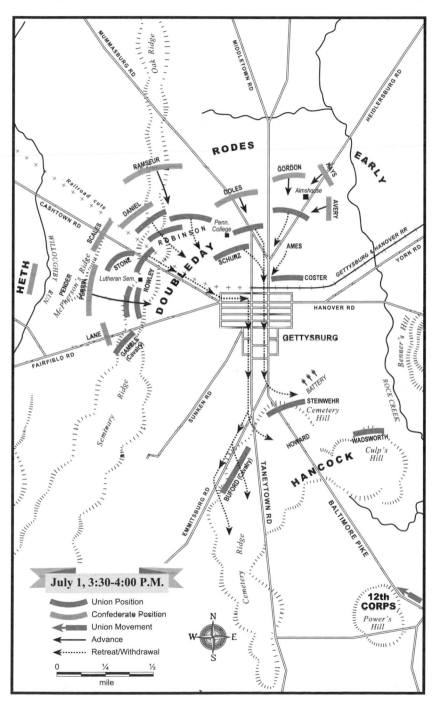

July 1, 3:30-4:00 P.M.

Union Position
Confederate Position
Union Movement
Advance
Retreat/Withdrawal

0   ¼   ½
mile

with Baxter's brigade having been joined by the other brigade of John Robinson's division, the Union position on the Mummasburg Road was finally overwhelmed by the combined pressure of two of Rodes's three fresh brigades, along with survivors of Iverson's and O'Neal's debacles, who joined the attack without awaiting orders from their wretched brigade commanders. The fight was fierce, and Federals of the brigades of Cutler, Baxter, and Gabriel Paul made Rodes's Confederates pay dearly for the position. In the end they could not hang on, and the Rebels swept forward toward the town.[20]

At about the same time, the Eleventh Corps line in the open fields north of Gettysburg collapsed in the face of an attack that came mostly from another direction. By no one's planning but by the aggressive improvisation that had become habit among the generals of the Army of Northern Virginia, that force's key component parts were now converging simultaneously on the battlefield from different directions in a manner that was as perfect as anything Napoleon ever planned. Early had been near Heidlersburg that morning on his way to a convergence with the rest of Richard Ewell's Second Corps, when he had received word that most of the rest of the army would be marching toward Gettysburg. Without hesitation, Early put his division on the march for that town as well. They would be moving on what was known locally as the Heidlersburg or Harrisburg Road, approaching Gettysburg from the northeast—right on the flank of the Eleventh Corps line. About two miles from town, Early received a dispatch from his corps commander, Ewell, notifying him that Rodes was engaged with the enemy and directing him to pitch in as soon as possible.[21]

The Union line there was held by the division of twenty-nine-year-old Harvard graduate and New York lawyer Francis Channing Barlow. Enlisting as a private in April 1861, Barlow had risen rapidly through the ranks to become colonel of the Sixty-first New York just one year later, and before that year was out he was a general. He had transferred from the Second to the Eleventh Corps just three months before the battle of Gettysburg. It had not been a happy assignment either for Barlow or for his new soldiers. Many, though by no means all, of the corps's regiments were composed of German-Americans who did not trust Barlow or their corps commander, Howard. The feeling was mutual. Worse, the whole army tended to think that the "Dutchmen," as they contemptuously called the Germans, were inferior soldiers. This bias sprang partially from ethnic prejudice and was partially the result of the disastrous battle of Chancellorsville, two months before, when the Eleventh Corps had fortuitously felt the brunt of Stonewall Jackson's last great flanking maneuver. Still, though morale in the hard-luck Eleventh Corps may not have been quite what it was in the jaunty First, its soldiers were ready to give a good account of themselves if only their generals would give them a fair chance.[22]

Barlow's division held the extreme right flank of the Union line north of Gettysburg, and he decided to anchor that flank on a little knoll, where he placed his division's only battery of artillery. Just beyond the knoll—and thus beyond the end of Barlow's line—was Rock Creek, which Barlow hoped might provide some additional cover for his flank. To occupy that knoll, however, Barlow had to move his line well forward of where Carl Schurz, commanding the corps temporarily while Howard exercised overall command of the battlefield, had wanted him to put it. The entire Eleventh Corps line was already stretched far too thin, but that could not be helped if the First and Eleventh Corps were going to try to keep the Rebels out of Gettysburg. Barlow's move made the situation worse by stretching the line farther. Aside from that grave fact, Barlow's knoll would have been a fairly good place to confront the Confederates of Rodes's division coming down from the neighborhood of Oak Hill, northwest of the Eleventh Corps.[23]

Disastrously for Barlow and the chronic hard-luck soldiers of the Eleventh Corps, the primary assault on their line developed not from Rodes's position on Oak Hill but rather from Early's division sweeping down the Heidlersburg Road directly onto the flank of the corps at Barlow's knoll. To make matters worse, woods along Rock Creek screened Early's approach so that the first real warning that Barlow had of the attack was when Early's artillery opened up on him from just across the creek. Barlow's single battery, commanded by nineteen-year-old Lieutenant Bayard Wilkeson, fired back gamely, but the more numerous Confederate guns began to pound it to pieces. Wilkeson himself, gallantly directing his guns astride a magnificent white horse, went down under the impact of a shell that killed his horse and almost removed Wilkeson's leg. Knowing it would have to come off, he saved the surgeons the trouble and finished the job with his penknife.[24]

Then, about half an hour into the one-sided artillery duel, Early's infantry started forward. The Georgia brigade of John B. Gordon, Early's right flank brigade, splashed through the creek and charged out of the trees scarcely a hundred yards from the knoll, which suddenly became the center of a fierce, close-range fight. Flanked, Barlow's men never had a chance. George P. Doles's brigade of Rodes's division moved in to help their fellow Georgians, striking the front of Barlow's position while Gordon hit the flank and rear. Barlow's Yankees, Germans and natives alike, made Gordon's Confederates pay heavily for this little hummock of Pennsylvania soil. "We had a hard time moving them," admitted one of Gordon's men. "We advanced with our accustomed yell, but they stood firm until we got near them. . . . They were harder to drive than we had ever known them before. Men were being mown down in great numbers on both sides." "We feared that Gordon would be borne back," a soldier in the neighboring Louisiana brigade later recalled, "but in a few minutes the firing ceased, & the smoke lifting from the field, revealed to our sight the defeated Federals in disorderly flight." Thirty percent of Gordon's men fell before the knoll was theirs. Then the tide of battle rolled on toward the Union flank and rear, leaving the grassy hillock strewn with the fallen of both sides, including the badly wounded Barlow.[25]

Brigadier General Alexander Schimmelfennig's division of the Eleventh Corps tried to stop the Confederate onslaught in the fields north of town but was thrashed by a more or less equal number of Confederates. Doles's brigade and Early's division fought with the skill and drive that were trademarks of the Army of Northern Virginia, inflicting fearful losses on the brave but hapless bluecoats. In the ranks of the 157th New York, Jonathan Boynton had been fascinated as he watched the skillful artillery duel that had preceded the Rebel onslaught. Then his regiment was swept into the fight with dizzying speed. The 157th moved up to support a Union brigade to their right front. In rapid succession came orders: "Fire," "Fire at will," and then "Charge bayonets." Boynton got separated from his comrades and swept up by the onrushing Confederates. He obeyed their summons to surrender, and as they marched him off to the rear, one said, "Yank, don't be skeered. We won't hurt you all."[26]

The remnants of Barlow's division tried to rally near the almshouse on the northern outskirts of Gettysburg. They, too, were crushed almost at once. The shattered remnants of two divisions of the Eleventh Corps streamed into the town with Early's and Doles's troops in hot pursuit.[27]

Still hoping that Slocum would arrive in time to save the Union position north and west of Gettysburg, Howard had delayed issuing an order to fall back until 4:00 P.M., and by that time events on the battlefield had already made that order obsolete. The Eleventh Corps north of town was crumbling, and the First Corps line was gradually being pushed back off McPherson's Ridge. Howard's pressing need now was to hold back the Confederate pursuit long enough for his retreating troops to get through Gettysburg and regroup on the hills south of it: Cemetery Hill on the southern outskirts of town, and Culp's Hill just east of Cemetery.[28]

On the west side of town, Doubleday was already dealing with that problem. He ordered James Wadsworth's and Thomas Rowley's divisions, along with the First Corps artillery, to pause on Seminary Ridge and make a stand there to delay the Confederate pursuit. Robinson's division had thrown up some makeshift breastworks there while waiting in reserve near the seminary that morning, and now those piles of fence rails, along with some nearby stone fences, offered a welcome place for Doubleday's battered but unbroken regiments to turn and fight again. One by one the regiments drifted out of the carnage on McPherson's Ridge and took up their positions along the seminary line. As the 143d Pennsylvania neared the seminary, an overwrought battery commander called out, "My God, boys, save my guns." The Pennsylvanians, who had been planning to stop there anyway, went into line in a peach orchard near the guns.[29]

The Second and Seventh Wisconsin were among the last to retire, falling back in good order and pausing to fire repeatedly. Halfway across the swale between the two ridges, Major John Mansfield, now commanding the Second after its colonel and lieutenant colonel had been carried to the rear, badly wounded, faced the regiment about and actually advanced briefly toward the Confederates on McPherson's Ridge. Once again, however, he found his left flank threatened and had to fall back to join the line on Seminary Ridge. Some of Buford's cavalry moved into position to cover the new line's left flank.[30]

While Doubleday's Federals caught their breath on Seminary Ridge and braced for the next onslaught, Heth's division, utterly spent, halted atop McPherson's Ridge. It would do no more fighting this day. Through its thinned ranks, however, passed the solid lines of Major General William Dorsey Pender's fresh division. Having followed Heth up the Chambersburg Pike to Gettysburg that day, Pender's formation was now ready to pick up the fight where Heth left off. Pender's three brigades (Hill kept Pender's fourth brigade back in reserve) now swept down the slope of McPherson's Ridge toward the bluecoats waiting across the swale along Seminary Ridge.[31]

As the Rebel line strode down the slope, twenty-one Union cannon roared out in a single salvo. Canister and shell ripped through the gray-clad ranks, and men went down by tens, dozens, and scores. Battle flags fell and rose again. The troops, Carolinians to a man, did their best to close the yawning gaps Yankee cannon were plowing through their lines, and they kept on coming. At two hundred yards they paused to cross a fence. From behind the Union breastworks, the ranks of blue-coat infantry rose up and loosed a sheet of fire. That one volley brought down thirty-four of the thirty-nine men of Company K, Fourteenth South Carolina, and scores in other units as well.[32] "Their ranks went down like grass before a scythe," a soldier of the Nineteenth Indiana later recalled.[33] "They lay in piles before us," wrote a Wisconsin soldier.[34] On the north end of the ridge, near the Chambersburg Pike and the seminary itself, the remnants of the Iron Brigade, along with the Bucktails and the artillery, stood firm and stopped Colonel Alfred M. Scales's North Carolina brigade in its tracks. Scales fell, wounded, and the survivors of his brigade went to ground, daring neither to advance nor retreat. The brigade was all but shot to pieces, every field officer down but one, and, in Scales's own words, "only a squad here and there marked the place where regiments had rested."[35]

Farther south, however, Colonel Abner Perrin's South Carolina brigade faced a thinner line of defenders and fewer cannon. The Palmetto State soldiers also had in Perrin an excellent leader, who ordered them not to stop in the open and exchange fire with the defenders but to plunge ahead all the way through the enemy position. Then Perrin led them in, brandishing his sword and spurring his horse through the ranks and on toward the Union line. The South Carolinians followed with a shout and surged up the gentle slope of the ridge. The makeshift breastworks did not extend all the way across Perrin's front, and the Carolinians were able to flank them on the south. After a stout resistance, the defenders had to give way.[36]

Back at the north end of the ridge, Scales's men rallied and came on again. The Union defenders in that sector, including the Bucktails, the Iron Brigade, and much of the First Corps artillery, held on doggedly. The fighting became hand-to-hand and muzzle-to-muzzle. "This gun is mine," shouted a North Carolinian, laying his hand on the muzzle of one of the Second Maine Battery's 12-pounder cannon. "D—n you, take it then," roared a Maine artillerist a few feet away as he yanked the lanyard, discharging the loaded cannon and scattering pieces of the bold Rebel across the slope.[37] Yet the steadfastness of the defenders could at most delay the inevitable. Flanked on both ends of their line, seeing the Eleventh Corps and the rest of the First Corps in retreat, the blue-coat soldiers around the seminary made their own escapes as best they could, joining the other Federals heading into Gettysburg.[38] Hundreds of wounded Union soldiers could not make the retreat with their comrades and had to be left behind to face capture. Among those taken prisoner was old John Burns, hobbled by three wounds, one in the foot.[39]

While the First Corps made its stubborn stand on Seminary Ridge, the situation on the north side of Gettysburg was growing more desperate as the badly beaten divisions of Barlow and Schimmelfennig streamed into the town. The blue-clad troops obviously would not rally anywhere short of Cemetery Hill, and unless something was done to check the headlong Confederate pursuit, many of the fleeing Federals would be swept up trying to get through the constricted streets of Gettysburg. Though loath to weaken his grip on vital Cemetery Hill, Howard now saw no alternative but to commit one of the two brigades of Adolph von Steinwehr's division that he had hitherto held in reserve there. Colonel Charles R. Coster's brigade accordingly got the order, and its four regiments formed up and marched down the hillside into Gettysburg and up Stratton Street. A growing stream of wounded and then unwounded bluecoats flowed past them in the opposite direction. Coster dropped off one regiment near the center of town and took the other three to the north side of Gettysburg, where they took position along a stout post-and-rail fence in a brickyard. Beyond the fence were fields of ripe wheat and, out of sight just beyond a gentle rise of ground, the onrushing Rebels of Early's division.[40]

In the center of Coster's line, Sergeant Amos Humiston and his comrades of the 154th New York knelt behind the fence and steadied their rifles on the rails, determined to make the first volley count. Early's men topped the rise and came on fiercely. The New Yorkers blasted a volley into their faces. The gray-clad line wavered, then came on again. Doggedly the men of the 154th stuck to their rail fence, loading and firing as fast as they could. Along the regiment's line, Lieutenant Alanson Crosby noted that the men of his company were as "firm as the Pyramids" and "fighting with desperation." Five minutes passed that seemed like so many hours. Then disaster struck. Out of sight to either side because of the uneven ground, the other two regiments of Coster's brigade had come to grief. Early's long, powerful lines overlapped their flanks; flowed around them; struck them front, flank, and rear; and squashed them like bugs. Coster ordered retreat, but the 154th, already deep in a pocket with Rebels on three sides, did not get the word.

The regiment fought on, a shrinking knot of men clustered around their colors in the drab surroundings of a small-town brickyard. Rebels surged over the fences, and a desperate melee ensued. Order disintegrated, and the New Yorkers now needed no one to tell them the time had come to go. Like the men of their sister regiments, they now had three choices: surrender, run the gauntlet to escape, or fight to the death. Some chose one way, some another. Dozens died fighting for the flags, and all of Coster's regiments somehow brought their colors back to Union lines. Individual soldiers who chose to make their escape dashed for the brickyard gate and then back along Stratton Street. The Rebels were already surging through the street by the gate, and the New Yorkers had to force their way through with bayonets. Most of the men never made it more than a few steps beyond the gate.[41]

The scarce fugitives fled through the northern outskirts of Gettysburg toward the relative safety of Cemetery Hill. Amos Humiston, who had survived the slaughter in the brickyard, was among them. He ran up Stratton Street, over a little brook called Stevens Run, and across the railroad tracks. Others were running and dodging too, and the Rebels were after them, shooting and yelling. Just ahead, York Street crossed Stratton; Humiston had now made it halfway across the west side of town. Then, about a quarter-mile from the brickyard, he was hit and went down with a serious wound. Nearby was a fenced lot with some brush and small trees, offering cover from the pursuing Rebels as well as from the sweltering late-afternoon sun. Somehow he managed to struggle inside the enclosure and pull himself into the shade, shelter, and stillness of the bushes. The noise of shooting and yelling in the street began to seem more distant—presently much more distant. Humiston pulled out the photo of Frank, Alice, and Fred, gazed on it, and thought of home.[42]

Other Union soldiers were working their way through various parts of Gettysburg toward the haven of Cemetery Hill. It was a somewhat disorderly affair, as units already disrupted by heavy combat and defeat now funneled through a puzzling network of narrow streets. Many units, like the Fourteenth Brooklyn of Cutler's brigade, kept up a solid front as they retreated before overwhelming Confederate numbers, but the congestion and confusion of Gettysburg's streets broke up their formations. The Confederates already held the north side of town even as the troops of the First Corps moved into it from the west. "The streets were crowded with retiring troops, batteries, and ambulance trains," a Union officer recalled.[43] A Gettysburg woman, looking down from her upstairs window, thought there were so many men in the street below that she could have walked across it on their heads.[44] The Rebels were firing down the streets from the north side of town and pressing southward to bag all the prisoners they could.[45] Some Federals blundered up blind allies and were captured by the pursuing Rebels or had to hide out in sheds or behind woodpiles for the duration of the Confederate occupation. Among the latter was Brigadier General Schimmelfennig.[46]

Like most other regiments, the 143d Pennsylvania lost its cohesion in the chaos, and Simon Hubler found himself fleeing down a side street along with two Union soldiers from other regiments. As they approached an intersection, Rebels burst into view on the cross street. "Halt, you Yankee sons of b———," shouted the graycoats. Hubler and his comrades ran harder. The Confederates fired. Hubler felt a bullet cut through his hair just above his left ear and then heard a crack "like a pistol shot" as the same bullet struck the head of one of the Union soldiers at his side. The Federal, a big, strapping fellow, sprawled onto the street. Hubler glanced down only long enough to see the man's brains oozing out before leaping over the body and continuing his own flight. Another Rebel bullet struck his cartridge box, convincing Hubler he had been shot in the hip. To his relief and surprise, however, he could still run, and he did—harder than ever.[47]

Not all was confusion and headlong flight as the two corps pulled back through the town. A battery of Union artillery unlimbered near the central square and gave the pursuing Rebels a few rounds of canister before carrying on the retreat.[48] The Sixth Wisconsin had continued to operate in the neighborhood of its morning triumph at the railroad cut. When orders came to withdraw to Seminary Ridge and then through the town to Cemetery Hill, Colonel Dawes faced his regiment by the rear rank and marched it off still in line of battle, "with the flag of the Union and of Wisconsin held aloft." The Rebels seemed almost to have cut off retreat entirely, but most of the regiment's members were able to stick to the colors, and together they found a way through town. While marching through the streets of Gettysburg the scrappy Badger State soldiers returned Confederate fire and gave "three cheers for the good and glorious cause for which we stood in battle."[49]

Their sister regiment, the Seventh Wisconsin, also came off the field with its organization intact. Serving as the corps's rear guard, the Seventh marched through Gettysburg with colors flying. When color bearer Daniel McDermott fell, wounded, he asked his comrades to lay him on the caisson of the battery just ahead of the regiment, and from that perch he continued to wave the tattered flag on its shattered staff while the caisson rumbled along the cobblestones in front of the regiment.[50] Like other regiments, however, the Seventh lost members all along the way—to wounds, exhaustion, or the confusion of the retreat. A combination of the latter two combined to doom the Seventh's Horace Currier to capture. "Perfectly exhausted" and "used up," he became separated from the regiment, and the Rebels took him prisoner on the outskirts of Gettysburg.[51]

The citizens of Gettysburg were sober but sympathetic. Numbers of them braved the danger of stray shots to offer drinks of water to the soldiers. Rufus Dawes remembered an old man who met the retreating remnant of the Sixth Wisconsin "with two buckets of fresh water." To the soldiers, who "were almost prostrated with over-exertion and heat," it was a gift of "inestimable value."[52] A member of the Seventy-sixth New York recalled a young woman who stood along the street with a bucket of cold well water at her side and a cup in each hand, ladling out drinks to the soldiers as fast as she could while tears ran down her face.[53]

As the retreating units reached Cemetery Hill, they glimpsed the welcome sight of Brigadier General Orland Smith's brigade of the Eleventh Corps, the only fresh Union brigade on the field, presenting a solid front on the hillside where it had waited in reserve for most of the day. General Howard and other officers moved about the hilltop getting the survivors of the day's fighting into position on either side of Smith's brigade, ready to repel the next Confederate assault. Gamely, the weary remnants of once-proud regiments filed into their assigned positions and sagged to the ground in exhaustion. Ordnance officers issued new supplies of ammunition, and the men refilled their cartridge boxes. The eighty men still around the colors of the 121st Pennsylvania soon felt refreshed enough to sing hymns as they waited in line of battle for what the evening, or the following morning, might bring their way.[54]

The day had not gone as Howard had hoped. Some would later question his judgment, but no one ever questioned Oliver O. Howard's bravery. Amid the buzzing bullets of Confederate sharpshooters in the town and under the imminent threat of overwhelming attack, his courage and calmness were contagious. Meeting a regiment just reaching Cemetery Hill, Howard ordered the color bearer to turn around and plant his flag on a stone wall at the base of the hill and the edge of town, where the men were to rally. "All right," the sergeant replied, "if you will go with me I will!" Howard took the flag himself, walked down to the desired position, and rallied the regiment there. An officer of the Twenty-fifth Ohio wrote that the general's performance in this crisis "taught me what a cool and confident man could do."[55]

Presently, Howard was joined by Winfield Scott Hancock, on the errand to which Meade had dispatched him at midday. His arrival created an awkward situation, since Howard outranked Hancock, but Meade's order placed Hancock in command over him. By the most reliable accounts of the exchange, Howard took the surprising development in stride, but he was deeply humiliated at what appeared to be Meade's lack of confidence in him. Later that evening, after things had quieted down, Howard sadly wrote to Meade that being placed under Hancock "has mortified me and will disgrace me." He had, he maintained, done as well as any of the Army of the Potomac's corps commanders would have done in similar circumstances. Howard may have been right about that, though, in truth, except for selecting Cemetery Hill as a fallback position, he had not done very well. He had allowed the Eleventh Corps to deploy badly, had withheld reinforcements until they were too late to do much good, and had delayed ordering the retreat until his troops were already giving way and had no choice but to withdraw with considerable disorder and heavy losses. Bright and dedicated, Howard was nevertheless slow to develop his skills as a corps commander, and Gettysburg had been another learning experience for him.[56]

In fairness, the situation had been all but impossible. Reynolds, not Howard, had made the decision to try to hold Gettysburg. Union forces were woefully inadequate for the task, but Howard had fought on throughout the day in constant expectation of the arrival of the Twelfth and Third Corps. He was unaware that Meade's orders were holding back those reinforcements and leaving the First and Eleventh Corps to fight their doomed battle north and west of Gettysburg.

As for Meade's decision to put Hancock temporarily in charge at Gettysburg, however, it was not, as Howard supposed, a particular statement of distrust for the Eleventh Corps commander. Meade had immense confidence in Hancock and believed that his recent conversations with that general gave the Second Corps commander a greater understanding of Meade's thinking than Howard or even Reynolds could have had. If Meade's sending Hancock to Gettysburg revealed a lack of confidence in anyone, it was, perhaps, Meade's lack of confidence in himself.[57]

Such considerations, however, would have been consciously deferred to some more suitable and peaceful future hour, as Howard and Hancock strove to ready the Federals on Cemetery Hill for the possibility of a renewed Confederate attack. Three to four hours of daylight remained after the battered remnants of the First and Eleventh Corps began to take up their positions in and around the town's burying ground. Howard was as cool as a steel blade, calm and reassuring, while Hancock was animated, voluble, and, as always, thoroughly inspiring to the troops. The Union commanders wisely saw the need to hold neighboring Culp's Hill as well, just to the east of Cemetery Hill, and sent two divisions of the First Corps over to take possession of its previously unoccupied slopes.

Encouragingly, help was on the way. Howard had that afternoon sent renewed and more urgent messages to Slocum, four miles out the Baltimore Pike at Two Taverns. Howard's first afternoon message must have reached Slocum about the time the fighting flared up at Gettysburg, providing the roar of distant battle to underscore the urgency of Howard's request. The combined effect was enough to nerve Slocum to set aside Meade's orders and go at last to Howard's aid. He lost no time in getting his Twelfth Corps on the road for Gettysburg. No sooner had the corps taken up its march than an order arrived from Meade urging Slocum to make for Gettysburg as rapidly as possible. The message was too late to change anything, but it no doubt made Slocum feel a good deal better about what he had decided to do. By late afternoon the Twelfth Corps was getting close to the east side of town while the Confederates were driving in the Union lines north and west of Gettysburg. At Howard's request, Slocum split up his corps's two divisions and sent them toward opposite ends of what had been the Union line, one to extend the left flank of the First Corps and the other to extend the right flank of the Eleventh. Before the new troops could come into their widely separated positions, however, Union forces were streaming back through the town in full retreat. Brigadier General Alpheus S. Williams's division, which had been heading for the right of the old Eleventh Corps position, actually began deploying in preparation to attack the flank of Early's Confederates north of town until it became apparent that in doing so, Williams's small division would be entirely on its own. The obvious course for the Twelfth Corps now was to buttress the new Union position rather than attempt to salvage the old.[58]

Confusion continued, however, regarding Slocum's own whereabouts. Apprised of Hancock's presence on Cemetery Hill with orders giving him command of the field, Slocum apparently assumed that his own presence was not required there and so remained with his troops. In fact, Meade had not intended the order to place Hancock over the very senior Slocum but rather only over Howard and, if necessary, Sickles. Had Meade hastened to the field in person, as Lee had done when he discovered that part of his army was engaged, much of the confusion and hard feelings about the Union command at Gettysburg that day could have been avoided. Eventually the generals got the mess straightened out, and Slocum duly took overall command of the Union forces around Gettysburg, the sixth Union officer to hold that responsibility since sunrise. Slocum still had very little idea of what Meade expected of him and wrote in a brief dispatch to the army commander late that evening: "Unless I receive orders from you before Midnight I shall assume that the other Corps are coming up and that the battle is to be fought here tomorrow."[59]

About the same time that evening, Daniel Sickles and the Third Corps approached the Gettysburg area from the south on the Emmitsburg Road. Like Slocum, Sickles had found himself in a difficult situation that day, receiving desperate requests for aid from Howard at Gettysburg but being bound by orders from Meade to stay where he was (Bridgeport, Maryland) preparatory to falling back to Pipe Creek. After some hesitation and attempts to contact

Meade for clarification, Sickles put his corps on the road for Gettysburg, marching through Emmitsburg and over difficult roads made muddy by intermittent light rain. His leading troops arrived at the battlefield shortly after 6:00 P.M.[60]

With the Third Corps approaching and the Twelfth Corps not yet in position, the combined First and Eleventh Corps strength on Cemetery and Culp's Hills was probably a little less than 7,000 men. That included the 2,200 fresh troops of Orland Smith's brigade and fewer than 5,000 veterans of the day's fighting north and west of Gettysburg, a sad remnant of the 14,200 First and Eleventh Corps soldiers who had gone into action on the other side of town. Bolstering the Union defenses on the hills were some forty-three pieces of artillery, weapons that were at their best in breaking up attacks and had a good field of fire down the gentle slopes below them. The question for Howard, Hancock, and all the rest of the Federals south of Gettysburg that late afternoon and evening was whether the Confederates would attack and, if so, whether they could be repulsed.[61]

That was also the question for Lee and his lieutenants. Unlike Meade, Lee was now present on the battlefield in person, having arrived at the peak of the afternoon's Confederate success. Clearly, four of his army's nine divisions had combined to win a spectacular victory over a somewhat smaller Union force at Gettysburg. But how badly were the Union forces beaten? What additional force might be coming up behind them? And, for that matter, where was the rest of Meade's army? Only two of Meade's seven corps were accounted for in the prisoners taken that day. Where were the other five? The Army of Northern Virginia owed its victory this day to the fact that its various formations had arrived in the space of a few hours on almost all sides of a beleaguered and outnumbered enemy. What if the tables should presently be turned and Lee should find himself in the midst of a massive concentration of the Army of the Potomac? Above all, where was Stuart, who should have been bringing Lee the information he needed? "I cannot think what has become of Stuart," Lee had said to a subordinate earlier that day. "I ought to have heard from him long before now." Without the intelligence for which he counted on Stuart, Lee mused, "I am in ignorance as to what we have in front of us here. It may be the whole Federal army, or it may be only a detachment."[62]

There was much for Lee to think about. If later generations would ruminate at length on how he could have won the war in a single midsummer's afternoon, Lee, as he stood near the place where the Chambersburg Pike crossed Seminary Ridge and gazed through his field glasses across the Gettysburg plain toward the heights where the Federals were gathering beyond, had to bear in mind that he was also the man who could lose the war before sundown. He knew his own army was not all up yet. Most of it was strung out on the pike in a traffic jam that stretched all the way back to Chambersburg. Longstreet's corps was bringing up the rear and would not be available until morning, some parts of it not until a good deal later than that. Lee did not know how close Meade's army was to concentrating at Gettysburg, and so he chose caution. He had six fresh brigades available on Seminary Ridge: five of Major General Richard H. Anderson's division, along with Brigadier General Edward L. Thomas's brigade of Pender's division, which Hill had kept back in reserve. He could have launched them in an all-out assault on the Cemetery Hill position with at least a two-to-one superiority in numbers. Instead, he opted to keep them in reserve.[63]

To Ewell, on the north side of Gettysburg, Lee sent a discretionary order to attack the hill if he thought the prospects looked good for taking it. Ewell and his two division commanders who were present at that time, Rodes and Early, thought they might accomplish something if supported by a simultaneous attack by Hill's troops on their right, but Lee had already decided against that. Without such help, Ewell was doubtful. Rodes's and Early's divisions had seen hard fighting that day, and Johnson's division, just getting out of the traffic jam on the Chambersburg Pike, would not be available for action until 7:00 P.M. The Union front on Cemetery Hill was clearly gaining strength and solidity, making the delay crucial. Ewell was also concerned that he could find no good positions from which to use artillery against Cemetery Hill. He considered launching Johnson's division when it came up, in an attempt to take wooded Culp's Hill, just east of Cemetery Hill, but finally decided against that too. A number of Second Corps personnel, from staff officers to soldiers in the ranks, muttered that things would have been different if Stonewall Jackson had been present. But Stonewall was dead, and the world will never know what would have happened had he been in Ewell's place at the head of his old Second Corps on July 1.[64]

For more than a century since that day, the wistful defenders of the Lost Cause, eager to maintain the myth of Lee's invincibility,

have blamed Ewell, Early, Hill, Anderson, and others for failing
Lee by not having the nerve to carry out the assault that he did not
see fit to order unequivocally.[65] The fact remains, however, that Lee
was in command and present in person on the battlefield. If he had
been sure that the army should attack, he could have ordered it.
Such an attack might have brought good or bad results for Lee. His
men might have been repulsed with heavy losses, or they might
have succeeded—also no doubt with heavy losses. For good or ill,
however, the Army of Northern Virginia rested on its arms that
evening because that was Robert E. Lee's decision.[66]

The day's fighting was over, and as darkness fell, the generals
made their plans for the morrow. At 10:00 P.M., Meade finally decided to go to Gettysburg himself after several of his generals, including Hancock, had urged that it would be a good place to fight.
He arrived around midnight and approved his subordinates' arrangements. If, as he dryly noted, it was too late to make changes,
that was his own doing. His performance as an army commander
that day had been uneven. Wedded to his Pipe Creek plan, he nevertheless allowed Reynolds to bring on a pitched battle well to the
north. While the First and Eleventh Corps fought for their lives
around Gettysburg, Meade's orders to the commanders of the Third,
Fifth, and especially Twelfth Corps kept potential reinforcements
halted only a few hours' march from the battlefield. The Army of
Northern Virginia, an experienced winning team, had taken advantage of the Army of the Potomac's new commander and uncertain generals by getting to the battlefield first with the most men.

On the other hand, Meade had finally adjusted to the new situation, and if he had shown too much readiness to send others to
the battlefield rather than going himself, he had at least sent very
good men in Reynolds and Hancock. If Meade's overall arrangements had not produced victory in the first day's fighting, they
had at least staved off major disaster and put his army in a good
place to recover from its July 1 setback. Whereas Lee's army was
currently being delayed in completing its concentration at Gettysburg because of the miles-long traffic pileup on the Chambersburg
Pike, Meade's corps were converging rapidly using several of the
roads that led to Gettysburg. By the time Meade reached the battlefield, the First and Eleventh Corps had been joined by the Third
and Twelfth. The Second and Fifth were only a few miles off and
would be on hand an hour or two after dawn. The Sixth Corps, at
13,000 men the largest formation in the Army of the Potomac, was

still about thirty miles away at Manchester and about to embark on one of the epic forced marches of the war as it raced for Gettysburg the next day. In all, Meade would have on the morning of July 2 about 63,000 of the approximately 76,000 soldiers remaining in the Army of the Potomac. By evening he could expect to have the rest. Lee, whose July 1 casualties had been about two-thirds of those suffered by Meade's army, would have about 58,000 of the roughly 68,000 he could still number in the Army of Northern Virginia.

Lee, for his part, had no doubt about his general intentions for the morrow, even if some specifics remained to be worked out. He had decided hours before Meade reached the battlefield. James Longstreet appeared at Lee's Seminary Ridge headquarters before sundown, and to his most senior lieutenant, Lee had revealed his determination to attack the enemy next day. Longstreet protested, arguing instead for turning the Army of the Potomac by marching around it to the south, thus compelling the Federals to attack. Lee was not convinced. July 1 had been a success, the beginning of the kind of success he had envisaged before the campaign started, catching the Union corps by ones and twos as they rushed north to defend their home country. Lee meant to push his advantage. "If the enemy is there tomorrow," he told Longstreet, "we must attack him."[67]

NOTES

1. *OR*, vol. 27, pt. 2, p. 552.
2. *OR*, vol. 27, pt. 2, pp. 552–53.
3. *OR*, vol. 27, pt. 2, pp. 444, 553–54; Baxter, "Death's Mission," 49–52, first quotation from p. 49, second quotation from p. 52.
4. *OR*, vol. 27, pt. 2, pp. 444, 553–54; quotation from Pfanz, *Gettysburg—The First Day*, 178.
5. Rod Gragg, *Covered with Glory: The 26th North Carolina Infantry at Gettysburg* (New York: HarperCollins, 2000), 31–32.
6. Pfanz, *Gettysburg—The First Day*, 194–95.
7. Simon Hubler Narrative, Simon Hubler Papers.
8. Martin, *Gettysburg, July 1*, 371–76.
9. Venner, *The 19th Indiana*, 65.
10. Simon Hubler Narrative, Simon Hubler Papers.
11. *OR*, vol. 27, pt. 1, pp. 247–48, 330; George W. Soult Diary, July 1, 1863, George W. Soult Papers, Civil War Miscellaneous Collection, USAMHI; Simon Hubler Narrative, Simon Hubler Papers; Coddington, *The Gettysburg Campaign*, 293.
12. *OR*, vol. 27, pt. 1, p. 268; Venner, *The 19th Indiana*, 6, 68–69.
13. *OR*, vol. 27, pt. 1, p. 315.

14. Venner, *The 19th Indiana*, 8, 74–77.

15. *OR*, vol. 27, pt. 1, pp. 268–69; Venner, *The 19th Indiana*, 77–83.

16. Gragg, *Covered with Glory*, 5, 117–30.

17. Ibid., 130–36, 140; William F. Fox, *Regimental Losses in the American Civil War, 1861–1865* (Albany, NY: Albany Publishing Company, 1889), 556.

18. Roswell L. Root to "Dear Grand Father," August 23, 1863, Roswell L. Root Papers; George W. Soult Diary, July 1, 1863, George W. Soult Papers.

19. Simon Hubler Narrative, Simon Hubler Papers; *OR*, vol. 27, pt. 1, p. 339.

20. *OR*, vol. 27, pt. 2, p. 554.

21. *OR*, vol. 27, pt. 2, pp. 468–69; Harry W. Pfanz, *Gettysburg: Culp's Hill and Cemetery Hill* (Chapel Hill: University of North Carolina Press, 1993), 38.

22. Coddington, *The Gettysburg Campaign*, 305–6.

23. *OR*, vol. 27, pt. 1, p. 728.

24. Martin, *Gettysburg, July 1*, 282; *OR*, vol. 27, pt. 1, p. 728.

25. *OR*, vol. 27, pt. 1, pp. 712–13; pt. 2, pp. 468–69; Martin, *Gettysburg, July 1*, 283–96; first quotation from p. 286; second quotation from Seymour, *Civil War Memoirs*, 70–71.

26. Jonathan W. W. Boynton Reminiscences, Boynton Papers, Civil War Miscellaneous Collection, USAMHI.

27. *OR*, vol. 27, pt. 1, pp. 712–13.

28. Pfanz, *Gettysburg—The First Day*, 294.

29. Simon Hubler Narrative, Simon Hubler Papers; *OR*, vol. 27, pt. 1, p. 339.

30. *OR*, vol. 27, pt. 1, p. 274; pt. 2, p. 657.

31. *OR*, vol. 27, pt. 2, pp. 656–57.

32. Martin, *Gettysburg, July 1*, 402–4.

33. Venner, *The 19th Indiana*, 86.

34. Robert B. V. Bird to "Frend Rosey," August 21, 1863, Bird Family Papers.

35. *OR*, vol. 27, pt. 2, pp. 657, 660–62, 670.

36. Pfanz, *Gettysburg—The First Day*, 310–12; *OR*, vol. 27, pt. 2, p. 667.

37. Simon Hubler Narrative, Simon Hubler Papers.

38. Robert B. V. Bird to "Frend Rosey," August 21, 1863, Bird Family Papers.

39. Pfanz, *Gettysburg—The First Day*, 312–20; Martin, *Gettysburg, July 1*, 375–76.

40. *OR*, vol. 27, pt. 1, p. 721.

41. Martin, *Gettysburg, July 1*, 306–16; Pfanz, *Gettysburg—The First Day*, 258–68.

42. Dunkelman, *Gettysburg's Unknown Soldier*, 120, 130.

43. *OR*, vol. 27, pt. 1, p. 277.

44. Martin, *Gettysburg, July 1*, 441–42, 451.

45. *OR*, vol. 27, pt. 1, p. 277.

46. Pfanz, *Gettysburg—The First Day*, 328–29.

47. Simon Hubler Narrative, Simon Hubler Papers.

48. *OR*, vol. 27, pt. 1, p. 757; Martin, *Gettysburg, July 1*, 317; Pfanz, *Gettysburg—The First Day*, 327.

49. Dawes, *A Full Blown Yankee of the Iron Brigade*, 176–78.

50. *OR*, vol. 27, pt. 1, p. 277; Pfanz, *Gettysburg—The First Day*, 326.

51. Horace Currier Diary, July 1, 1863, Horace Currier Papers, State Historical Society of Wisconsin, Madison.

52. Dawes, *A Full Blown Yankee of the Iron Brigade*, 178; *OR*, vol. 27, pt. 1, p. 277.

53. Martin, *Gettysburg, July 1*, 447.

54. Dawes, *A Full Blown Yankee of the Iron Brigade*, 178–79; Pfanz, *Gettysburg: Culp's Hill and Cemetery Hill*, 53–54; Martin, *Gettysburg, July 1*, 472.

55. Pfanz, *Gettysburg: Culp's Hill and Cemetery Hill*, 53.

56. Pfanz, *Gettysburg—The First Day*, 338–40; Martin, *Gettysburg, July 1*, 334–35; Pfanz, *Gettysburg: Culp's Hill and Cemetery Hill*, 88–96.

57. *OR*, vol. 27, pt. 1, pp. 296–97.

58. Martin, *Gettysburg, July 1*, 478–80; *OR*, vol. 27, pt. 1, pp. 126, 758–59; pt. 3, p. 465.

59. *OR*, vol. 27, pt. 1, p. 696; Pfanz, *Gettysburg—The First Day*, 339–40; Pfanz, *Gettysburg: Culp's Hill and Cemetery Hill*, 97–105; Henry W. Slocum Letter, July 1, 1863, Pearce Civil War Collection, Navarro College, Corsicana, Texas.

60. Martin, *Gettysburg, July 1*, 541–44; *OR*, vol. 27, pt. 1, pp. 16, 144, 369, 482.

61. Pfanz, *Gettysburg—The First Day*, 334–35.

62. Quoted in Martin, *Gettysburg, July 1*, 340.

63. Ibid., 512.

64. *OR*, vol. 27, pt. 2, p. 445; Seymour, *Civil War Memoirs*, 72; Martin, *Gettysburg, July 1*, 554–69; Pfanz, *Gettysburg: Culp's Hill and Cemetery Hill*, 72–76.

65. Bowden and Ward, *Last Chance for Victory*, 178–209.

66. Brooks D. Simpson, " 'If Properly Led': Command Relationships at Gettysburg," in *Civil War Generals in Defeat*, ed. Steven E. Woodworth (Lawrence: University Press of Kansas, 1999), 161–68.

67. James Longstreet, *From Manassas to Appomattox: Memoirs of the Civil War in America* (Bloomington: Indiana University Press, 1960), 357–58. See also Gary W. Gallagher, " 'If the Enemy Is There, We Must Attack Him': Lee and the Second Day at Gettysburg," in *The Second Day at Gettysburg*, ed. Gary W. Gallagher (Kent, OH: Kent State University Press, 1993), 1–32.

CHAPTER SIX

FORWARD AND TAKE THOSE HEIGHTS!

THURSDAY, JULY 2, 1863, dawned warm and humid at Gettysburg. Morning mists covered the fields and thick clouds filled the sky, while a heavy dew or light, misting rain dampened the thousands of men sleeping in the fields outside of town, both those who would shortly awake to the sounds of drums and bugles and those whom only the Last Trump would ever waken again. The temperature was a muggy 74 degrees at 7:00 A.M., with a light breeze from the south. It was going to be a hot day.[1]

Lee was eager to renew the successful battle of the previous day. When he mentioned that eagerness to Longstreet, however, the general whom Lee had once described as his "old warhorse" balked again. Longstreet brought up the same objections he had raised the evening before and offered as a counterproposal a vague plan for disengaging from the enemy, swinging far to the south of the Army of the Potomac. Moving between it and Washington, he would take up a position the Yankees would have to attack, as they had done with such spectacular lack of success and ruinous casualties at the battle of Fredericksburg, down in Virginia seven months before. It was the sort of plan that sounds good until someone actually starts to consider the practical details involved in implementing it.

First, it was based on Meade's sitting still while the Confederates marched to gain the advantage on him. Second, it was a rather obvious ploy, and Meade could be expected to think of it and plan countermeasures, as in fact he did. Third, it required that such an alert Union cavalryman as John Buford suddenly become slothful and inefficient and abandon his habit of active scouting that would undoubtedly have revealed any such Confederate move before it got well under way. Finally, Longstreet's plan would have made it impossible for Lee to feed his troops. The Army of Northern Virginia had no real supply lines during this campaign but rather was living off the land, as many a sorrowful Pennsylvania farmer and storekeeper could attest. An army can live off the land as long as it stays spread out and keeps moving. Once it draws together and halts—as it must do in order to fight a battle and as Lee's army was even then doing at Gettysburg—it can wait only a few days before hunger starts gnawing at the soldiers' bellies. Assuming the Army of Northern Virginia could have given Meade the slip, dispersed its own columns to forage in its southward and eastward march, and then seized the kind of position of which Longstreet dreamed, it could have remained in that position only a few days before hunger forced it to move on. Thus, even in the unlikely event that the first steps of Longstreet's plan would actually work, it stood a very poor chance of producing the results he envisioned. The dynamic of the campaign was such that the Confederates were obliged to maintain the initiative or else accept failure and retreat.[2]

Lee recognized these factors and continued to insist that he wanted to attack the enemy at Gettysburg that morning, "as early as practicable."[3] He was not quite sure, however, exactly where he would launch that attack, nor can we be quite sure of all the processes that went into the decision and of what passed between Lee, Longstreet, and the rest of the Confederate brass that morning amid the jungle of conflicting claims that sprouted up in later years.

Lee did visit his several corps commanders, continuing discussions that he had begun the evening before. He did not get especially encouraging reports from any of the lieutenant generals. In discussions with Lee the previous evening, Ewell claimed that little could be done on his front. He encouraged Lee to attack on the opposite flank, the Confederate right. Lee sensibly suggested that in that case, Ewell's corps should be pulled back out of Gettysburg and moved to a position where he could be of more help in such an attack, but Ewell and his division commanders multiplied lame excuses until Lee gave up and left the Second Corps where it was. At most, Ewell thought, he might be able to take Culp's Hill as long as the Yankees had not occupied it. In Lee's morning discussions with Ewell, the corps commander explained that the Yankees were indeed present on Culp's Hill, in force. Otherwise, their conference was in most ways a rehash of the previous evening's session, with Lee finally agreeing that the primary attack would not be made in this sector.[4]

Ambrose Hill, still ailing, commanded the corps that had taken the heaviest losses on July 1. At least two of his three divisions,

Heth's and Pender's, had been savaged the previous afternoon and were in poor shape for any serious use on this day. Neither the Third Corps nor its commander was a prime candidate for a leading role in Lee's July 2 operations.

Longstreet was Lee's most experienced corps commander, but he was also a man steadfastly opposed to making any attack at Gettysburg. Worse, he disliked and distrusted Lee, largely because he was jealous of him. To Lee's plans for the day, Longstreet continued to respond with a stubborn series of objections. His next was that not enough of his First Corps had reached the field of battle. Seven of Longstreet's eleven brigades were on hand before midmorning, having marched across South Mountain the day before, camped near Marsh Creek in the wee hours, and hiked the four or five remaining miles to the battlefield early on July 2. The division of Major General George Pickett, three brigades of Virginians, was marching from Chambersburg and could not possibly be available for fighting that day. The remaining brigade, Brigadier General Evander Law's of Hood's division, had been detailed to guard some of the army's wagon trains and was pressing toward Gettysburg by a prodigious twenty-four-mile forced march that had started shortly after 2:00 A.M. Private W. C. Ward of the Fourth Alabama remembered it as "the most fatiguing march of the war." The rising sun illuminated the Alabamians tramping over South Mountain and heading down toward Cashtown. The brigade would arrive about noon. Longstreet wanted to wait until both Law and Pickett were available, which ruled out action on July 2.[5]

Lee was not to be put off in that manner. Instead, he placed at Longstreet's disposal Major General Richard H. Anderson's division of the Third Corps, the only one of Hill's divisions to escape heavy losses on the previous day. Anderson and his men were familiar with Longstreet, to whose corps they had belonged up until the army reorganization a few weeks before. Anderson's five brigades would bring the strength of Longstreet's attacking column up to twelve brigades, one more than the pre-battle full strength of the First Corps.

By about midmorning, Lee had settled on a plan of attack. When it came to tactics, he did not believe in tampering with success. When a particular plan worked well for him in one battle, he was very likely to try it in the next, and such was the case here at Gettysburg. At his previous battle, Chancellorsville, in May, Lee had achieved spectacular results by means of an assault on his

opponent's flank. Stonewall Jackson, Lee's most trusted lieutenant, had led a large column on a long march through seemingly
impassable woods and thickets to descend like a thunderbolt on
the flank of the unsuspecting Union line, sending the bluecoats fleeing. Though Jackson was dead now, Lee set about to reproduce the
glorious victory of Chancellorsville here in the rolling fields and
woodlots around Gettysburg. While Ewell's corps made a diversion against Culp's Hill and Cemetery Hill—with the option to con-
vert the diversion to a real attack if opportunity should beckon
—Longstreet would deliver the real decisive blow by leading his
corps on a roundabout march that would place Confederate troops
on the vulnerable Union southern flank.

The location of that flank Lee determined by consulting with
Captain Samuel R. Johnston of his staff, who had scouted out the
terrain on the Union left in an early morning ride. From Meade's
position on Cemetery Hill, two lower ridges radiated to the south
and southwest. The one to the south, Cemetery Ridge, ran for about
a mile until it gradually lost itself in the gentle undulations of Pennsylvania farmland. Farther south stood two conical hills, Little
Round Top and Round Top. The latter was heavily wooded, but
the west face of Little Round Top was cleared. The southwest ridge,
nameless and somewhat less defined, lay roughly along the course
of the Emmitsburg Road as it angled southwest out of Gettysburg
for about a mile or so. South of this latter ridge, and thus directly
west of Little Round Top, lay rugged Houck Ridge. Steeper and
higher than either Cemetery Ridge or the one that carried the
Emmitsburg Road, Houck Ridge was nonetheless lower than Little
Round Top. It ran north to south and terminated at its south end in
a jumble of boulders and outcroppings known locally as Devil's
Den.

Johnston reported that he and several other staff officers had
ridden down Seminary Ridge and then across the Emmitsburg Road
and all the way to the summit of Little Round Top. How they did
this without encountering or even seeing any of the numerous
Union troops that were in the area remains a mystery to this day.
Lee himself was surprised at Johnston's report. "Did you get there?"
he asked incredulously, pointing at Little Round Top on the map
he and Johnston were studying. Johnston assured him he had.[6]

On the basis of Johnston's report and other data he received
that morning, Lee concluded that the Union line ran along the
Emmitsburg Road for a short distance and then ended. Longstreet's

flanking column thus needed only to march a few miles southward on the west side of Seminary Ridge—out of the Yankees' view— then cross over to the east side and sweep northeastward up the Emmitsburg Road, rolling up the Union line as they came.

Lee had some difficulty getting his idea across to his officers. Longstreet's senior division commander, Major General Lafayette McLaws, who was to lead the march, wanted very much to examine the terrain and seemed not to understand that Johnston had already been over the ground and back again. He kept suggesting that he go along with Johnston to scout the lay of the land. Longstreet, perhaps hoping Lee would give up his plan as impractical, insisted just as persistently that he would not have McLaws leaving his division for any purpose, including looking over the ground. When Lee tried to explain to McLaws how he wanted his division to deploy, Longstreet interrupted by directing McLaws to deploy it parallel to the Emmitsburg Road. "No, General," said Lee, who must by this time have been wondering if even Longstreet actually understood the plan. "I wish it placed just the opposite"— that is, perpendicular to the Emmitsburg Road.[7]

At 11:00 A.M. Lee gave the order for the attack. Longstreet asked if he could wait until Law's brigade came up, and Lee agreed. Longstreet, however, still sullenly unenthusiastic about the planned attack, used that permission as an excuse to delay preparations and the positioning of other troops that could just as well have been taken care of before Law's brigade reached the battlefield. It was nearly noon when the Alabamians arrived, having marched the twenty-four miles from New Guilford, Pennsylvania, over South Mountain, since 3:00 that morning. Then more delay followed while Anderson's division of A. P. Hill's corps got into position. Hill was sluggish today, suffering from a flareup of his old illness, and should have had his troops in position sooner. Then one of his brigades fought a brief but sharp skirmish with a Yankee reconnaissance probe and drove the bluecoats away to the east.[8]

Finally, Longstreet's march got under way, but before it had gone far another problem developed. The road on which the column was marching took the head of McLaws's division over a rise and into plain view of a Union signal station that had lately appeared on the summit of Little Round Top. Longstreet did nothing until the column neared the top of the hill; then he halted the troops and deliberated about the loss of secrecy. Though a short detour could have gotten his men around the knoll unseen by the Yankees on Little Round Top, Longstreet decided instead to march his corps on a four-mile roundabout that would begin by retracing their steps almost back to the starting point of the afternoon's march.[9]

By the time Longstreet had decided on this course of action, Hood, whose division was bringing up the rear, had with his customary impetuosity neglected to halt when McLaws's troops did, and so had badly entangled the front of his column with the rear of the leading division. More time passed while the officers sorted things out, and soldiers of Brigadier General George T. "Tige" Anderson's Georgia brigade took advantage of the halt to loot a nearby farmhouse. A few roguish Georgians even ransacked the wardrobes and then cavorted across the yard in hoop skirts, crinolines, and fancy bonnets, to the howls of their comrades' laughter. Then came the order to fall in, and some Pennsylvania woman's best clothes landed in the dust as the men scrambled back into ranks and continued their march.[10]

The sun had dropped about halfway down the western sky as Longstreet's divisions approached the jumping-off point for their attack, moving through an extensive woodland belonging to a farmer named Pfitzer. At the head of the column, Longstreet and McLaws conferred about how to deploy. "There is nothing in your front," Longstreet assured his division commander. "You will be entirely on the flank of the enemy."[11] Longstreet, who had not bothered with any reconnaissance, and McLaws, whom Longstreet had not allowed to make any reconnaissance, were both in for some surprises about the position of their enemy. The situation had never been quite as they imagined it, and it had been rapidly evolving even as they made their roundabout march.

On the Union side of the lines, Meade was having difficulties with a subordinate who made Lee's vexations with Longstreet seem mild by comparison. As the remaining units of the Army of the Potomac arrived that morning, Meade assigned them their places in a position that came to resemble a fishhook. Culp's Hill was the barb, and Cemetery Hill the bend. From that bend the long, straight shank of the hook ran southward along Cemetery Ridge. Little Round Top was the eye of the hook. On the far right of the Union line, Slocum's Twelfth Corps held Culp's Hill. On its left was a division of the battered First Corps, and after that the Eleventh Corps on Cemetery Hill. Next in line, trailing down the slope to Cemetery Ridge and southward for some distance along the ridge, came the Second Corps. On the left of the Second Corps stood the Third

Corps, which, in theory at least, continued the line all the way to Little Round Top. The Fifth Corps Meade held in reserve, and the Sixth Corps was making its marathon march from Manchester and could not be expected to reach the field until late in the day.

Dan Sickles was not satisfied with the position Meade assigned to his corps. Some question remains as to whether he ever got his troops into exactly the position Meade wanted them. They were definitely in the vicinity of lower Cemetery Ridge, and Sickles wanted them moved. The position had its drawbacks. It was low—lower than the high ground along the Emmitsburg Road and Houck Ridge, both several hundred yards out in front of the line. Fairly extensive patches of woods on and immediately in front of this sector of Cemetery Ridge left very poor fields of fire for artillery.

To Sickles's mind this disadvantage was a conclusive reason to advance his corps to that high ground along the Emmitsburg Road and Houck Ridge, but he was wrong in much the same way Barlow had been wrong the day before in advancing to the little knoll north of town where his division had come to grief. Although it was certainly desirable for a defensive position to occupy strong ground, it was absolutely indispensable for the position to be coherent and sufficiently manned. No amount of good ground would compensate the defenders if they found themselves scattered and unable to support each other in a position too extensive to be held in strength. The ground south of Gettysburg was very favorable for defense but not perfect. That meant that in order to keep the defensive position compact and coherent, some parts of the line would lie on weak ground, but the overall position would be stronger than it would have been if Union troops were spread out on every hilltop in the neighborhood. Such a portion of weak ground was lower Cemetery Ridge, and with his amateurish lack of appreciation for the big picture, Sickles did not see why his troops ought to stay there.

Sickles was also haunted by memories of Chancellorsville, where his corps had suffered almost as badly as the Eleventh. He was wary of another broad flanking movement that might come crashing down upon the end of his line at any moment, and he remembered a piece of high ground—a good artillery position called Hazel Grove—that his corps had held and then abandoned before the Confederates moved in and used it to blast the Army of the Potomac. Sickles was determined nothing like this should happen again.

So first by sending a staff officer, and then by visiting head-quarters himself, he tried to get Meade to come down and look at his position and order the Third Corps to advance and take the high ground. Meade was busy—not to say preoccupied—with his right wing and not particularly interested in Sickles's concerns. During the morning hours, Meade worried that Lee might launch an attack in the Culp's Hill sector, where the Baltimore Pike, Meade's indispensable line of supply and communication, lay un-comfortably near the front. When Lee showed no propensity to try to fulfill Meade's forebodings there, the Union general contem-plated launching an attack of his own from the vicinity of Culp's Hill. He alerted Slocum to have his wing of the army, the Twelfth and Fifth Corps, ready for the assault, but upon further investiga-tion decided that the prospect was not promising and abandoned the plan. Meanwhile, he could not be bothered with the concerns of a corps commander in a quiet sector. Meade knew where he wanted the Third Corps and told Sickles. Thereafter he seemed to consider the matter settled.[12]

Sickles did not. If Meade was too busy to go, could Sickles have chief engineer Major General Gouverneur K. Warren? No, Warren was busy too, so Sickles requested and finally got chief of artillery Henry J. Hunt. With Sickles, Hunt rode over the ground and had to admit that some of the terrain along the Emmitsburg Road offered good positions for artillery. However, it was far too extensive a position for the Third Corps to occupy. As Hunt prepared to leave the sector, Sickles eagerly asked if he should advance to take up the new line. "Not on my authority," Hunt replied, and he rode off to report to Meade.[13]

About noon, Sickles authorized Colonel Hiram Berdan to take a battalion of the First U.S. Sharpshooter Regiment, supported by the Third Maine Regiment, and probe west to see if the Confeder-ates were present in force on the part of Seminary Ridge west of the Third Corps's position. Berdan and his troops found out soon enough. Shortly after entering the woods that cloaked the crest of Seminary Ridge, they encountered the southernmost extension of Major General Richard Anderson's Confederate division, a brigade of Alabamians under the command of Brigadier General Cadmus Wilcox. A short, sharp fight ensued before the Federals fell back to make their report to Sickles. That clinched it, as far as he was con-cerned. If the Rebels were that far south on Seminary Ridge, they must be making for that coveted high ground along the Emmitsburg

Road, and Sickles was determined to have it first, with orders or without.

Early in the afternoon, Sickles sent the two divisions of his corps forward to take up the new line. In its final form, the line started near the buildings of the Codori farm on the Emmitsburg Road and ran southwest along the road for about a mile to a large peach orchard owned by a farmer named Sherfy. From the Sherfy orchard (henceforth known to history as the Peach Orchard), Sickles's line bent back at almost a 90-degree angle, running southeastward across an open field, down a rocky, wooded hillside to the valley of the West Fork of Plum Run (also known as Rose's Run), across a field of ripening wheat (henceforth the Wheatfield), then up Houck Ridge and along the ridge to where it ended in the pile of boulders known as Devil's Den. And where the ridge ended, so did Sickles's line, unsupported—"in the air," in the military parlance of the time— perched atop its rocky eminence half a mile in front of Little Round Top, where it was supposed to be. Likewise, the other end of Sickles's line, up near the Codori farm, was equally in the air, hanging out in the middle of a wide, open field half a mile from the left of the Second Corps, with which Sickles's corps was supposed to connect. The line was twice as long as the one Meade had assigned for the Third Corps and about twice as long as the corps could reasonably hold. Especially in the sector from the Peach Orchard to Devil's Den, the line was dangerously thin, with sometimes wide gaps between brigades. The Third Corps had no reserves left at all.

While Sickles was getting his men into their new, unauthorized position, he received two invitations from Meade to stop by army headquarters and discuss things. Now it was Sickles's turn to be too busy, and he declined to go. Then came a peremptory order from Meade. All corps commanders were to report for a conference with the commanding general. Before Sickles could reach the meeting, events developed rapidly. As the officers began to assemble at the farmhouse that Meade had made his headquarters, Meade's chief military engineer, Major General Warren, mentioned that the Third Corps was entirely out of position. This was news to Meade, whose notoriously ungovernable temper now rose toward one of its classic eruptions.

Sickles, however, would escape a tongue lashing. By the time he reached headquarters, heavy gunfire had broken out in his corps's sector. Meade met him as he rode up and told him not to dismount but to get back to his troops and direct the defense. It was too late now to put the Third Corps where it should have been. The Rebels were upon them, and they would just have to fight it out, with the rest of the Army of the Potomac supporting them as best it could. Meade gave orders for the Second and Fifth Corps to support Sickles, and the conference of corps commanders broke up before it got started, with the officers riding off to look to their own sectors and Meade hastening to the army's left to see what sort of mess Sickles had made and what could be done about it.[14]

The second day's fight, like the first, thus developed in a way that was not quite what either of the commanding generals had intended. When Longstreet's Confederates reached their attack position in Pfitzer's and Biesecker's Woods a little less than a mile west of the Round Tops, they found the situation in front of them much different than they had expected. They were supposed to be on the flank of the Union army. All they should have needed to do was deploy a line straddling the Emmitsburg Road and facing northeast, then march right up the road, rolling up the Union line. Instead, they found the Union defenders almost as far south as Little Round Top and several hundred yards west of it, in a sprawling position that rambled over hill and dale but was definitely in front of them and more or less facing toward them. What followed would have to be a frontal attack, not a flank attack as Lee had envisioned.

So Longstreet's corps deployed facing east, rather than northeast, and prepared to advance. On the right was Hood's division, its front line composed of Evander Law's footsore Alabama brigade on the right and Jerome Robertson's redoubtable Texas Brigade on the left. About two hundred yards behind them waited the Georgia brigades of Henry "Rock" Benning and Tige Anderson. Longstreet's left division was McLaws's, with its front line composed of Joseph B. Kershaw's South Carolina brigade on the right and William Barksdale's Mississippi brigade on the left. Two more Georgia brigades, those of Paul J. Semmes and William T. Wofford, formed McLaws's second line. Still farther left, Anderson's division was ready to go in when its time came. The attack was to begin on the right, with the brigades attacking one after another from right to left until all were engaged. Meanwhile, alert Union artillerymen at a battery on the bald end of Houck Ridge, just above Devil's Den, and at several more batteries in the Peach Orchard, opened fire on the Confederate troops along Seminary Ridge. Several batteries of Longstreet's artillery unlimbered and replied,

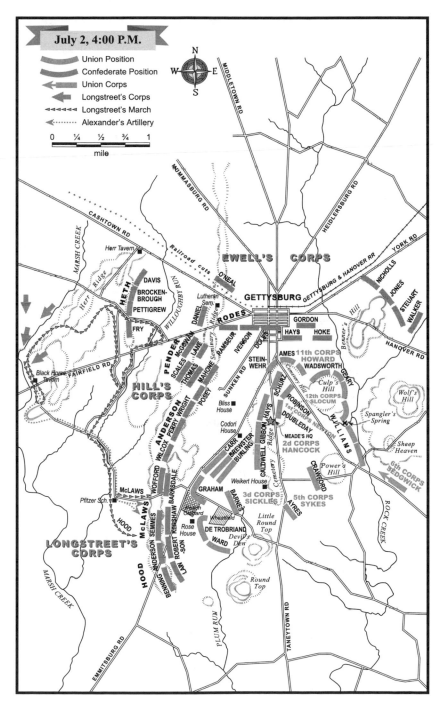

July 2, 4:00 P.M.

Union Position
Confederate Position
Union Corps
Longstreet's Corps
Longstreet's March
Alexander's Artillery

0   ¼   ½   ¾   1
mile

hoping to beat down the Union fire before the Confederate infantry began its advance.

While the troops were coming into line and the cannon thundered away, Hood, whose division was to launch the attack, sent scouts forward and learned that it might be possible to march around the south end of Round Top and get into the Union rear. The idea intrigued him, and he appealed repeatedly to Longstreet for permission to try it. Now it was Longstreet's turn to be realistic. Too many unknowns attended the plan, which in any case would have left McLaws's division unsupported on its right. Besides, Hood's division would have needed several hours to execute the maneuver, and the sun was already halfway down the western sky. Longstreet insisted that Hood attack the enemy in front of him.

Hood rode to the front of his division's line and called out to the Texas brigade he had once commanded, "Fix bayonets, my brave Texans; forward and take those heights!" As the Confederate and Texas flags at the center of each regiment's line sloped forward and the men stepped out, the First Texas's Lieutenant Colonel Phillip A. Work shouted, "Follow the Lone Star Flag to the top of the mountain!" On the Texans' right, Law's Alabama brigade strode forward through a field of standing wheat amid a chorus of Rebel Yells, their weariness forgotten as they raised "that wild, indescribable battle yell that no one having heard ever forgot." The time was approximately 4:30 P.M.[15]

The Union artillery began hitting them from the moment they started their advance, and gray-clad bodies littered the division's track. "Men were falling, stricken to death," recalled a member of the Fourth Alabama. The passing shells sounded like partridges in flight but burst, spraying lethal fragments. Junior officers urged the men forward, but they needed little encouragement. Private Rube Franks of the Fourth Alabama called to his fellow soldiers, "Come on, boys; come on! The Fifth Texas will get there before the Fourth! Come on, boys; come on!" A shell fragment struck down the exuberant soldier, but the Alabama line strode onward.[16]

Also among the first to fall was Hood himself, knocked out of the fight with a nasty shrapnel wound in the left arm. His division would have to make its attack without his direction. Already the rough, uneven terrain, houses, barns, and patches of woods, combined with the inevitable confusion of battle, had begun the process of shuffling the divisions' formations. Law shifted two of his Alabama regiments to the left to counter the Union battery above

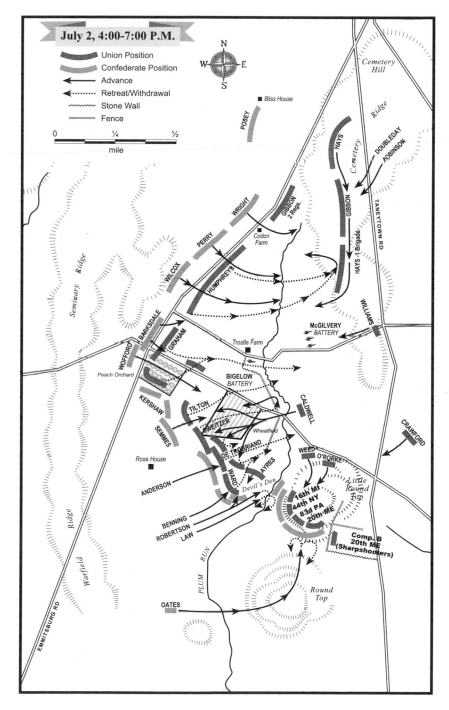

July 2, 4:00–7:00 P.M.

Union Position
Confederate Position
Advance
Retreat/Withdrawal
Stone Wall
Fence

0   ¼   ½
mile

N W E S

Cemetery Hill

Bliss House

POSEY

Cemetery Ridge

WRIGHT

GIBBON 2 Regts.

PERRY

Codori Farm

VILCOX

HUMPHREYS

HAYS

DOUBLEDAY
ROBINSON

GIBBON

HAYS - 1 Brigade

TANEYTOWN RD.

WILLIAMS

McGILVERY BATTERY

WOFFORD
BARKSDALE
GRAHAM
Peach Orchard

Trostle Farm

BIGELOW BATTERY

KERSHAW

TILTON

SWEITZER

Wheatfield

CALDWELL

CRAWFORD

SEMMES

DE TROBRIAND

Rose House

WARD

AYRES

WEED
O'RORKE

Little Round Top

ANDERSON

Devil's Den

16th ME
44th NY
83d PA
20th ME

Comp. B
20th ME
(Sharpshooters)

BENNING
ROBERTSON
LAW

Semiary Ridge

Warfield Ridge

PLUM RUN

EMMITSBURG RD.

OATES

Round Top

Devil's Den, but that turned out to be in the Texas Brigade's sector, and the two regiments found a place in the middle of that brigade's line, between the First and Fourth Texas regiments. Union skirmishers fell back before the Confederate advance. Law's three right regiments followed them up and over Round Top, then wheeled left and headed down the slope toward neighboring Little Round Top to the north. The Texas Brigade, along with the other two regiments of Law's Alabamians, bore a bit farther left and headed in the general direction of Devil's Den.[17]

The sound of Longstreet's cannon and the Union guns with which they were dueling in the Peach Orchard and atop Devil's Den had alerted Meade to impending trouble for his ill-deployed left flank, leading him to break up the meeting of corps commanders and send Sickles galloping back to his command. Meade was soon headed in that direction himself, along with most of his staff. He dispatched Warren to ride ahead and survey the ground and the situation.

The thirty-three-year-old Warren, a bridegroom of fifteen days, was high-strung, headstrong, and somewhat erratic. He could be brilliant at times, and this was one of those times. He galloped through Sickles's sector to what should have been the southern anchor of the Union line. Little Round Top, recently logged and devoid of trees on its top and western face, appeared to be the key terrain feature in that sector, and though Sickles had been ordered to hold the hill, a few signalmen were now the only Yankees on its rocky, bald top. At once, Warren decided that Little Round Top was vital. If this hill fell into Confederate control, he believed, the battle of Gettysburg would be all over but the shouting. The Taneytown Road would be lost and the remaining Federal position fatally compromised. In that case, it was easy to imagine a defeated Army of the Potomac fleeing toward Washington via the Baltimore Pike.

Warren also recognized that Sickles's ill-chosen position left the hill wide open to Confederates sweeping around the south end of Devil's Den. "The discovery was intensely thrilling to my feelings and almost appalling," Warren later wrote. As Hood's division prepared to begin its advance, Warren made an instant decision. Without taking time to consult with Meade or anyone else, he immediately dispatched his aide, Lieutenant Ranald S. Mackenzie, to find troops to put on Little Round Top. Mackenzie went first to Sickles, but the Third Corps commander had not a man to spare. The lieutenant rushed on and appealed to Major General George Sykes, whose

Fifth Corps had, on Meade's orders, moved up to support the Third. Sykes agreed to send a brigade of his lead division and ordered a staff officer to summon it.[18]

Major General Gouverneur K. Warren. Library of Congress, Prints and Photographs Division, LC-B8172-1757

The staff officer, a captain, reached the head of Brigadier General James Barnes's division column, but Barnes, who should have been there, was not in evidence. Instead, the commander of Barnes's lead brigade, Colonel Strong Vincent, impatiently demanded of the captain, "What are your orders? Give me your orders." "Genl. Sykes directs Genl. Barnes to send a brigade of his division to occupy that hill yonder," replied the staff officer, pointing toward Little Round Top. "I will take the responsibility myself of taking my brigade there," replied Vincent. Turning to Colonel James C. Rice, commanding the brigade's lead regiment, Vincent ordered, "Colonel, bring the brigade as quickly as possible on to that hill. Double quick where the ground will permit." Vincent sent his staff officers galloping down the column to give the word to the colonels of the other regiments and then, taking his brigade color bearer, rushed ahead toward Little Round Top to select a position for his troops.[19]

Meanwhile, pandemonium was erupting along the Third Corps line from Devil's Den to the Wheatfield. Two regiments of Law's Alabamians, along with the First Texas and the Third Arkansas from the Texas Brigade, charged toward the ridge top above Devil's Den and the small gorge just east of there, where the east branch of Plum Run squeezed between the encroaching slopes of Round Top and the tumbled boulders of Devil's Den. The Fourth Maine defended the gorge while the 124th New York and the four 10-pounder Parrott guns of Captain James E. Smith's Fourth New York Battery perched atop Devil's Den.[20]

The 124th had been recruited the previous summer in rural Orange County, New York, and its men were nicknamed "the Orange Blossoms." The regiment's right, connecting with the rest of Brigadier General J. H. Hobart Ward's brigade, lay in an extensive forest called Rose's Woods. The left, connecting with Smith's battery, lay behind a low stone wall that formed one side of a triangular field, about 150 yards to a side, covering about three acres of the hillside in front of them. At the foot of the slope was the west branch of Plum Run. The Texans and Arkansans splashed through the run and charged up the slope, yelling like fiends. The 124th met them with rifle fire, and Smith's cannoneers fired canister into the advancing ranks. A seesaw battle followed for control of the various walls edging the triangular field, lending a strange geometrical dynamic to the struggle for the south end of Houck Ridge. The Third Arkansas, advancing through Rose's Woods, ran into the other regiments of Ward's brigade and took flank fire from the Seventeenth Maine Regiment of Colonel Philippe Régis de Trobriand's brigade, where the Union line angled westward at the Wheatfield. The baffled Arkansans had to fall back.[21]

Next in line, the First Texas fought bitterly for the triangular field. For the outnumbered Orange Blossoms of the 124th New York, the situation rapidly became desperate. Some of the Texans later claimed that the muzzle flash of their rifles had singed the New Yorkers' uniforms. At the start of the fight, the regiment's Colonel A. Van Horne Ellis and Major James Cromwell had been on foot. It was safer that way. Now, Ellis had their horses brought forward, and he and Cromwell mounted up. To a captain who remonstrated at what good targets the colonel and major would make on horseback, Ellis replied, "The men must see us today."[22]

Then, as the crisis seemed to approach, Ellis gave the signal. He and Cromwell led their men over the wall and down the slope. For a few moments all was glorious victory for the Orange Blossoms as the First Texas broke and fled before them. Then, at the far side of the triangular field, the Texans turned and blasted a volley into the faces of their pursuers. Cromwell, a magnificent figure on his iron-gray horse, crumpled to the ground. The Orange Blossoms surged forward to recover his body, and the rocky field became a fiery cauldron of battle. One participant recalled that all was "roaring cannon, crashing rifles, screeching shots, bursting shells, hissing bullets, cheers, shouts, shrieks and groans."[23]

Once again the Texas line seemed to recede. Perhaps, after all, the panting, sweating, powder-grimed Orange Blossoms had won a victory against all odds. Then, emerging from the thick smoke and passing through the Texans' line, strode a solid gray-clad line of battle, fresh and unbloodied, two ranks deep, shoulder-to-shoulder and stretching out of sight in the battle smoke in either direction. Benning's Georgia brigade had moved up from its reserve position and was going into action to renew the momentum of the Confederate assault. The Georgia line swept the scattered Orange Blossoms before it like the first chill blast of a violent spring storm. Colonel Ellis fell dead with a bullet in his brain, and the survivors of the 124th, now scarcely one hundred strong, fell back to the crest of Houck Ridge, struggling to delay the Confederate advance. Smith's gunners, having served their cannon to the bitter end, now found it too late and had to leave behind three of their guns.[24]

While Smith's battery and the 124th New York fought to hold the west face of Houck Ridge at Devil's Den, the Fourth Maine succeeded in checking the Alabamians who strove to push through the rocky Plum Run gorge. The scene of that fight, a brush- and boulder-studded slope at the base of the Round Tops, was already earning its later title as "the Slaughter Pen." The Fourth's Colonel Elijah Walker soon realized, however, that the Rebels were surging up over the nose of the ridge on his right and through the boulder heap of Devil's Den itself. Flanked and in desperate straits, Walker responded with the sublime audacity that seemed almost commonplace on both sides this afternoon. He ordered his regiment to wheel to the right, fix bayonets, and charge. "I shall never forget the 'click' that was made by the fixing of bayonets," the colonel wrote years later. "It was as one."[25]

The Fourth Maine surged to the top of the ridge, but there it, too, met the onrushing wave of Benning's Georgia brigade. The fighting became hand-to-hand on the ridge top and in Devil's Den. The Maine men were soon joined by reinforcements of their own, one regiment from the other end of Ward's line and another from de Trobriand. The oversized Fortieth New York took up the position the Fourth Maine had just left, covering the Slaughter Pen and Plum Run gorge. The Ninety-ninth Pennsylvania, led by Major John W. Moore with the shout of "Pennsylvania and our homes!" charged into Devil's Den alongside the Fourth Maine and drove the Georgians and Alabamians out of the boulders and off the ridge. Meanwhile, the Fortieth New York charged the Confederates who were trying to press through the gorge and drove them back but could not dislodge them. One Confederate counted seven separate charges by the Fortieth. The two sides blazed away at each other there until the Slaughter Pen was more thickly strewn with bodies than with boulders.[26]

This new-won Union grip on the south end of Houck Ridge and Plum Run gorge proved short-lived. Benning's Georgians, together with the Alabama regiments and the First Texas, regrouped and came on again. The remaining brigade of Hood's division, Tige Anderson's Georgia brigade, plowed into de Trobriand's brigade, preventing it from supporting Ward with flank fire. Thus relieved, the Third Arkansas also joined the assault on the north end of Ward's line. All together it was too much. The Union line fell back, leaving Houck Ridge in Confederate hands. The Fortieth New York, threatened flank and rear, abandoned the position it had tenaciously defended. The Confederates now owned the triangular field, Devil's Den, Plum Run gorge, and the Slaughter Pen, for whatever they might be worth, but fighting still was furious on either side of the position, in northern Rose's Woods and the Wheatfield to the north and on the slopes of Little Round Top to the east.[27]

The fighting was still raging along Houck Ridge when Colonel Vincent and his color bearer arrived atop Little Round Top. Vincent, who had celebrated his twenty-sixth birthday a fortnight before, was a Harvard graduate who had been a lawyer in Erie, Pennsylvania, before the war. He had led Erie's own Eighty-third Pennsylvania Regiment before rising to command the brigade. As Vincent and the color bearer sat their horses on Little Round Top surveying the country and the battle raging about half a mile away, shells began to explode around them, coming from Longstreet's guns over on the Emmitsburg Road. Vincent turned to the color bearer: "They are firing at the flag. Go behind the rocks with it." Boulders were plentiful on Little Round Top, and the color bearer had no difficulty complying. Vincent selected a position for the brigade, and when Colonel Rice led it up the hill, it could go straight into place.

Confederate casualties in one small corner of the Slaughter Pen at the foot of Little Round Top. Library of Congress, Prints and Photographs Division, LC-B8171-0265

The brigade's line curved around the south and southwest slopes of Little Round Top. The Sixteenth Michigan held the difficult position on the bare ground of the southwest slope. Then came the Forty-fourth New York, the Eighty-third Pennsylvania, and finally the Twentieth Maine, in the scant shelter of the open woodlands of the south slope. In altitude the line slanted downward from the Sixteenth Michigan's position, a little way below the crest, down and around to the Twentieth Maine's just above the saddle between the Round Tops. Colonel Vincent sent his horse to the rear and prepared to direct the brigade on foot.[28]

As it did to all the other soldiers of the Army of the Potomac, this battle meant something special for Vincent and his men. On a Northern hillside, beneath a Northern sky, it was easy to remember why they must fight. Vincent's brigade had received many reminders in the past twenty-four hours. While the battle had raged at Gettysburg on July 1, Vincent's men, along with the rest of the Fifth Corps, had marched toward the field. They had slept in Maryland the night of June 30, and on the morning of July 1, as they marched across the state line into Pennsylvania, a thrill ran up and down the brigade column. They were in a free state now, on Northern soil. Excitement ran highest in the ranks of the Eighty-third Pennsylvania. They might still be a long way from Erie, their hometown, but this was their home state. Vincent sent word back down the column "to hang out the banner on the outward wall." Color sergeants uncased their flags, battle-stained Stars and Stripes torn by the bullets of past engagements. The fifes and drums struck up "Yankee Doodle," then still America's favorite patriotic air. Pennsylvanians, New Yorkers, Michiganders, and Maine men sang, cheered, and yelled themselves hoarse. Along the Fifth Corps column the contagion spread, as one Pennsylvanian recalled, "from regiment to regiment, and from brigade to brigade, until every banner was flying, every fife screaming, and every drum beating."[29]

Nightfall found them still marching between Hanover and Gettysburg, spurred on by word from the battlefield of the first day's reverses and the death of Reynolds. Still, in the little villages through which they passed, women came out to wave flags by lantern-light and sing "The Star-Spangled Banner" and other patriotic songs. The soldiers cheered and waved their caps as they strode along. The march had finally ended on the edge of the battlefield about 2:00 that morning.[30]

Thoughts of all the songs and cheers and waving flags may have flitted through the minds of Vincent's men in the ten minutes or so they waited in line of battle on the slopes of Little Round Top. "Scarcely had the troops been put in line," recalled the Eighty-third Pennsylvania's Captain Amos Judson, "when a loud, fierce, distant yell was heard." It was as though all the demons of Hell had broken loose and "joined in the chorus of one grand, universal war-whoop." The Fifteenth and Forty-seventh Alabama had swept over the crest of Round Top and now surged down the north face toward Vincent's left. The Fourth Alabama and the Fourth and Fifth Texas charged across a shoulder of Round Top, just above the Plum Run gorge, and stormed onward toward the center and right of Vincent's position. When Judson first spotted them, they appeared to be about a quarter of a mile away, advancing at the double-quick with bayonets fixed, "coming down upon us." Vincent took one look at the oncoming Confederate tide and turned to Captain John M. Clark, one of the officers of the brigade staff. "Go and tell Gen. Barnes to send me reinforcements at once," Vincent instructed. "The enemy are coming against us with an overwhelming force." Clark hurried off, and Vincent prepared to face the Confederate onslaught.[31]

The Texans struck first, along with the Fourth Alabama, charging up the hill toward the center of Vincent's line. The attackers passed out of sight behind a fold of ground near the base of the hill. The Eighty-third Pennsylvania and the Forty-fourth New York braced themselves. "There they come," cried a member of the Forty-fourth. New Yorker Charles Sprague saw the Texans and Alabamians on the lower slope of Little Round Top, "dodging zig-zag among the trees." "On came the enemy," recalled Captain Judson of the Eighty-third, "running and yelling like fiends." The Yankees crouched behind the numerous small boulders, outcroppings, and rock ledges along their line and loosed a deadly volley that cut down dozens of attackers. After a furious exchange of fire, the attackers fell back.[32]

The Rebels rallied at the foot of the hill and came back up again, working their way through the rocks, firing as they came. "Hundreds of them approached even within fifteen yards of our line," recalled Captain Judson. The regiment's drummers laid aside their instruments and picked up rifles and cartridge boxes from the fallen. New Yorker Ezra Sprague recalled the thick bank of gunsmoke just in front of his regiment's line and how "a red star of flame would jump right out of the smoke at every discharge" of an enemy rifle. Eventually, the bluecoats' tenacious defense forced the Texans back down the hill a second time. They came back a third. Still, the Union line held.[33]

Ammunition ran short in the Forty-fourth New York, and men began scavenging rounds from the cartridge boxes of the dead and wounded. Frasier Rosenkranz's rifle became so hot that he could not use it, so he "snatched one from a dead man" and went on firing. On the slope below, the Texans sought every bit of shelter

they could find. "Every tree, rock and stump . . . was soon appro-
priated," wrote Val Giles of the Fourth Texas. Giles recalled how
he and another soldier had laid claim to a "moss-covered old boulder about the size of a 500-pound cotton bale." The Texans and
Alabamians had little organization left and even less momentum,
but they stubbornly clung to the hillside and fought bitterly. "There
seemed to be a viciousness in the very air we breathed," Giles later
wrote. The lines were still not more than fifty yards apart, and, as
Giles explained, "Everything was on the shoot. No favors asked,
and none offered."[34]

While its center held strong, Vincent's brigade faced disaster
on both its flanks. Out on the extreme Confederate right, the Fifteenth and Forty-seventh Alabama, having gone right over the peak
of Round Top, were a bit later in hitting the Union line than the
other Confederates to their left. When they did, they plunged
straight across the shallow saddle between the Round Tops and
slammed into the line of the Twentieth Maine, Vincent's left-flank
regiment. The fighting soon became as intense here as on the front
of the hill. The outnumbered Maine men hung on doggedly. The
Confederates, led by twenty-nine-year-old Alabama lawyer Colonel William C. Oates, swung out and struck the Twentieth Maine's
exposed flank.

Across the way, the Twentieth's commander, thirty-five-year-
old Bowdoin College professor Joshua Lawrence Chamberlain, was
startled when one of his officers pointed out a Confederate movement in the woods beyond the enemy line that was engaging his
men. Chamberlain climbed atop a rock and recognized Oates's
movement for what it was. He responded by stretching his own
line to match and then refusing his left flank—that is, swinging the
left half of his line backward like a gate on its hinges. Oates's men
attacked front and flank, more fiercely than before, pressing in to
point-blank range. Here and there, gray-clad platoons or companies broke into the Union line. Maine men and Alabamians came
to blows with bayonets, rifle butts, and fists. The struggling lines
surged up and down the slope, a few yards one way and then the
other. The Rebels drove the Twentieth's line back a dozen yards or
so by main force but could not break it.[35]

The situation was rapidly becoming desperate for Chamberlain. A third of his men were down, and the survivors were frantically rummaging through the cartridge boxes of their fallen
comrades in search of ammunition. The Alabamians fell back, as

they had several times before during the fight, each time regrouping and attacking with renewed vigor. Convinced his regiment could not hold off another attack, Chamberlain decided not to wait to receive it. He ordered his men to fix bayonets, and he later reported that the word "ran like fire along the line, from man to man, and rose into a shout." Then he sent the refused left wing swinging forward into line with the rest of the regiment again. The whole line swept downhill, driving startled and exhausted Alabamians before it. Many Rebels surrendered, and the rest fled back over Round Top. Vincent's left, and the Army of the Potomac's, was secure.[36]

The west face of Little Round Top, much as the attacking Texans would have seen it. Library of Congress, Prints and Photographs Division, LC-B8171-7318

Meanwhile, a crisis just as dire threatened the right flank of Vincent's brigade. The Sixteenth Michigan had the worst position of any of the brigade's regiments. Yet someone had to hold the open crest on the west side of the hill, and that job had fallen to the men from the Great Lakes State. They fought stoutly, but the relentless fury of the Texans' assault began to tell. By this time, Devil's Den and the rest of Houck Ridge had fallen to the Rebels, and the Forty-eighth Alabama, Third Arkansas, and possibly other regiments added their weight to the assault and began to work around the Sixteenth's right flank. The Michigan regiment's lines wavered and began to crumble, and the Confederates closed in for the kill.[37]

Major General Joshua Lawrence Chamberlain. Library of Congress, Prints and
Photographs Division, LC-B8172-1859

In the meantime, Gouverneur Warren had been busy. Some time
after dispatching the request to Sickles and Sykes that had finally
brought Vincent's brigade, the chief engineer had galloped off himself in search of troops to secure Little Round Top. The first blue-
clad column he encountered was Brigadier General Stephen H.
Weed's brigade of Romeyn Ayres's division, another element of the
Fifth Corps moving up to support Sickles as per Meade's orders.
Weed was off somewhere investigating where to bring his brigade
into action, but Warren had commanded this brigade himself before being promoted to his present post, and the officers and men
knew and trusted him.

Dead on the wooded southern slope of Little Round Top, where the Twentieth Maine fought. Library of Congress, Prints and Photographs Division, LC-B8171-0252

Warren spurred his horse down the hill toward the head of the brigade's column, shouting all the way. Pulling up at the head, Warren wasted no time on pleasantries. To Colonel Patrick O'Rorke, commanding the lead regiment of the brigade, he called, "Paddy, give me a regiment!" The twenty-seven-year-old O'Rorke was a sometime apprentice stonecutter who had changed career paths, entered the United States Military Academy, and graduated first in the West Point class of 1861. Now he tried to explain about his orders and General Weed's expectations. Warren had no time. "Never mind that!" he barked. "Bring your regiment up here and I will take the responsibility." That was good enough for O'Rorke. Directed by one of Warren's aides, he took his regiment, the 140th New York, up the back slope of Little Round Top at the double-quick.[38]

As O'Rorke and his men surged over the crest, the Sixteenth Michigan was just beginning to give way. With frantic haste and heedless of the niceties of formation, the young colonel chivvied his men into a semblance of line beside the Sixteenth. The Rebels were now only forty feet away. "Here they are, men," shouted

O'Rorke. "Commence firing!" A Confederate shot O'Rorke dead, and the 140th New York returned the fire with a crashing volley. The Confederate line staggered but then poured its deadly fire into the badly exposed ranks of the 140th. Rushed into battle, deprived of their colonel, and hit hard by enemy fire, the regiment started to waver. Colonel Vincent saw the crisis from where he had been directing his brigade's fight and rushed over to try to rally the 140th. While doing so, he fell with a bullet in the abdomen, but the New York line steadied and held.[39]

The Confederate tide ebbed back down the hillside, leaving behind many men who were too pinned down to make their escape. Sergeant Consider Willett of the Forty-fourth New York led a squad forward and rounded up ninety prisoners. As one of the cornered Confederates stood up in front of Captain Albert N. Husted, begging him not to shoot, a Confederate bullet from somewhere down the slope slammed into the surrendering Rebel's back, toppling him over directly in front of the startled New Yorker.[40]

Meanwhile, more help was on the way for the embattled defenders of Little Round Top. Lieutenant Charles E. Hazlett's Battery D, Fifth U.S. Artillery, was even then wrestling its six 10-pounder Parrott guns up the back slope of the hill. The west face was neither as steep nor as rocky as the rugged east face, but it was challenge enough to force Hazlett's artillerists and some passing infantry to join their muscle to that of the straining teams and manhandle the half-ton cannon into place by brute force. The narrow and rocky summit was not an ideal artillery position, and guns deployed there could not be depressed enough to help beat off the Confederates on the slope below. Nonetheless, Hazlett could slam his shells into Devil's Den, and, as he told Warren when the chief engineer pointed out the problems of the position, "The sound of my guns will be encouraging to our troops and disheartening to the others." So up the guns went, and shortly after the 140th New York had helped Vincent's brigade beat off the last Confederate assault, the Parrotts were banging out their defiance to the Rebels across the way.[41]

While Hazlett's sweating artillerists were heaving their guns into position, the remaining three regiments of General Weed's brigade moved up to join their comrades of the 140th New York, extending its line northward along the west face of Little Round Top. Soon another battery of artillery was going into position on the hill's northern flank, and the hill seemed secure against any number of Confederates—more than secure against the badly spent remnants that clung stubbornly to its slopes and crouched behind boulders in the Slaughter Pen and Devil's Den. The Confederates were not used to being thwarted, and they seethed with frustration at the Yankees they could not seem to move. Val Giles of the Fourth Texas later said that he and his comrades knew they "were whipped, and all were furious about it." Giles consoled himself in later years by claiming that the Federals were whipped, too, but on the evening of July 2, every man in the vicinity in blue, gray, or butternut knew who had possession of Little Round Top and what it meant.[42]

The angry Confederates kept up a steady sniping fire against the summit of Little Round Top. They felled General Weed as he directed his brigade there. Then Lieutenant Hazlett bent over the fallen general to hear some last message, but Hazlett, too, was shot and collapsed across his superior officer. Both were soon dead, but too many Yankees now held Little Round Top to be driven off by snipers.[43]

The issue was no longer in doubt on Little Round Top, but the fierce fighting that had begun along the slopes of Houck Ridge had radiated by now to other sectors as well. North of Little Round Top and Devil's Den that fighting was even now rising toward a climax that had the potential to cancel Union success on this rocky hilltop at the southern end of the battlefield.

NOTES

1. Pfanz, *Gettysburg: The Second Day* (Chapel Hill: University of North Carolina Press, 1987), 58.

2. Bowden and Ward, *Last Chance for Victory*, 226, 230–38.

3. Pfanz, *Gettysburg: The Second Day*, 28.

4. Pfanz, *Gettysburg: Culp's Hill and Cemetery Hill*, 71–87.

5. Robert K. Krick, " 'If Longstreet Says So, It Is Most Likely Not True': James Longstreet and the Second Day at Gettysburg," in *The Second Day at Gettysburg*, ed. Gary W. Gallagher (Kent, OH: Kent State University Press, 1993), 57–62; Coles, *From Huntsville to Appomattox*, 205–6.

6. Pfanz, *Gettysburg: The Second Day*, 105–7.

7. Ibid., 110.

8. Krick, "James Longstreet and the Second Day," 70–71; Pfanz, *Gettysburg: The Second Day*, 110.

9. Krick, "James Longstreet and the Second Day," 71–72.

10. Warren Wilkinson and Steven E. Woodworth, *A Scythe of Fire: The Civil War Story of the Eighth Georgia Regiment* (New York: HarperCollins, 2002), 230–31.

11. Pfanz, *Gettysburg: The Second Day*, 122.

12. Pfanz, *Gettysburg: Culp's Hill and Cemetery Hill*, 117; William Glenn Robertson, "The Peach Orchard Revisited," 47.

13. Pfanz, *Gettysburg: The Second Day*, 97; William Glenn Robertson, "The Peach Orchard Revisited," 47–48.

14. Pfanz, *Gettysburg: The Second Day*, 138–40.

15. Coles, *From Huntsville to Appomattox*, 104, 208; Pfanz, *Gettysburg: The Second Day*, 149–68.

16. Coles, *From Huntsville to Appomattox*, 208.

17. Ibid.; Valerius Cincinnatus Giles, *Rags and Hope: The Recollections of Val C. Giles, Four Years with Hood's Brigade, Fourth Texas Infantry, 1861–1865*, ed. Mary Lasswell (New York: Coward-McCann, 1961), 179; Pfanz, *Gettysburg: The Second Day*, 167–76.

18. David M. Jordan, *"Happiness Is Not My Companion": The Life of General G. K. Warren* (Bloomington: Indiana University Press, 2001), 90–92.

19. Oliver Norton to Frank Huntington, September 28, 1888, Oliver Norton Papers, Civil War Miscellaneous Collection, USAMHI.

20. *OR*, vol. 27, pt. 1, pp. 493–94, 588–89; Pfanz, *Gettysburg: The Second Day*, 185.

21. *OR*, vol. 27, pt. 1, pp. 493–94, 588–89; Pfanz, *Gettysburg: The Second Day*, 179–83.

22. Pfanz, *Gettysburg: The Second Day*, 187.

23. Ibid.

24. *OR*, vol. 27, pt. 1, p. 589; Pfanz, *Gettysburg: The Second Day*, 187–92.

25. Pfanz, *Gettysburg: The Second Day*, 193.

26. *OR*, vol. 27, pt. 1, pp. 494, 526–27; Pfanz, *Gettysburg: The Second Day*, 195–96.

27. *OR*, vol. 27, pt. 1, pp. 526–27; Pfanz, *Gettysburg: The Second Day*, 196–200.

28. Oliver Norton to Frank Huntington, September 28, 1888, Oliver Norton Papers; Amos H. Judson, *History of the Eighty-third Regiment Pennsylvania Volunteers* (Erie, PA: B. F. H. Lynn, 1865), 67.

29. Judson, *History of the Eighty-third*, 66.

30. Ibid.

31. Albert N. Husted, "Gettysburg in Perspective," posted on Web site "The Normal School Company: Company E of the 44th New York," created by graduate research seminar directed by Professor Allen Ballard, State University of New York at Albany, p. 3; Judson, *History of the Eighty-third*, 67.

32. *OR*, vol. 27, pt. 1, pp. 616–18; Judson, *History of the Eighty-third*, 126–27; Charles Ezra Sprague, "Holding Little Round Top," posted on Web site "The Normal School Company: Company E of the 44th New York," created by graduate research seminar directed by Professor Allen Ballard, State University of New York at Albany, p. 8.

33. *OR*, vol. 27, pt. 1, p. 630; Judson, *History of the Eighty-third*, 126–27; Sprague, "Holding Little Round Top," p. 8.

34. *OR*, vol. 27, pt. 1, pp. 616–18; Frasier Rosenkranz to "Dear Cousin," July 20, 1863, Frasier Rosenkranz Papers; Giles, *Rags and Hope*, 179–81.

35. *OR*, vol. 27, pt. 1, pp. 623–24.

36. *OR*, vol. 27, pt. 1, pp. 616–18, 624.

37. *OR*, vol. 27, pt. 1, p. 628; Oliver Norton to Frank Huntington, September 28, 1888, Oliver Norton Papers; Giles, *Rags and Hope*, 182; Pfanz, *Gettysburg: The Second Day*, 227.

38. Jordan, "*Happiness Is Not My Companion*," 93; Pfanz, *Gettysburg: The Second Day*, 225–26.

39. Pfanz, *Gettysburg: The Second Day*, 230; Judson, *History of the Eighty-third*, 67; Oliver Norton to Frank Huntington, September 28, 1888, Oliver Norton Papers.

40. Husted, "Gettysburg in Perspective," p. 3.

41. Pfanz, *Gettysburg: The Second Day*, 223.

42. Giles, *Rags and Hope*, 182–83.

43. Pfanz, *Gettysburg: The Second Day*, 240.

CHAPTER SEVEN

ONE MORE CHARGE
AND THE DAY IS OURS

SHORTLY AFTER BENNING'S Georgia brigade had gone forward to support the Texans in their assault on Devil's Den, Tige Anderson's Georgia brigade had advanced as well, likewise in answer to a request for support from Brigadier General Jerome Robertson, commander of the Texas Brigade. Anderson's men moved across open fields under heavy artillery fire. Their position on the left of Hood's second line put them uncomfortably close to the massed Union batteries in and just east of the Peach Orchard, whose guns now fired southwestward, enfilading the Georgians' line as they marched across wheat fields and clambered over the post-and-rail fences along the Emmitsburg Road. All the way, shell bursts cut down men by ones and twos, leaving them in crumpled heaps along the brigade's line of march or draped limply over the top rail of a fence. Lieutenant Colonel John C. Mounger of the hard-hit Ninth Georgia was one of many officers who strove to reform his men as quickly as possible after they had crossed the road and the fences. "Boys, guide right!" shouted Mounger, who then disappeared in a flash, a roar, and a cloud of smoke, dust, and flying fence rails and body parts. The shaken survivors formed up and pressed on.[1]

The Eighth Georgia was also taking a pounding as it crossed the open fields. One shell struck Sergeant Travis Maxey full in the chest, disintegrating him from the waist up and so dousing Sergeant Jeff Copeland in blood that Captain John Reed thought Copeland was wounded and gaped in amazement as the gory soldier kept pace with the regiment as if nothing had happened. Other shells opened holes in the line, but the men stepped over the mangled bodies of their comrades, closed the gaps, and moved on.[2]

"Double-quick!" came the order, and the men trotted forward across gently rising ground toward the small orchard of a farmer named Rose. They passed through the orchard, leaving the Rose farm buildings on their left and entered the extensive woodlot known as Rose's Woods, driving Union skirmishers before them. They descended a steep rocky slope into the green, shadowy valley of the west branch of Plum Run, sometimes also called Rose's Run. Across the valley the ground rose steeply toward Houck Ridge, on the Georgians' right front, and more gradually toward the Wheatfield, opposite the brigade's center and left. In both locations Union troops waited.

These Federals were the ones who had defeated the Third Arkansas, on the left of the Texas Brigade, and kept alive Union hopes of holding the Triangular Field and Devil's Den. In the woods on northern Houck Ridge was Ward's brigade, and along a stone fence where the Wheatfield bordered Rose's Woods was the Seventeenth Maine Regiment, part of the brigade commanded by Colonel Philippe Régis de Trobriand. The Seventeenth was ready to pour an enfilading fire into any troops that advanced against Ward on Houck Ridge. Anderson's brigade eliminated that problem, at least, by storming toward both Union positions at the same time.

At the right end of Anderson's line, the Fifty-ninth Georgia joined the Texas Brigade's Third Arkansas Regiment in attacking the north end of Ward's line on Houck Ridge. With the addition of the large Georgia regiment and the subtraction of the flanking fire from the Seventeenth Maine—now very much occupied—the Confederate attackers soon began to gain the upper hand in the struggle for Houck Ridge. This was all the more true once the Texans, along with the Georgians of Benning's brigade, overran Devil's Den. The Union position on Houck Ridge finally crumbled under the pressure added by Anderson's attack.

The Wheatfield was another matter. Anderson's other three regiments all charged across the low, marshy ground in the bottom of the ravine of the west fork of Plum Run toward the low stone wall on the edge of the Wheatfield and a wooded, stony hill (the Stony Hill, of course) just beyond the western corner of the field. In front of them was a single regiment, the Seventeenth Maine. The Georgians heavily outnumbered the defenders, but the position proved deceptively strong. Fifty yards or so in front of the Seventeenth Maine's stone wall was the west fork of Plum Run, a muddy stream a few inches deep flowing between banks a couple of feet high in most places. In those areas the Georgians used it as a ready-made trench as they crouched and exchanged fire with the Maine men behind the stone wall. As dozens of them were hit and fell into the sluggish stream, they soon dyed its shallow waters red.[3]

To the right of the Seventeenth Maine, on the Georgians' left, lay a 150-yard gap in the Union line that would have been fatal to Federal hopes of holding the Wheatfield except that it was covered by a vicious crossfire from the Maine men along the stone wall and the other regiments of de Trobriand's brigade on the other side of the gap, on the slopes of the Stony Hill. To further complicate the Georgians' task, the west fork of Plum Run here flattened out into a soggy morass that blocked the Georgians' forward progress, preventing them from charging through the gap. Instead, the brigade remaining—the Ninth Georgia and left companies of the Eighth—had to stand in the boggy ground along the run and shoot it out with Yankees behind the stone wall, to their right front, and on the Stony Hill, to their left front.[4]

The Georgians tried valiantly to push across the bog. The Eighth Georgia's color bearer, Sergeant Felix King, led the way but was shot down with a severe leg wound. Lying on the ground, the badly wounded sergeant kept waving the flag above him until one of the Eighth's lieutenants took it from him—only to be shot down in turn. The Georgians tried to work their way forward through the morass, but the intense crossfire dropped a number of them into the mud and water. The upper portion of one gray-clad corpse remained half upright, so deeply mired it could not topple over.[5]

The fight raged on, and the woods filled up with low-hanging powder smoke. Eventually Anderson's left succeeded in working its way through the deadly bog and took control of an alder thicket beyond it, on the corner of the Wheatfield and squarely on the flank of the Seventeenth Maine. The rest of the Georgians charged the stone wall from in front. Astoundingly the Maine men held on. Refusing their right-flank companies, just as the Twentieth Maine was refusing its left companies about this time over on Little Round Top, the Seventeenth checked the Georgians' flanking maneuver. The Maine men, still crouching behind the stone fence, rose up and met the Georgians charging out of the woods in front of them. The lines met along the fence, and men thrust bayonets and swung rifle butts over its 3-foot height. Briefly the Eleventh Georgia planted its flag on the fence.

Once again, however, the Georgians had to fall back to the banks of the west fork, leaving behind their dead and wounded in front of the stone fence along with a single unwounded member of the Eleventh Georgia, a prisoner whom the Maine men had succeeded in grappling and dragging over to their side of the fence. Worse, fire from the Stony Hill became so severe that the Ninth Georgia, on Anderson's flank, had to refuse its own left wing in order to counter it. The captain upon whom command of that regiment had by this time devolved found the noise so intense that he had to convey his orders to his men by pantomime. Somehow he got the regiment into the new formation.[6]

It was all for naught. After perhaps half an hour of intense combat in the Plum Run bottoms, Anderson realized that his brigade could never batter its way into the Wheatfield by that route. The Seventeenth Maine's position along the stone wall was a strong one, but the real Yankee trump card was possession of the Stony Hill. From that vantage point, they could cover the Seventeenth's flank and pour a deadly cross fire on the Georgians in the bog below. Yet though the Stony Hill dominated the Wheatfield to the southeast, it was an insignificant rise when approached from the west. West of the Stony Hill, however, was McLaws's division's sector. So Anderson gave the order to fall back to the west edge of Rose's Woods, near the Rose farm buildings. Then, while a brief lull followed in this sector, he went to consult with officers of Brigadier General Joseph Kershaw's South Carolina brigade, the left brigade of McLaws's division, to see what could be done about the Stony Hill.[7]

The fact is that McLaws's division should have joined the attack long before. Indeed, Kershaw's brigade should have led the division into action by following just to the left of and a few hundred yards behind Robertson's Texans. Had that been the case, the Seventeenth Maine could never have inflicted flanking fire on Robertson's right regiment (the Third Arkansas). Houck Ridge would almost certainly have fallen thirty to forty-five minutes earlier than it did, with imponderable consequences. But McLaws was waiting together with Longstreet back on Seminary Ridge, and Longstreet, for reasons best known to himself, kept his left division idle while Hood's men struggled and died along Houck Ridge and in the valley of the west fork of Plum Run.

No one recorded what passed between Anderson and the South Carolinians. The Georgian returned to his brigade, where skirmish firing was still lively enough to keep up a steady but irregular ringing of the Rose farm bell as stray bullets struck it. Another Yankee skirmisher's bullet shortly struck Anderson in the leg. His men carried him off the battlefield, and command of the brigade passed all the way down to a lieutenant colonel.[8]

About 5:00 P.M., Longstreet finally gave his permission, and Kershaw's South Carolina brigade advanced with a parade-ground precision that revealed it as the splendidly drilled unit it was. Kershaw's men were even closer than Anderson's had been to the massed guns in and around the Peach Orchard, so the South Carolinians had to run a gauntlet not so much of shells but of the far deadlier canister. One South Carolinian remembered "the awful deathly surging sounds of those little black balls as they flew by us, through us, between our legs, and over us!"[9] Kershaw directed half of his brigade to veer to the left, directly toward the quarter-mile-wide space of open ground between the Peach Orchard and the Stony Hill where nothing but closely ranked Union batteries precariously held the ground without infantry support.[10] It took nerve to march toward the muzzles of those guns that had strewn the open fields with broken bodies, but the South Carolinians' iron discipline held firm as they continued to bear down on the artillery while the gunners frantically loaded and fired charge after charge of double canister. Then, when it looked as if the assault would be successful, a garbled order sent the well-drilled South Carolina formation wheeling directly across the fronts of the batteries, and the Union guns pounded it to pieces. The left-flank regiments of Kershaw's brigade were out of the fight for the time being, and, as Kershaw himself later wrote, "hundreds of the bravest and best men of Carolina fell, victims of this fatal blunder."[11]

While Kershaw's left regiments came to grief in front of the Union gun line, the right of the South Carolina brigade moved through the buildings of the Rose farm and straight toward the Stony Hill. Anderson's Georgians, now minus Anderson himself, advanced alongside Kershaw's men. Once again the sylvan stillness of Rose's Woods and the West Plum Run ravine exploded in the crashing rattle of 2,000 rifles and the yells, cheers, screams, groans, and muttered oaths of their users. At first, the results were the same. The Seventeenth Maine clung to its stone wall as tenaciously as ever. The defenders of the Stony Hill, the rest of de Trobriand's brigade and two small brigades of the Fifth Corps, fought hard and held off Kershaw. As it had elsewhere on the field that day, the fighting grew intense.[12] After several members of the Third South Carolina's color guard fell killed and wounded, someone shouted to Color Sergeant William Lamb, "Lower the colors, down with the flag!" so as not to draw fire. Lamb held the flag high and replied, "This flag never goes down until I am down!"[13]

Then, when it looked as if the defenders of the Stony Hill might drive off Kershaw's attacking force, the fortunes of battle shifted with startling suddenness. The two small Fifth Corps brigades helping to defend the Stony Hill belonged to the division commanded that day by Brigadier General James Barnes, who was nervous about the quarter-mile stretch devoid of Union infantry between his position and the Peach Orchard. His qualms compounded when he saw Kershaw's South Carolinians moving against both the Stony Hill and the unsupported artillery line. Although the Union batteries held their ground against all odds, Barnes, taking counsel of his fears, ordered his division to march to the rear, leaving de Trobriand's lone brigade to try to hold the Stony Hill and the Wheatfield against the combined forces of Anderson and Kershaw. Barnes deployed his division again some 300 yards to the rear, where things seemed safer.[14]

De Trobriand's men had put up a good fight, but they could not hope to hold on where they were. To the pressure from the Rebels in front was soon added that from Georgians and Texans moving north up Houck Ridge after driving off Ward's brigade. De Trobriand gave the command, and the brigade fell back in good order. Kershaw's men overran the Stony Hill, and Anderson's Georgians finally swarmed over the stone wall they had assaulted so long in vain, surging out into the by-now badly trampled Wheatfield.[15]

Ward's and de Trobriand's brigades belonged to the division of Major General David B. Birney. His division's defeat, Birney realized, endangered the remainder of the Third Corps line—Major General Andrew A. Humphreys's division in the Peach Orchard and along the Emmitsburg Road—as well as the whole Union position south of Gettysburg. Help was on the way in the form of the rest of the Fifth Corps and a division of the Second. For the moment, however, the victorious Confederates threatened to sweep across all the ground between the Peach Orchard and Little Round Top, severing Vincent's and Weed's brigades from the rest of the army and beginning the rolling up of the Army of the Potomac that Lee had intended all along.

Birney needed something to check the Confederate advance until reinforcements could come up, and he seized upon a regiment retiring from the fight in good order, looking as steady and battleworthy as ever: the sturdy Seventeenth Maine. Birney sent them charging back across the Wheatfield they had just left. The Maine men went in with a cheer and sent their old foes of

Anderson's brigade scampering back out of the Wheatfield. The Seventeenth then took up a position at the top of the ridge that ran through the middle of the Wheatfield and fired down on the Georgians who crouched behind the stone wall—the same one the Georgians and New Englanders had fought over for the past hour—at the low southwest end of the field. Birney ordered another of de Trobriand's regiments, the Fifth Michigan, to join the Seventeenth Maine in the Wheatfield and try to hold off Kershaw's South Carolinians pressing forward from the Stony Hill.[16]

Just when it seemed the South Carolinians' advantage in numbers and position might crumple the Michigan outfit and leverage their Maine friends out of the Wheatfield at last, the tide of battle took another sudden drastic shift as new Union troops arrived on the scene, relieved de Trobriand's weary men, and advanced to meet the Confederates. The new troops made up the division of Brigadier General John C. Caldwell, a part of Hancock's Second Corps. A thirty-year-old schoolteacher from East Machias, Maine, Caldwell had enlisted at the beginning of the war and risen rapidly in rank. A popular and efficient officer, Caldwell commanded one of the most renowned divisions of the Army of the Potomac. It had been Hancock's before Caldwell took over, and Israel B. Richardson's before that. All three men were tough, aggressive officers who had imbued the division with spirit and discipline. It had broken the Confederate line at the Bloody Lane at Antietam and performed prodigies of valor before Marye's Heights at Fredericksburg.[17]

When the fighting began on the Union left on the afternoon of July 2, Caldwell's division was waiting at the left end of the Second Corps sector near the middle of Cemetery Ridge. Almost immediately Caldwell got orders to join the fight and actually marched the division a short distance to the left before it was recalled to its original position. Apparently someone further up the chain of command assumed at first that the Fifth Corps would be sufficient reinforcements for Sickles. Caldwell's men, however, were experienced soldiers and knew, as the roar of battle grew and spread to the south of them, that their turn would likely come soon enough.[18]

One of Caldwell's brigades was the famed Irish Brigade, five regiments of Irish Americans from New York, Massachusetts, and Pennsylvania. No braver soldiers ever shouldered muskets in any army, but their conspicuous valor had cost them such high casualties in previous battles that their numbers now were scarcely those of a single good-sized regiment. As the men of the Irish Brigade, along with the rest of the division, waited with combat clearly impending, Catholic Chaplain William Corby asked their commander, Patrick Kelly, if he could give the brigade general absolution. Kelly agreed and called the troops to attention. Corby stepped to the top of a 3-foot-high boulder and raised his right hand. The men knelt and removed their caps.[19]

Seeing the religious preparations in the Irish Brigade spurred Lutheran Chaplain John H. W. Stuckenberg of the 145th Pennsylvania, a part of Colonel John R. Brooks's brigade. In peacetime, Stuckenberg had been a pastor in the 145th's hometown of Erie and had known many of the regiment's men and their families. Now he asked Colonel Hiram L. Brown of the 145th if he could hold a brief worship service for the regiment. Brown, too, readily agreed and had the men called to attention. Stuckenberg made "a few remarks" and then led the men in prayer. "The occasion was a very solemn one," the chaplain wrote. "It was the last prayer in which some of our regt. joined."[20]

When the order came down from Meade to Hancock to send a division to support the hard-pressed Union left, Hancock dispatched Caldwell, and the latter moved his division quickly to the scene of the fighting. Realizing he had no time to arrange his division in its accustomed formations, Caldwell rapidly threw his brigades into line and launched them at the Rebels, who were threatening the Wheatfield and the Stony Hill. Soon, fighting was raging hotter than ever across the bloody Wheatfield.[21]

Caldwell's four small brigades totaled somewhat fewer men than the original combined strength of Anderson's and Kershaw's brigades, but Caldwell's men went in hard, as was their custom. Colonel Edward E. Cross's brigade, on the left of Caldwell's line, struck not only Anderson's Georgians but also troops from Benning's and Robertson's brigades, who had moved up Houck Ridge from Devil's Den. Cross soon fell, mortally wounded, but his men pushed the Rebels back into Rose's Woods and held them there. On Caldwell's right, Brigadier General Samuel K. Zook's brigade and Kelly's Irish Brigade converged on the Stony Hill. Kershaw's South Carolinians fought fiercely. Zook fell early in the fight, but his men and the Irish kept the pressure on the South Carolinians.[22]

Anderson's Georgians, ensconced in the fastness of Rose's Woods, proved stubborn. Caldwell responded by committing his small reserve brigade, that of Brooks. Though scarcely half the size of one of the Confederate brigades, Brooks's formation provided the crucial extra impetus to tip the balance toward the Union in this sector. Fighting hard all the way, Brooks's men drove the Rebels back through Rose's Woods, across the west branch of Plum Run, and up the rocky west slope of its ravine. Anderson's men tried to make a stand at the top of the slope, on the west edge of Rose's Woods. By this time, Anderson's Georgians were being joined by elements of their fellow Georgians from Paul J. Semmes's brigade, one of McLaws's two reserve brigades now committed to action. Nonetheless, Brooks's Federals chased the Confederates from that line as well, clear out of Rose's Woods and into the open fields. Semmes fell, mortally wounded, while trying to rally his troops. The Yankees finally stopped at the lip of the ravine, just where Rose's Woods gave way to the open fields toward the Emmitsburg Road, and Anderson's Georgians took shelter behind a stone fence another 200 yards to the west.[23]

The retreat of Anderson's brigade finally made Kershaw's position untenable. The South Carolinians clung to the Stony Hill until they were almost surrounded but finally had to fall back to the vicinity of the Rose farm. From the north edge of Devil's Den all the way to the Stony Hill, almost half a mile to the north, Caldwell's division had now won back all the ground the Confederates had taken in the hour of hard fighting since Anderson's brigade had started its advance. The trouble for Caldwell now was to hold what he had won. Anderson and Kershaw were rapidly regrouping and would obviously be joined by Semmes's brigade and possibly by additional troops in their next big push. Caldwell consulted with the commanders of two nearby divisions of the Fifth Corps about supporting his own badly exposed division, but neither Fifth Corps commander Sykes nor Third Corps commander Sickles was exercising much leadership at this point. The two divisions of the Fifth Corps moved up somewhat haltingly on either side of Caldwell's line, but before they could solidify the position, events farther up the line once again rearranged the Wheatfield sector with earthquake suddenness.[24]

Longstreet was allowing far too much delay between the attacks of his brigades. He had held back McLaws's right front brigade, Kershaw's, so that Anderson's had been unsupported on its left and had fought to a bloody and futile standstill along the edge of the Wheatfield. Then, Longstreet delayed the advance of McLaws's left front brigade so that Kershaw in turn was unsupported on his left, where he was mercilessly hammered by many of the forty Union cannon concentrated in the salient, or outward-jutting angle, of the Union line that was capped by the Peach Orchard.[25]

Directly in front of the Peach Orchard and its deadly Union batteries was McLaws's left front brigade, a solid mass of Mississippians commanded by forty-one-year-old Brigadier General William Barksdale. A lawyer, newspaperman, and politician before the war, Barksdale had also been a fire-eater, one of the coterie of fanatical pro-slavery agitators whose efforts had finally plunged the nation into civil war. Not shrinking from the full implications of the position he had taken, Barksdale had raised a regiment and had fought at Bull Run and at most of the Confederacy's other battles in the eastern theater. After two years of combat he had gained a general's commission and an enviable reputation as one of the Army of Northern Virginia's premier brigade commanders. His hard-driving aggressiveness and consistent success in battle almost made men forget his portly and ungainly appearance.[26]

Barksdale waited fretfully while the Confederate artillery began its long duel with the Union guns in the Peach Orchard salient. He watched with intense impatience as first Hood's division and then Kershaw's and Semmes's brigades of his own division marched forward across the open fields toward Houck Ridge and Rose's Woods. As the bombardment entered its second hour, Barksdale sought out both McLaws and Longstreet and pleaded to be sent into the fight. "I wish you would let me go in, General," Barksdale begged. "I would take that battery in five minutes." "Wait a little," was Longstreet's reply, and Barksdale had to summon what little patience he could muster while Anderson, Kershaw, and Semmes struggled for Rose's Woods, the Wheatfield, and the Stony Hill.[27]

At last, Longstreet believed the time was right and gave the word to McLaws. McLaws sent an aide galloping to Barksdale, who was overjoyed to get the order to advance. The brigade surged forward, raising the Rebel Yell, and slammed into the Union line at the Peach Orchard. The Federals there, like the rest of the Third Corps, were spread thinner than they should have been. Barksdale's Mississippians waded into them ferociously. As Charles N. Maxwell of the Third Maine recalled it, the Confederates paused, lying down in the grass in front of the Peach Orchard. Then they advanced in earnest. "At last they came close upon us," Maxwell wrote. "A great part of our men were shot down." The two sides traded volleys at little more than twenty yards; then Maxwell and his comrades thought they heard an order to fall back and did so rapidly, hotly pursued by the enemy. The Union line in the Peach Orchard collapsed.[28]

That collapse reverberated along the Union line, back to the Stony Hill, through the Wheatfield and Rose's Woods, to Houck Ridge. McLaws's remaining brigade, four Georgia regiments under Brigadier General William T. Wofford, followed a little behind Barksdale and to his right, bearing down on the Stony Hill. Seeing these new Confederate formations go forward, Kershaw, Semmes, and the remnants of Anderson's brigade joined the advance. The South Carolinians swept over the Stony Hill, crushing the right flank of Caldwell's thin line and driving off a small division of the Fifth Corps. With the Stony Hill gone, the rest of Caldwell's line was doomed, and the resurgent tide of Confederate success rolled southward. Anderson's and Semmes's Georgians stormed Rose's Woods and the Wheatfield and, along with elements of Benning's and Robertson's brigades, swept onward to the crest of Houck Ridge. Caldwell's survivors, together with nearby remnants of units belonging to the Fifth and Third Corps, fled east, across the marshy valley of the east branch of Plum Run toward the low southern end of Cemetery Ridge.

Meanwhile, Barksdale's brigade, from the site of its breakthrough at the Peach Orchard, turned north to roll up the rest of the Third Corps line. That line was held by Humphreys's division, strung out along the Emmitsburg Road for about three-quarters of a mile from just north of the Peach Orchard to a little south of the Codori farmhouse and barn. Humphreys's division never had a chance. The next phase of the Confederate attack was following without the delay that had held back Kershaw and Barksdale earlier that afternoon. Now, Richard H. Anderson's Confederate division, next on McLaws's left, was launching its own attack, with its right brigades leading off. These two brigades, one of Alabamians under Brigadier General Cadmus Wilcox and another of Floridians under Colonel David Lang, struck Humphreys's line in front just as Barksdale was hitting it in flank. Humphreys's troops fought stoutly, and Humphreys himself was magnificent, calmly mounted amid the storm of enemy fire, galloping from one threatened sector of his line to another. None of that could avail, however, and the division grudgingly but steadily fell back, frequently pausing to turn and fight before taking up the retreat again.[29]

Barksdale, all fire and drive, urged on his men. "Crowd them," he called to two of his colonels. "We have them on the run." Conspicuous on horseback, he rode in front of his line and pointed grandly to the front with his sword. "Brave Mississippians," he shouted, "one more charge and the day is ours." They made that charge and others after it, but slowly the momentum drained out of the Mississippians' incredible assault. Barksdale fell, grievously wounded, and by this time many of his men were down as well. Fatigue, confusion, and disorganization among the attackers did the rest while the Union line, bolstered by reinforcements, began to solidify in front of them. The advance finally stalled in the broad, shallow swale that here formed the valley of the east fork of Plum Run. By that time Sickles, too, was among the fallen, struck in the leg by a cannonball and carried to the rear for amputation.[30]

The fresh Union troops that had helped stall Barksdale's advance came from Hancock's Second Corps. Having—on Meade's order—already dispatched Caldwell's division into the maw of the ferocious battle on his left, Hancock responded to the crisis of Humphreys's division by sending a brigade of Brigadier General John Gibbon's division, the center division of his corps and of the army. Then, once again on Meade's order, Hancock rode over to take command of the Third Corps and try to extricate what was left of it from its dire situation.[31]

Hancock was shortly to find that the situation was even worse than he imagined. The Confederate attack was not over. Anderson's whole division was slated to go in, and it had five brigades, three of which had not yet charged. The next to join the attack was Brigadier General Ambrose Wright's Georgia brigade. What was about to give Hancock a nasty surprise, however, was the fact that since the Third Corps had collapsed, the Confederate brigades of Wilcox, Lang, and Wright were bearing down on a stretch of Cemetery Ridge that was very lightly held. Caldwell's division had been there before being sent to Sickles's aid, but now the only Yankees there were the pitiful remnant of Humphreys's division along with a few scattered Second Corps units sent over from Gibbon's division.

Hancock discovered this when in the gathering dusk and thick smoke he and an aide rode toward what they thought was a retreating Union formation moving out of some thickets in the Plum Run swale. The troops, who were in fact Wilcox's Alabama brigade, loosed a fusillade of shots at the Union officers, wounding Hancock's aide. Hancock wheeled his horse and galloped back to Cemetery Ridge to organize a defense. There he was horrified to find only a small body of blue-clad troops drawn up on the ridge, with no others in sight. "My God!" shouted Hancock. "Are these all of the men we have here? What regiment is this?" "First Minnesota," responded Colonel William Colvill. Actually only eight companies of the First Minnesota were present, some 262 officers and men. Hancock knew more reinforcements were on the way—a division of the Twelfth Corps, two from the First, the entire Sixth Corps—but this crisis was immediate. Wilcox's Alabamians, five regiments strong, were less than 200 yards away and coming fast. Hancock pointed to one of the battle flags of the advancing line of Alabamians. "Advance, colonel," he roared, "and take those colors!"[32]

Colvill and his Minnesotans tried. Another of the handful of western regiments in the mostly eastern Army of the Potomac, the First Minnesota was a veteran outfit that been at First Bull Run and had missed little of the eastern theater's bloody fighting since that time. Cut from the same cloth as the Iron Brigade, it was a collection of lumberjacks and hardy pioneer farmers of the northern prairies. Now, facing fivefold their numbers, the Minnesotans advanced. With bayonets fixed and arms at "right shoulder shift" they charged down the gentle slope at double-quick time in crisp alignment. The Alabamians gave them a volley. Dozens of westerners toppled, but the rest charged on. Faster and faster they went, as the strip of grass separating them from the Alabama line shrank. Then rifles came down from right shoulders and bayonets came level, thrust forward, as the Minnesotans lunged the last few yards.

It was too much for the Alabamians of Wilcox's front-line regiments. Fatigued, disorganized, and winnowed by casualties, they broke for the rear and rallied on the brigade's second line. Colvill halted his Minnesotans along the course of Plum Run. So heady was the feeling of invincibility, rushing forward behind leveled bayonets, shoulder-to-shoulder with 200 other brave men, that many of the Minnesotans subsequently expressed regret at the "halt" order. If Colvill had let them, they maintained, they could have torn through the whole Confederate army, or as much of it as was in front of them. Colvill, however, had reason for his order. The much heavier Alabama line had regrouped on its supports and was coming on again. The westerners took cover behind boulders, outcrops, or humps in the creek bank and began picking off the oncoming Alabamians.

They held on for a time, but the graycoats were too many for them at last. The Alabamians poured around both flanks of the rapidly dwindling little band of Minnesotans. After fifteen minutes,

Colvill, who was wounded and could not flee, ordered those who still could to head for Cemetery Ridge. They were almost surrounded and had to run a gauntlet of Confederate fire. Forty-seven men made it back to their starting point. The First Minnesota had suffered 82 percent casualties, the highest rate for any Union regiment in a single engagement during the entire war, but they had bought the time Hancock needed. Wilcox's own ranks were thinned, with many key officers down. Stunned by the ferocity of the First Minnesota's counterattack and aware that Union reinforcements were beginning to move into the area, Wilcox ordered his brigade to fall back on Seminary Ridge.[33]

Farther north, Lang brought his brigade to the foot of Cemetery Ridge, encountered modest Union resistance, and decided to fall back. He felt he was overextended, and, like Wilcox, he had no supporting troops available behind him. Still farther north, Wright's Georgians struck another gap in the defenses of Cemetery Ridge near the Union center. The left of Wright's brigade attacked the southern extremity of Gibbon's division's line while a couple of Georgia regiments on the right of the brigade actually charged onto a deserted stretch of Cemetery Ridge. They were in the heart of the Federal defensive position. As Wright later reported with understandable overstatement, "We were now complete masters of the field, having gained the key, as it were, of the enemy's whole line."[34] Not quite; but in a small way, at least, they had cut the Army of the Potomac in two—or would have if they had been ten times more numerous. As it was, however, Gibbon's infantry and artillery struck hard at Wright's northern flank while rallying Third Corps troops hit him from the other side. Then the First Corps column hove into sight at the double-quick, hurrying toward the breach. General Meade, who happened to be nearby and had watched the struggle, momentarily appeared ready to lead the counterattack, but if that was his intent, he soon thought better of it.[35]

On the other side of the lines, the Confederate brigade commander had seen enough. With no support in sight and darkness and Yankee reinforcements closing in, Wright, like Lang and Wilcox, ordered a retreat. He did not get off without severe punishment, as counterattacking Union regiments claimed well over 200 Georgians captured. With Wright's repulse, the attack of Anderson's division flickered out. For reasons that have never been adequately explained, Anderson's remaining two brigades never advanced at all.[36]

The wave of Confederate success that had rolled northward from the point of Barksdale's Peach Orchard breakthrough had now finally spent itself and ebbed back toward Seminary Ridge through the gathering dusk and ragged clouds of sulfurous gunsmoke. However, the simultaneous wave of Rebel triumph that had rolled southward from the Peach Orchard was at that moment cresting where the valley of Plum Run's east fork separated Houck Ridge from Little Round Top. When Kershaw, Semmes, Anderson, and Wofford joined Barksdale's advance, they had crushed and dispersed the thin Union line that Barksdale had torn loose from its moorings at the Peach Orchard. From the Stony Hill, down across the bloody and trampled Wheatfield, through the gloomy depths of Rose's Woods, and along the whole length of Houck Ridge, the only remaining Federals were the dead and wounded. The resurgent Confederates now prepared to storm down into the marshy valley of Plum Run—a vale that had already earned its post-battle epithet, "the Valley of Death." Beyond the Valley of Death was the northern shoulder of Little Round Top and one last chance to tear off the flank of the Army of the Potomac and unravel its line.

The Wheatfield. Library of Congress, Prints and Photographs Division, LC-B8171-0227

Confederate battle flags clustered along the top of Houck Ridge, where remnants of regiments commanded by captains and lieutenants gathered for the final push. At least fourteen of those twenty-one regimental flags represented Georgia outfits. Men from the rugged mountains of north Georgia, the red-clay hills of the pied-mont, the black dirt of the cotton belt, the sandy soil of the wiregrass region, and the cultured environs of Savannah wiped the grime of sweat and powder residue from their eyes, bit off the ends of new cartridges, and prepared for renewed action alongside South Caro-linians and Texans.[37]

Just above the distant crest of South Mountain the sun was a lurid red disk through the hanging clouds of powder smoke as the Rebel line, their backs to the setting sun, swept down the slope of Houck Ridge and into the Valley of Death. The discordant chorus of Rebel Yells rose through the gloom as it had dozens of times that afternoon. From the opposite side of the valley came the deep bari-tone of a Union cheer. Then, charging down off the far slope, a solid blue-clad line surged forward to meet ragged Confederate forma-tions. Unlike the powder-blackened Rebels clustered in small knots behind their many flags, these Yankees were fresh troops, a full brigade of the storied and veteran Pennsylvania Reserves Division, the last uncommitted reserve of the Fifth Corps. Along with them charged elements of the Sixth Corps, finally getting into the fight after their prodigious march. Behind the charging Pennsylvania Reserves and their Sixth Corps comrades, regiment after regiment of Federals rose into view as they marched forward over the crest of the ridge just north of Little Round Top and into a new and mas-sively solid battle line on the forward slope. The two lead divi-sions of the Sixth Corps, the most powerful in the Army of the Potomac, were ready for action.[38]

The Confederates in the Valley of Death turned back in retreat. Wofford, whose brigade was the freshest, wanted to press on, but an order from Longstreet, arriving at this opportune moment, com-pelled him to turn back. Elsewhere on the Confederate line, a glance was all that was necessary to tell veterans what their chances were. Captain George Hillyer, commanding what was left of the Ninth Georgia, remembered years later how they had come to the foot of Little Round Top, looked up at the powerful Union forces guard-ing it, and by general consensus turned their backs on the hill. As Hillyer started back, a captain of the Eleventh Georgia met him with the words, "If you have been in there any further and could not do anything, there is no use for me to go."[39] So they all turned away, and the Pennsylvania Reserves, led by their exultant divi-sion commander, Brigadier General Samuel W. Crawford, hurried them along. The Union troops retook much of Houck Ridge, while

Robertson's Texans and Benning's Georgians held on to Devil's Den; Anderson's and Semmes's troops fell back to the valley of the west fork of Plum Run; and Kershaw's retreated to the vicinity of the Stony Hill.[40]

As darkness and relative silence fell over the smoking carnage of the southern half of the battlefield, the sound of gunfire was reaching a crescendo well to the north, almost at the outskirts of Gettysburg, on the slopes of Culp's Hill and Cemetery Hill. There, a separate struggle was in progress, as a planned diversionary attack had grown to pose its own serious threat to the Union position. During that afternoon, while Longstreet had moved into position and finally launched his assault on the Union left, Ewell had waited to make his diversion on the Union right, around Culp's Hill and Cemetery Hill. Late in the afternoon, as Longstreet was launching his assault, Ewell's left-flank division commander, Major General Edward Johnson, began carrying out the diversion by sending a battalion of artillery to take up a position on Benner's Hill, east of Gettysburg, from which to bombard the Union forces on Cemetery Hill.

The eighteen guns, under the command of nineteen-year-old "boy major" Joseph W. Latimer, rolled up the hill at a rattling gallop and swung into battery. The Union guns on Cemetery Hill were more numerous and possessed superior ammunition. Skillfully and bravely served by their blue-clad crews, the Union batteries blasted the hapless Confederate gunners and their equipment mercilessly, while Confederate infantrymen looked on, from a distance, in awe-struck admiration for the courage of Latimer and his gun crews. "The shot and shell could be seen tearing through the . . . batteries," wrote a Louisiana soldier, "dismounting guns, killing and wounding men and horses, while ever and anon an ammunition chest would explode, sending a bright column of smoke far up towards the heavens." One of Latimer's gunners noted, "It was like the enemy had our range before the first shot was fired." As the pounding continued, the Confederate fire became less accurate. After about an hour, Latimer ordered the battalion to withdraw out of range except for a single battery that he kept with him on the exposed hilltop to check any possible Union infantry attack. As the thunder of the guns gradually subsided, one of the last shots exploded near the young major, mortally wounding him.[41]

It had been a very unpleasant hour for the Union troops on Cemetery Hill. "We had nothing to do but lay and take it," wrote a staff officer on the hill. "It was terrible, but the majority of the shots were too high."[42] Yet diverting as the episode might have been for the Union and Confederate troops on or within sight of Cemetery Hill, it had failed to get Meade's attention. In fact, Meade now seemed as narrowly focused on his left wing as he had previously been on his right. To be sure, he now had much better reason to think as he did, for the attack on the Union left was indeed Lee's major effort. Still, Meade's concern for the safety of his left now almost led him into making an error on his right, and all that prevented serious trouble there was the level head of Henry W. Slocum.

Meade, in his urgency to send reinforcements to Sickles's endangered sector, dispatched a steady stream of reinforcements to the embattled left: a division of the Second Corps as well as all of the Fifth Corps and the Sixth, too, when it arrived. In addition to these troops, Meade also gave orders for the entire Twelfth Corps to march from the army's right to its left. The Fifth and Sixth Corps were in reserve and could readily be spared. The division of the Second Corps left a hole in the line that the First Minnesota paid a high price for plugging. Had the Twelfth Corps gone as ordered, it would have left Culp's Hill entirely unoccupied with results that could have been disastrous for the Army of the Potomac. Realizing the danger, Slocum, though losing no time in putting the head of his column on the march, appealed to Meade to let him leave a division on Culp's Hill. Meade would not go that far but did let Slocum keep a brigade. That was the only force holding the vital hill during the late afternoon and evening hours. As it turned out, the rest of the Twelfth Corps was not really needed on the left but could have proved very valuable on Culp's Hill.[43]

The sun was almost setting, and the banks of smoke from Latimer's brave but doomed artillery bombardment had scarcely dissipated when General Johnson proceeded to the next stage of the diversion that Ewell, pursuant to Lee's orders, had directed. Through the gathering twilight, Johnson's division advanced toward the east face of Culp's Hill and plunged into the deeper gloom of the thickly forested slope.[44]

Awaiting them in line near the hill's crest were the five New York regiments of George S. Greene's brigade. At sixty-two, Greene was one of the oldest generals at Gettysburg and certainly one of the most capable brigade commanders. In defending Culp's Hill against such long odds, Greene had a couple of important advantages. One was that throughout much of the day his brigade and

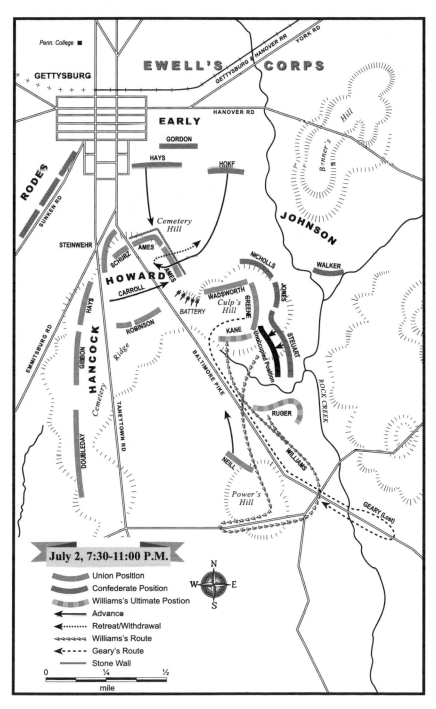

Penn. College ■

GETTYSBURG

EWELL'S CORPS

GETTYSBURG & HANOVER RR
YORK RD

EARLY

HANOVER RD

GORDON

HAYS

HOKE

Benner's
Hill

RODES

SUNKEN RD

Cemetery
Hill

JOHNSON

STEINWEHR

AMES

SCHURZ

AMES

NICHOLLS

WALKER

HOWARD

CARROLL

JONES

BATTERY

WADSWORTH

Culp's
Hill

GREENE

STEUART

ROBINSON

KANE

Unoccupied Position

EMMITSBURG RD

HAYS

Ridge

BALTIMORE PIKE

ROCK CREEK

GIBBON

HANCOCK

Cemetery

TANEYTOWN RD

RUGER

DOUBLEDAY

WILLIAMS

NEILL

Power's
Hill

GEARY (Lost)

July 2, 7:30–11:00 P.M.

Union Position
Confederate Position
Williams's Ultimate Postion
Advance
Retreat/Withdrawal
Williams's Route
Geary's Route
Stone Wall

N
W   E
S

0   ¼   ½
mile

other troops on Culp's Hill had worked hard at building breastworks. They felled trees, rolled the logs into place in front of their
line, and dug and piled the dirt in front of them. By the time of the
Confederate attack their entrenchments were such as to multiply
the fighting strength of Greene's small command by a factor of
three.[45] Greene's other advantage was that because of the curving
Union "fishhook" position, he could get reinforcements quickly. In
response to Greene's call for help, reinforcements swarmed in from
the whole northern arc of the Union position—three regiments from
the First Corps, on the saddle between Culp's Hill and Cemetery
Hill; four from the Eleventh Corps on Cemetery Hill itself; and
another one from the Second Corps on upper Cemetery Ridge. The
fresh troops stumbled through the darkening woods at the best pace
they could manage, steering usually toward some staff officer's idea
of where they were needed. Enough of them arrived and got into
the fight, however, to render vital help to Greene's hard-pressed
brigade.[46]

The fight on Culp's Hill that night was a confused scuffle on
boulder-strewn, forested slopes that were soon as dark as midnight.
Yet it was important, too, for if the Confederates gained complete
control of Culp's Hill, they stood a fair chance of either unraveling
the rest of the Union line or cutting off the Union's primary line of
supply and retreat—or both. Lee would no doubt have been happy
to accept decisive victory on the Union right rather than the left.
The outcome of the battle could well depend on which side could
succeed in driving back the mostly unseen enemies behind the rows
of stabbing muzzle flashes in the darkness of Culp's Hill's woodland slopes.

Each side blundered through lack of knowledge of the other's
whereabouts. There were friendly-fire incidents as well as times
when one side or the other held its fire in the mistaken belief that
friends, rather than foes, were the source of the noises a few yards
to the front. The Confederate line overlapped Greene's small force
and, despite his best efforts to stretch his line, succeeded in taking
possession of a large portion of the breastworks that the rest of the
Twelfth Corps had abandoned when it departed on its errand to
the Union left.[47] Culp's Hill is a two-humped affair, with its higher
northern summit connected to a lower southern summit by a shallow saddle. The northern summit is the part of Culp's Hill that
connects to Cemetery Hill via another saddle to the west. By dint of
Greene's skill and his men's stout fighting, the Federals managed

to hold onto the northern summit, but Johnson's Confederates took control of the southern summit, the point and barb of the Army of the Potomac's fishhook-shaped position.[48]

The firing on Culp's Hill had more or less settled down when at about 10:00 P.M. the missing Twelfth Corps troops came marching back from their evening's excursion, mostly ignorant of the fact that the enemy now held their previous positions. This occasioned more confused and violent encounters. The surprised Yankees at first thought they were receiving fire from their comrades in Greene's brigade, and only with much difficulty and some losses did the Union officers get the situation sorted out. By about midnight, the displaced Twelfth Corps troops, mostly Brigadier General John W. Geary's division, had come to accept the fact that they would have to find themselves other quarters for the remainder of the night, while both sides understood that the matter was not settled and would be taken up again at first light.[49]

While Greene and Johnson still struggled for control of Culp's Hill, Ewell prepared to launch the next phase of his attack. Early's division, minus Gordon's brigade, which had taken a beating north of town the day before, formed up on the outskirts of Gettysburg in preparation for a direct assault on Cemetery Hill. In her house at Stratton and High Streets, Gettysburg resident Mrs. Robert Shead was so near the Confederate ranks that she could hear the men talking excitedly about how they were going to "take that hill and capture the guns that have been shelling our lines all day." Distressed, Mrs. Shead turned to her husband. "Robert," she said earnestly, "let us go to God in prayer [and] . . . ask him to help our boys keep their battery." So the Sheads knelt and began to pray.[50]

At Early's order, his two brigades surged upward toward the Union positions on Cemetery Hill. On the Confederate right, Brigadier General Harry T. Hays's Louisiana brigade struck the Union defenses from due north while Colonel Isaac E. Avery's North Carolina brigade, on Hays's left, approached the hill from the northeast. The Louisianans and North Carolinians had had all day to contemplate the Federal defenses, and their mood when ordered to attack was somber but determined. "I felt as if my doom was sealed and it was with great reluctance that I started my skirmishers forward," recalled Lieutenant Joseph Jackson of Hays's brigade.[51] The Union guns opened up on them at once, tearing holes in the ranks. Colonel Avery fell, unnoticed by his men in the gathering darkness. As the battle swept on ahead of him, the dying colonel pulled a pencil and a scrap of paper from his pocket and scrawled a brief note to his friend, Major Samuel Tate: "Major: Tell my father I died with my face to the enemy. I. E. Avery."[52]

A depression in the ground gave the attackers shelter for part of the advance. Then they closed in on the Union infantry line behind a stone fence at the base of the slope. The fight was short and sharp. Louisianan William J. Seymour remembered many of his comrades falling here, but the Union defenders, members of the battered Eleventh Corps, finally gave way and fled up the hillside, with the Confederates in hot pursuit. At the Union batteries near the crest, the blue-jacketed artillerists stuck to their guns doggedly, firing load after load of double canister. Yet nothing, it seemed, could stop the shadowy masses of Rebels swarming up the darkening slope. They dashed in among the cannon of several batteries, and the stubborn gunners met them swinging handspikes, rammer staffs, or their fists. Lieutenant Charles B. Brockway of the First Pennsylvania Light Artillery brained a Confederate with a large rock he picked up from the ground. Other officers, Union and Confederate, slashed at the enemy with their swords. A Rebel color bearer, waving his flag, leapt atop a Union gun only to be shot down. Some of the blue-clad gunners carried revolvers and used them. Meanwhile, Union infantry reinforcements were hastening to the scene.[53]

Early's men hung on in hopes that Rodes's division, scheduled to go in next on their right, would come up to turn the tide in their favor, but Rodes was unaccountably slow that evening. His division deployed in the gloaming, made a brief, abortive advance, and finally halted completely several hundred yards from the hill. The only new formation that did climb Cemetery Hill after Early's men got there wore blue uniforms. Colonel Samuel S. Carroll's brigade of the Second Corps charged up the Union side of the hill after being sent over from that corps's sector south of the hill. Carroll's four regiments of midwesterners fixed bayonets and stormed across the hilltop.[54] Farther to the Union left, units of the Eleventh Corps had rallied and pushed forward. The Union counterattack drove the Confederates out of the contested batteries and down the hill's northern slope. Hays's and Avery's battered survivors had no choice but to fall back to the town of Gettysburg, covered in their retreat by the complete darkness that had now settled over the field. In their house at Stratton and High Streets, Mr. and Mrs. Shead rose from their knees. Their prayers had been answered.[55]

Both on Culp's Hill and on Cemetery Hill, Ewell's attacks had come close to achieving dramatic, possibly even decisive, results far beyond a mere diversion. Meade had focused all his attention and reserves on Longstreet's main Confederate attack, and Ewell had almost—but not quite—made him pay for it. As it was, the Union lines had held in all sectors, from the crest of Little Round Top all the way around the fishhook-shaped position to the main summit of Culp's Hill. After two days of bloody fighting, the battle's final decision remained as uncertain as it had been before the first shot was fired.

NOTES

1. *OR*, vol. 27, pt. 2, p. 405; M. O. Young, "History of the First Brigade," handwritten manuscript, Georgia Department of Archives and History.

2. John C. Reed manuscript, Alabama Department of Archives and History; *Rome [Georgia] Courier*, July 21, 1863.

3. Wilkinson and Woodworth, *A Scythe of Fire*, 238–40.

4. John C. Reed manuscript, Alabama Department of Archives and History; Pfanz, *Gettysburg: The Second Day*, 253.

5. John C. Reed manuscript, Alabama Department of Archives and History; E. J. Magruder to John Towers, January 19, 1888, private collection of Zack Waters, Rome, Georgia.

6. John C. Reed manuscript, Alabama Department of Archives and History; Pfanz, *Gettysburg: The Second Day*, 247–51; Address given by Judge George Hillyer, Atlanta, August 2, 1904, printed in the *Walton [County] Tribune*.

7. Wilkinson and Woodworth, *A Scythe of Fire*, 246–47.

8. Pfanz, *Gettysburg: The Second Day*, 252; *OR*, vol. 27, pt. 2, p. 359.

9. Pfanz, *Gettysburg: The Second Day*, 254–55.

10. *OR*, vol. 27, pt. 2, p. 368.

11. Pfanz, *Gettysburg: The Second Day*, 256; D. Scott Hartwig, " 'No Troops on the Field Had Done Better': John C. Caldwell's Division in the Wheatfield, July 2, 1863," in *The Second Day at Gettysburg*, ed. Gary W. Gallagher (Kent, OH: Kent State University Press, 1993), 145.

12. Wilkinson and Woodworth, *A Scythe of Fire*, 248.

13. Pfanz, *Gettysburg: The Second Day*, 257–58.

14. *OR*, vol. 27, pt. 1, p. 520; Pfanz, *Gettysburg: The Second Day*, 259–60; Hartwig, "Caldwell's Division in the Wheatfield," 145.

15. Pfanz, *Gettysburg: The Second Day*, 264–66.

16. *OR*, vol. 27, pt. 1, p. 520; Pfanz, *Gettysburg: The Second Day*, 265–66.

17. Hartwig, "Caldwell's Division in the Wheatfield," 136–46.

18. Pfanz, *Gettysburg: The Second Day*, 267–68.

19. Ibid., 268.

20. John Henry Wilburn Stuckenberg, *I'm Surrounded by Methodists: Diary of John H. W. Stuckenberg, Chaplain of the 145th Pennsylvania Volunteer*

Infantry, ed. David T. Hedrick and Gordon Barry Davis, Jr. (Gettysburg, PA: Thomas Publications, 1995), 71.

21. Hartwig, "Caldwell's Division in the Wheatfield," 150–52.

22. Pfanz, *Gettysburg: The Second Day*, 275–82.

23. Ibid., 282; Hartwig, "Caldwell's Division in the Wheatfield," 160–65; L. L. Cochran, "The Grandest Tragedy This Continent Has Ever Known," *Civil War* 69 (August 1998): 61–63.

24. Hartwig, "Caldwell's Division in the Wheatfield," 165–71.

25. Pfanz, *Gettysburg: The Second Day*, 318–20.

26. Sifakis, *Who Was Who in the Civil War*, 31; Pfanz, *Gettysburg: The Second Day*, 318.

27. Pfanz, *Gettysburg: The Second Day*, 320.

28. *OR*, vol. 27, pt. 1, p. 533; Lydia Minturn Post, ed., *Soldiers' Letters from Camp, Battle-field and Prison* (New York: Bunce & Huntington, 1865), 260–63; Pfanz, *Gettysburg: The Second Day*, 327.

29. *OR*, vol. 27, pt. 1, pp. 533, 559; Pfanz, *Gettysburg: The Second Day*, 344–72.

30. Coddington, *The Gettysburg Campaign*, 405–17; Pfanz, *Gettysburg: The Second Day*, 349.

31. *OR*, vol. 27, pt. 1, pp. 370–71; Pfanz, *Gettysburg: The Second Day*, 373–80.

32. Richard Moe, *The Last Full Measure: The Life and Death of the First Minnesota Volunteers* (New York: Henry Holt, 1993), 268; Pfanz, *Gettysburg: The Second Day*, 410–11.

33. Moe, *The Last Full Measure*, 268–75.

34. *OR*, vol. 27, pt. 2, p. 623.

35. Pfanz, *Gettysburg: The Second Day*, 421.

36. *OR*, vol. 27, pt. 2, pp. 623–24; Pfanz, *Gettysburg: The Second Day*, 386–89, 420.

37. Address given by Judge George Hillyer.

38. Pfanz, *Gettysburg: The Second Day*, 399.

39. Address given by Judge George Hillyer.

40. Pfanz, *Gettysburg: The Second Day*, 401.

41. First quotation from Seymour, *The Civil War Memoirs*, 74; *OR*, vol. 27, pt. 2, pp. 446–47, 456; second quotation from Peter Tomasak, "Glory to God! We Are Saved: Night Assault at Gettysburg," *North & South* 1, no. 5 (May 1998): 34; Pfanz, *Gettysburg: Culp's Hill and Cemetery Hill*, 178–89.

42. Jacob F. Slagle to "Dear Brother," September 13, 1863, Jacob F. Slagle Papers.

43. *OR*, vol. 27, pt. 1, p. 759; Pfanz, *Gettysburg: Culp's Hill and Cemetery Hill*, 190–200; Bowden and Ward, *Last Chance for Victory*, 321.

44. *OR*, vol. 27, pt. 2, p. 447; Pfanz, *Gettysburg: Culp's Hill and Cemetery Hill*, 205–11.

45. *OR*, vol. 27, pt. 1, pp. 826, 856.

46. *OR*, vol. 27, pt. 1, pp. 826, 856–57; Pfanz, *Gettysburg: Culp's Hill and Cemetery Hill*, 211–15.

47. *OR*, vol. 27, pt. 1, pp. 826, 856.

48. Pfanz, *Gettysburg: Culp's Hill and Cemetery Hill*, 215–23.

49. *OR*, vol. 27, pt. 1, pp. 847, 857; Pfanz, *Gettysburg: Culp's Hill and Cemetery Hill*, 223–34.

50. Tomasak, "Glory to God! We Are Saved," 37.

51. Seymour, *Civil War Memoirs*, 75.

52. Pfanz, *Gettysburg: Culp's Hill and Cemetery Hill*, 258–59.

53. Seymour, *Civil War Memoirs*, 75; *OR*, vol. 27, pt. 2, pp. 480–81; Pfanz, *Gettysburg: Culp's Hill and Cemetery Hill*, 270–71; Tomasak, "Glory to God! We Are Saved," 38–44.

54. *OR*, vol. 27, pt. 1, pp. 456–57.

55. Pfanz, *Gettysburg: Culp's Hill and Cemetery Hill*, 273–75; Seymour, *Civil War Memoirs*, 75–76; Tomasak, "Glory to God! We Are Saved," 37.

CHAPTER EIGHT

STAY AND FIGHT IT OUT

AS THE FIGHTING sputtered out along the dark slopes of Culp's Hill and Cemetery Hill, the battlefield grew silent save for the occasional crackle of rifle fire from nervous pickets and the mournful cries of the wounded. This day had left some 10,000 of them scattered across the Pennsylvania landscape or gathered into makeshift field hospitals in houses, churches, or barns. To a Union soldier at his post on Cemetery Ridge, the sound made by the wounded in the fields in front of him was "a low, steady, indescribable moan."[1]

By the light of a bright moon, stretcher bearers and others moved about the battlefield, trying to aid the wounded and, if possible, get them to the field hospitals. Soldiers felt responsible for the men of their own company—often their hometown friends from before the war—and whenever they could they made their way in ones and twos back to the scene of the day's fighting in search of their fallen comrades. The wounded were counting on it. One of those who lay suffering on the field that night was Private John B. Stowe of the Ninth Massachusetts Battery. "The night was long and dark to me," he recalled. "I thought if the boys could, they would come for me."[2] In the Little Round Top sector, an informal truce prevailed as both sides voluntarily refrained from firing at those who walked between the lines seeking wounded friends.[3]

Somewhere in the darkness between the Peach Orchard and Cemetery Ridge, a man began to sing. In a fine tenor voice he ran through a succession of old, familiar hymns while hundreds on both sides listened. Back along the west fork of Plum Run, where the Ninth Georgia had settled down for the night, Captain George Hillyer listened to the hymns and thought the singer must be a member of McLaws's division. Yet no listener could be certain. The wounded of both sides lay intermingled throughout that sector.[4]

Over on the saddle between Culp's Hill and Cemetery Hill, Sergeant Simon Hubler of the 143d Pennsylvania could hear someone crying for water. Thousands were making the same appeal all across the battlefield, but this man was closer, and Hubler wanted to help. His comrades told him he would be killed in the attempt, but Hubler stubbornly found a canteen that still had some water in it and crept forward. Following the sound, he discovered a badly wounded Confederate and helped him drink until he had drained the canteen. The wounded man asked who he was, and Hubler replied that he belonged to the Pennsylvania Bucktail Brigade. The Rebel remarked that even though he was a Yank, he had a good heart. The next morning, Union skirmishers found the thirsty Confederate dead.[5]

The field hospitals were scenes of appalling suffering throughout the night. Overworked surgeons plied their bone saws nonstop, and piles of amputated arms and legs rose outside each makeshift operating room. Anesthetic ran out, and the night was horrible with the screams of the victims, each held to the operating table by three or four burly men while the surgeon did what had to be done. In a Confederate hospital at the Planck farm, Lieutenant Fred Bliss of Savannah, Georgia, knew he could not survive. Dawn was just breaking over the Union lines to the east when Bliss asked the chaplain who had been sitting up with him, "Won't you turn me over?" The chaplain, aided by hospital orderlies, moved him from one side to the other so that he faced the soon-to-be rising sun and the enemy. "I did not wish to die with my back towards the field of battle," Bliss gasped.[6]

Inside Union lines near Little Round Top, badly wounded prisoner John W. Mosely of the Fourth Alabama received assistance from his captors in writing a final letter. "My Dear Mother," Mosely wrote, "I am here a prisoner of war and mortally wounded. I can live but a few hours more at farthest. I was shot within forty yards of the enemy's lines. They have been exceedingly kind to me." The dying young Alabamian was as confident as ever in the final triumph of the Confederate cause, both in this battle and in the war. "I . . . hope I may live long enough to hear the shouts of victory before I die. . . . Farewell to you all."[7]

The proud and the humble were alike in their deaths this night. Union soldiers found General William Barksdale where he had fallen the evening before at the culmination of his brigade's brilliant charge. He was grievously wounded by three bullets. The Yankees carried him to a Union field hospital at the Jacob Hummelbaugh farmhouse, where he spent his last hours.[8]

In raw statistics, the casualty toll from the second day's fighting was comparable to that of the first. About 9,000 Union soldiers had been killed, wounded, or captured as compared to some 6,000 Confederates. Both sides, to some extent, but the Army of the Potomac especially, had also suffered temporary losses due to men becoming separated from their units and scattered by the disruption of heavy combat. These men would return to the ranks in a few days, but for now they contributed nothing to their armies' fighting strength. Thus, although all the major units of both armies were now on the field (including even the errant Jeb Stuart, who had arrived with his Confederate cavalry late on July 2), each commander would have somewhat less than 60,000 useable troops available when the armies renewed the struggle the next morning.[9]

For Meade, the duties of that night began with determining whether the conflict indeed ought to be renewed when morning came. He summoned his corps and wing commanders to a council of war at his headquarters in the widow Lydia Leister's small farmhouse along the Taneytown Road, just behind the upper end of Cemetery Ridge. The meeting began with informal discussions, and Meade and some of the officers debated the advisability of falling back slightly to straighten out the line or possibly falling back all the way to Pipe Creek. Meade was prepared to do so. Finally, Chief of Staff Daniel Butterfield put the question to a vote. Overwhelmingly the generals concurred on holding the present position. Slocum summed up their determination when he said succinctly, "Stay and fight it out." In response to a second question, the generals voted just as heavily that the army should remain on the defensive.[10]

"Such then is the decision," Meade concluded, and the generals returned to their commands. As they did so, Meade approached Brigadier General John Gibbon, whose division held the center of the Second Corps line, which was the center of the army. At the moment, however, Gibbon commanded the entire Second Corps while Hancock served as a wing commander. "If Lee attacks tomorrow," Meade warned his subordinate, "it will be *in your front*." Gibbon wanted to know why Meade thought so. "Because," the army commander explained, "he had made attacks on both our flanks and failed and if he concludes to try it again, it will be on our centre." Gibbon said he hoped Lee would do just that. "We would defeat him."[11]

On the Confederate side of the lines there was at least no doubt that the battle should and would be renewed in the morning. The question was how. Lee knew exactly what he wanted to do. The attacks of July 2 had been poorly coordinated and disjointed, yet they had come tantalizingly close to success. Perhaps if similar attacks could be launched again, starting near the Peach Orchard and moving northward up the line in a series of well-coordinated hammer blows, the Army of the Potomac might crumble at last. Longstreet's entire corps was now on the field, completed late July 2 by the arrival of the small, three-brigade division of George E. Pickett. For July 3, therefore, Longstreet would take up where he left off the day before, now using all three of his First Corps divisions. Renewing the assault would be risky—as was everything else in war—but Lee had accomplished much through audacity and aggressiveness and knew that the Confederacy needed decisive results from this campaign.[12]

Simultaneous with Longstreet's renewed assault, Lee planned for Ewell to resume his attack on Culp's Hill that had seemed so promising at last light on July 2. The Baltimore Pike, Meade's chief supply artery, lay just beyond the hill, little more than a quarter-mile from Confederate positions. Thus, Lee hoped to crush both the right flank and the center of the Army of the Potomac. Both operations would begin at daylight on Friday, July 3, and Lee had appropriate orders sent to both Longstreet and Ewell so that they and their subordinates could use the night hours to make the necessary preparations.[13]

Longstreet had other ideas—of course—and apparently did not consider Lee's orders particularly binding. Before dawn that morning, while he should have been getting his troops into position to make the attack that Lee had ordered, he was instead planning an ill-conceived scheme based on hasty reconnaissance and aimed at flanking the Union line. Better scouting reports would have demonstrated the whole thing to be impossible, and in any case Longstreet had not gotten his corps correctly positioned even for his own lame idea, much less for the plan spelled out in Lee's orders. All of this Lee discovered, much to his surprise and dismay, when the two generals met at Longstreet's headquarters at about 4:45 on the morning of July 3. Expecting an attack to begin any minute, Lee was shocked to discover that Longstreet was as unprepared as he was unwilling.[14]

Meanwhile, Ewell had proceeded with preparations for the attack Lee had ordered him to make. The assault on Cemetery Hill had achieved limited success in the gathering darkness of the previous evening, but Ewell knew it would be suicidal to hit that position in daylight. Therefore he would strike his blow on Culp's Hill only, and to make that blow stronger he detached three brigades from Rodes's and Early's divisions and sent them to reinforce Johnson's division for the big push. Johnson, whose division had once been Stonewall Jackson's own, was also strengthened that night when one of his brigades, the renowned Stonewall Brigade at the head of which Jackson had won his famous nickname, reported back from detached duty guarding the division's supply wagons. In all, Johnson would have some 9,000 men to throw at the Union defenders of Culp's Hill, more than twice the force he had used the evening before.[15]

Ewell and Johnson, however, were not the only generals preparing to launch attacks in the Culp's Hill sector the next morning. Alpheus Williams was temporarily commanding the Union's Twelfth Corps while Slocum exercised wing command. Upon returning from the council of war at Meade's headquarters, Williams had discovered for the first time that his men had not been able to resume the positions they had left on Culp's Hill because the Confederates now occupied them. When Williams reported this disturbing news to Slocum, the latter grimly replied, "Well! Drive them out at daylight."[16]

Williams therefore spent the night getting his men and guns into position for an assault on the Confederate positions on lower Culp's Hill. The basic plan involved confronting the Rebels with two divisions. Brigadier General John W. Geary's division would use the leverage of the high ground around Greene's lines near the main summit of Culp's Hill to attack the lower summit, while Williams's own division, commanded on this occasion by Brigadier General Thomas H. Ruger, menaced the Confederates from the low ground just south of the hill. The Union lines would form a broad, spreading "V" with the Confederate positions on lower Culp's Hill between the two arms. The operation would be preceded by a short, sharp artillery bombardment.[17]

Promptly at 4:30 A.M. the Twelfth Corps artillery, twenty-six guns, split the pre-dawn stillness with an intense fifteen-minute barrage. At 4:45 A.M., right on schedule, the guns fell silent, and Geary's blue-clad infantrymen were about to go forward when from the slopes in front of them rose a high-pitched chorus of Rebel Yells. Johnson was launching his own attack, right into the teeth of Williams's bombardment and threatened advance. The Yankee soldiers gave up all ideas of attacking, hunkered down behind the breastworks on upper Culp's Hill, and loosed volley after volley at the charging Rebels. Gray-clad soldiers from some of the Army of Northern Virginia's most famous regiments scrambled forward relentlessly across the wooded, boulder-strewn slopes.[18]

For six hours both sides kept up the fight with stubborn fury. The Union entrenchments on upper Culp's Hill allowed Federal officers there to hold the position with half their troops. They rotated the other half of their regiments back into a sheltered hollow behind the firing line where they could clear the powder residue out of their rifles and replenish their supplies of ammunition. Each time a regiment with clean rifles and full cartridge boxes moved up to replace another in the firing line, it surged over the crest with cheers and took up the work with renewed vigor. Some regiments emptied their cartridge boxes several times, firing over 150 rounds per man. The 147th New York, on loan from the nearby First Corps lines, had refilled its cartridge boxes four times and fired 200 rounds per man by 10:00 A.M.[19]

The Confederates had no such luxury. They crept forward, using the cover of trees and rocks, firing back grimly with their fouled rifles and increasingly light cartridge boxes. The fire was so intense it seemed a miracle that anyone could live in the midst of it. A survivor described its sound as "one continuous roar." One Southern soldier recalled, "Had every lump of ice in a hail-storm been a bullet, the woods in our rear could not have been more effectually peeled & riddled & swept with lead & iron."[20]

At one point in the conflict a garbled message was interpreted by a Union brigade commander as an order to send two of his regiments charging straight across an open meadow near Spangler's Spring at the southeastern foot of lower Culp's Hill, on the extreme right of the Union line. At other times the bucolic meadow was a scene of the most profound serenity, but now it was a place of death, swept by Confederate fire. Receiving the order, twenty-four-year-old Lieutenant Colonel Charles R. Mudge of the Second Massachusetts knew someone had blundered. "Are you *sure* that is the order?" Mudge asked the staff officer who conveyed it to him. The man was sure. "Well," Mudge said, "it is murder, but it's the order." Theirs not to reason why, the men of the Second Massachusetts and Twenty-seventh Indiana rose and charged across the meadow. The gallant 650 men got to close quarters with nearly twice their number of Rebels and exchanged volleys at point-blank range. Soldiers of the Third Wisconsin, looking on from Union lines, saw the Massachusetts men "cut down in our front like grass before a prairie fire." Finally, the battered regiments fell back, leaving more than a third of their troops strewn across the meadow. Among them was young Mudge, dead.[21]

At least one of the Confederates who helped repulse the attack knew the ground here very well indeed. Twenty-two-year-old Private John Wesley Culp of the Second Virginia had grown up in Gettysburg and was cousin to the man who owned Culp's Hill. Some years before, young Culp had moved to Shepherdstown, Virginia, for the sake of a job as a carriage maker. When the war started, he had chosen to fight against his home and native state and had enlisted in the local Confederate regiment. One wonders what must have gone through his mind this morning, in his hometown, on Culp land, fighting in the ranks of an invading army. On the far right flank of Johnson's Confederate line, the Second Virginia had a relatively easy time of it that day, suffering a total of only twenty casualties, of whom just one was killed. That one was John Wesley Culp.[22]

Near the center of the contending lines, another and larger field stood in the midst of the surrounding woods on the southwest slope of lower Culp's Hill. A stone fence running through the middle of the field became a coveted prize between Rebel and Yankee, and the two sides took and retook the long, low pile of rocks. Finally, shortly after 10:00 A.M., the Confederates launched a final, all-out push to clear the Yankees off Culp's Hill and the surrounding terrain. Brigadier General George Steuart's brigade of Marylanders, Virginians, and North Carolinians swept across the open field, authoritatively seizing the disputed stone fence, but they were bucking a hurricane of Union rifle fire. "It was the most fearful fire I ever encountered," recalled an officer of Steuart's staff, "and my heart was sickened with the sight of so many gallant men sacrificed."[23]

Among the blue-clad defenders of this sector was a regiment of Union Marylanders called the First Maryland, Eastern Shore. Among the Rebel attackers in Steuart's brigade was the Confederate First Maryland Battalion, which had been recruited from the same part of the state. Many men in each of these regiments had relatives or neighbors in the other. Sergeant Robert W. Ross, who bore the colors of the First Maryland, Eastern Shore, was cousin to Sergeant P. M. Moore, who carried the flag of the Confederate First Maryland. Moore took four bullets and was left lying on the field. As Steuart's brigade fell back, a soldier of the Thirty-seventh Virginia later noted, "the dead lay one on top the other." Looking out across the open field, General Steuart could only murmur, "My poor boys! My poor boys!"[24] As this sector of the line began to grow quiet, members of the First Maryland, Eastern Shore, scrambled forward and, in the words of their commander, "sorrowfully gathered up many of our old friends & acquaintances, & had them carefully & tenderly cared for."[25]

Farther up the line, in the thick woods and boulders, the story of that final assault was much the same. Ewell's Confederates charged bravely but were mowed down by a fiery scythe of Union rifle bullets. By 11:00 A.M. the last Confederates—those who still could—were scrambling back down the slopes in retreat. Johnson, with more than a quarter of his force down, was ready to call it quits. Culp's Hill belonged exclusively to the Army of the Potomac. As the continuous rattling crash of massed volleys gave way to scattering shots and finally to an almost complete cessation of firing, the powder-blackened Federals realized what they had accomplished, and cheer after cheer rose from thousands of men all along the Union line on Culp's Hill.[26]

While the fight for Culp's Hill had raged, other parts of the battlefield had seen only minor skirmishing. Some of the skirmishers of Hancock's Union Second Corps, out in front of upper Cemetery Ridge, had gotten into a dispute with skirmishers of Hill's Confederate Third Corps over possession of a house and a large and sturdy barn between the lines. The barn was made of stone and wood, after the Pennsylvania fashion, and a Union soldier on Cemetery Ridge thought it was "an expensively and elaborately built structure, as barns go." It belonged to an unfortunate farmer named William Bliss, and though Bliss had never intended it for such work, it was a first-rate haven for sharpshooters. The firing around it heated up about midmorning, and soon both sides had thrown in their skirmish reserves, then more troops. Supporting artillery back on the ridges worked up to a full-throated roar. After charge and countercharge by infantry detachments from both sides, during which the buildings changed hands ten times, the Yankees finally set fire to them in order to deny them to the Confederate sharpshooters who had been picking off soldiers on Cemetery Ridge. Then that sector, too, grew quiet.[27]

During these same hours, along Seminary Ridge, Lee and Longstreet wrestled with the problem of what form the main Confederate attack should take. The sound of intense battle drifted across the fields from Culp's Hill, and Lee knew that his hopes for a coordinated, simultaneous offensive against both Union flanks could no longer be realized. His first reaction was to direct Longstreet to bring up Pickett's division from its position in the rear—something Longstreet should have done hours before—and go ahead with the attack on the Union center using the divisions of Hood (now commanded by Brigadier General Evander McIvor Law), McLaws, and Pickett. Longstreet balked again. Law's and McLaws's divisions were in bad shape after their fight on the previous evening; and besides, Longstreet maintained, if Hood and McLaws slanted left as Lee suggested, their right flank would be vulnerable to counterattack by the Union troops in the area of the Round Tops. Instead, Longstreet continued to urge his cherished idea of a movement around Meade's southern flank.[28]

Lee was adamant. "The enemy is there," he said, gesturing vigorously, "and I am going to strike him." Even if the chance for a coordinated attack had now been lost, Lee believed the previous evening's fighting had given him an advantageous position, and he was eager to exploit it. The high ground around the Peach Orchard would, he thought, be a commanding artillery position that would allow his guns to hammer the Union line much as the high ground around Hazel Grove had allowed them to do to the same army at Chancellorsville two months before.[29]

Faced with Longstreet's objections to the use of Law's and McLaws's divisions, Lee revised his plan. Law and McLaws could stay where they were, anchoring the Confederate right and pinning down the Union defenders of the Round Top sector. First, artillery in the new advantageous positions would blast the Union line, neutralizing the Federal artillery and demoralizing the bluecoat infantry; then, Pickett's division would spearhead the assault. As he had the day before, Lee planned to dip into A. P. Hill's Third Corps for the extra manpower Longstreet claimed he lacked. Yesterday, Lee had given Longstreet Anderson's division. This time he would give him most of Hill's other two divisions, Heth's and Pender's. Both savaged in the first day's fighting, these divisions had at least had a day to rest and recover. Lee earmarked all four of Heth's brigades and two of Pender's four for the new assault. In addition, Longstreet would have all five brigades of Anderson's division available to support the attack, particularly to guard the vulnerable flanks of the assault column. Robert Rodes, with three brigades positioned just to the left of the attacking divisions, would receive orders to pitch in as soon as he saw an opportunity.[30]

Partially because of the current location of the units assigned to the attack and partially out of respect for the strength of the Union position near the Round Tops, the new attack was to be aimed at the Union center, a long stretch of Cemetery Ridge with wide, open fields in front of it—no boulders, woods, ravines, or steep slopes to break up advancing formations. Lee had probably heard that Ambrose Wright's brigade had reached the crest of Cemetery Ridge the evening before. "It is not as hard to get there as it looks," Wright commented to Colonel Edward Porter Alexander of Longstreet's artillery. "The real difficulty is to stay there after you get there—for the whole infernal Yankee army is up there in a bunch." If Wright had gone there yesterday with one brigade and had to leave, Lee would send nine brigades today, with the rest of the army ready to support them.[31]

Stubbornly, Longstreet continued to object, but Lee was running out of patience. He made it clear he expected the attack to go forward as ordered. After spelling out to Longstreet the broad outlines of what he wanted, Lee, as was his custom, left it up to his subordinate to make the arrangements and carry out the operation.[32] Morosely, then, Longstreet set about making the preparations for an attack he bitterly resented having to make. From the outset he proceeded on the assumption that the attack would fail, and he made no provision for anything else. Troops would march forward, many of them would be shot, and the rest would march back. Lee would be taught his lesson. It was not that Longstreet intended to make the attack fail; it was simply that he never considered any other possibility.

To ensure that the inevitable disaster was no more extensive than necessary, Longstreet planned to use as few troops as possible. This meant leaving behind most of the supporting troops Lee had provided. Longstreet would have omitted the two brigades of Pender's division had Lee not specifically included them. Then, instead of using all five of Anderson's brigades, Longstreet decided to commit just two, and he did not bother to brief their commanders very thoroughly. Longstreet did brief Pickett, taking him to a vantage point in front of the woods on Seminary Ridge from which they could clearly see the Union line opposite and the solitary clump of trees. To Longstreet's intense disgust, Pickett "seemed to appreciate the severity of the contest upon which he was about to enter, but was quite hopeful of success." Longstreet did not want anyone to believe this attack would succeed.[33]

The morning passed while the various infantry formations slated for the attack marched to their jumping-off points. These had to be not only good places from which to begin an advance across the three-quarter-mile-wide valley between Seminary Ridge and Cemetery Ridge but also good places in which to ride out an artillery bombardment. It stood to reason that the heavy cannonade that was to precede the assault would draw substantial Union return fire. The waiting infantrymen needed to be sheltered as much as possible until the moment they began their advance. Pickett chose a deep swale in front of Seminary Ridge, and the other infantry commanders found similar positions in their sectors. Heth was still incapacitated with the wound he had received on the first day, so his division would be led by senior brigadier James J. Pettigrew. William Dorsey Pender, one of Lee's best division commanders, had been badly wounded by a shell near Gettysburg the day before, so his two brigades would be advancing under the command of Major General Isaac Trimble, a doughty old warrior who had served under Stonewall Jackson and was just returning to duty after a lengthy convalescence.

Shortly after 11:00 A.M. the last of the artillery pieces rumbled into its assigned position for the big bombardment, but the infantry still was not ready.[34] The sound of firing died down on Culp's Hill. Out in the shallow valley between the ridges, half a mile from either side's lines, the Bliss barn and house smoldered while skirmishers and their supporting infantry and artillery looked on in silence. A lull settled over the battlefield. The overcast drifted off, leaving a "few white, fleecy cumulus clouds floating over from the west." The sun blazed down on the green, hazy landscape of a hot, humid midsummer's noontime in south-central Pennsylvania, as quiet, for the time being, as the ripening wheat gently waving in the languid puffs of wind. It was a drowsy sort of time, especially for the great many men who had not gotten much sleep of late. Longstreet, like many others on both sides, napped.[35]

It was never completely quiet on the skirmish lines. For soldiers elsewhere on the field, the occasional distant crack of a rifle shot might have been faint enough to blend into the sounds of summer insects, but out where the exposed edges of the contending armies touched, the report of a rifle and the whine of its bullet passing close by were as starkly noticeable as they were deadly serious. Sharpshooters on both sides were playing for keeps.[36]

In Gettysburg, the civilians who had not fled to safer parts continued to seek shelter in their cellars for the most part. The town was a distinctly unsafe place to be. The Confederate front line actually ran through the town somewhat south of the central square. Rebels had barricaded the north-south streets and knocked holes in the walls of adjoining houses so that they could move back and forth along their line. From the windows of the houses or from holes they poked in the walls or roofs, Confederate sharpshooters fired southward toward Cemetery Hill.[37]

At the base of Cemetery Hill, only a few yards from the Union skirmish lines, stood a brick house occupied by two Gettysburg civilians who had no choice about fleeing their precarious position and two more who had chosen to stay with them. Mrs. Georgia Wade McClellan had given birth one week before and was recuperating. Her sister, Virginia "Ginnie" Wade, a young woman of twenty, and her mother were taking care of her and the baby boy. That morning, as Ginnie was in the kitchen making biscuits, a bullet cut through the wooden house door, passed through the open kitchen door, and struck her in the back, killing her. The only Gettysburg civilian to die in the battle, Ginnie had not lived long enough to receive the news that her fiancé, a soldier in a Pennsylvania regiment, had been killed by Ewell's troops at Winchester, Virginia, two weeks before.[38]

As the noon lull continued, several Union officers on the back slope of Cemetery Ridge sat down to a battlefield repast. John Gibbon's mess attendant had obtained "an old and tough rooster," stewed it, and rounded out the bill of fare with potatoes and coffee, all to be served atop a mess chest that would do for a table for the ranking guests. The lower-ranking officers sat cross-legged on the ground and held their plates in their laps. Hancock and Gibbon were there, along with aides and several other officers. Gibbon walked the few dozen yards over to Meade's headquarters and invited the commanding general. After some hesitancy, Meade agreed to join them. He was reluctant to leave headquarters, but there was really little for him to do there. A dispatch from Slocum announced that the Twelfth Corps had "gained a decided advantage" over the enemy in the Culp's Hill sector and could spare a brigade or two for service elsewhere on the battlefield if needed. Otherwise all was quiet. Having taken every sensible precaution he could think of,

Meade went off to enjoy his portion of the "old and tough rooster" as well as the camaraderie of his fellow officers. Once the meal was over, Meade hurried off to inspect his lines while Hancock, Gibbon, and the others sat around talking.[39]

About a mile or so due west of the little lunch group, on Seminary Ridge, Colonel Alexander was pondering a perplexing series of notes he had received from Longstreet. Alexander was in tactical command of the First Corps artillery this day and had been placing his batteries all morning in preparation for the big bombardment. That might have seemed responsibility enough for a twenty-eight-year-old colonel, but now Longstreet was making one final attempt to evade the task of carrying out—or refusing—Lee's orders, and that sidestepped responsibility appeared likely to land squarely on the shoulders of the young artillery officer. "If the artillery fire does not have the effect to drive off the enemy or greatly demoralize him so as to make our effort pretty certain," Longstreet had written in a note to Alexander about 11:30 that morning, "I would prefer that you should not advise Gen. Pickett to make the charge. I shall rely a great deal upon your good judgment to determine the matter, and shall expect you to let Gen. Pickett know when the moment offers."[40]

Alexander was shocked. Notwithstanding the obvious strength of the Union position, he had been blithely confident that the attack ordered by his superiors would succeed, but, as he later explained, "I was by no means ready to go for that place on my own judgment." He immediately wrote back to Longstreet pointing out that the artillery had enough ammunition for only one bombardment. When that was gone, the guns would be out of business; if the high command had any other options in mind, they had better consider those carefully before the bombardment began. Back came Longstreet's response at 12:15 P.M.: "The intention is to advance the Inf. if the Arty. has the desired effect of driving the enemy off or having other effect such as to warrant us in making the attack. When that moment arrives advise Gen. P. and of course advance such artillery as you can use in aiding the attack." It was rather ambiguous. Alexander, weighing Longstreet's instructions and the ammunition situation as best he could, decided that "if the artillery opened, Pickett must charge." To Longstreet he wrote, "When our artillery fire is doing its best I shall advise General Pickett to advance." When the time came for the bombardment to begin, the signal would be two shots in quick succession fired by the Washington Artillery of

New Orleans, whose guns were located not far from Longstreet's headquarters.[41]

While Alexander sweated out the unwonted responsibility in the sultry midday on Seminary Ridge, his most direct opponent, Union chief of artillery Brigadier General Henry Hunt, contemplated the situation from the other side of the broad, shallow valley. Clearly the Rebels were up to something. Hunt had taken careful note through the morning as battery after battery of Confederate artillery had wheeled into position on Seminary Ridge and on the high ground around the Peach Orchard. In Hunt's reckoning, this activity meant the Rebels were getting ready either to cover a withdrawal or to prepare for an assault—probably the latter. To be ready, Hunt carefully ordered all of the batteries of the artillery reserve, parked in the rear, to be ready to rush to the front at a moment's notice. To the batteries already in line along Cemetery Ridge and Cemetery Hill, Hunt gave orders that if the Confederates opened fire the Union gunners should wait fifteen minutes, then reply with deliberate, carefully aimed fire. Even the Army of the Potomac had no overabundance of artillery ammunition on hand and could not afford to waste it on inconsequential sparring between batteries when the Confederates might be preparing to launch something really big. Hunt wanted to be sure he had plenty of ammunition left to use against any gray-clad infantry who might be waiting to advance after the Confederate guns did their work.[42]

The infantrymen on both sides had little to do during the noon lull. Troops of Pickett's division rested in line in their somewhat sheltered swale. Part of the line ran through an apple orchard, and some of the soldiers of the First Virginia vented their youthful exuberance by pelting one another with green apples. That changed when their brigade commander, Brigadier General James L. Kemper, a politician and sometime speaker of the Virginia House of Representatives, had it announced throughout his regiments that they had special work to do that afternoon. "The commanding general had assigned our division the post of honor that day," as one of them recalled the announcement. Thereafter "an awful seriousness" came over the troops. As many of them recounted it later, their feelings were a mixture of foreboding and confidence. Success, they thought, was certain; personal survival, unlikely. "All appreciated the danger & felt it was probably the last charge to most of them," recalled Colonel Eppa Hunton of the Eighth Virginia of Richard B. Garnett's brigade. But, he added, "all seemed willing to die to achieve a victory there—which it was believed would be the crowning victory and the end of the war." Private Randolph Shotwell thought his comrades had no doubt "of sweeping everything before them."[43]

Pickett's division actually consisted of five brigades, but only three of them were in Pennsylvania this day. The other two had been held back by Jefferson Davis to help cover Richmond and its approaches against possible Union thrusts from the coast. The three brigades here at Gettysburg numbered 5,800 troops all told, Virginians to a man. All three brigades were veterans of the spring and summer 1862 Peninsula Campaign as well as various other actions, though since their organization as a division under Pickett's command, about ten months before coming to Gettysburg, they had seen very little combat. They had done their duty, but they were not among the more renowned units in this storied army—not yet. Besides the politician Kemper, the brigade commanders were West Pointers and Old Army men whose Confederate careers had been disappointing. Brigadier General Lewis Armistead had been criticized for his performance at Malvern Hill, a year and two days before. Garnett had been removed from the command of the Stonewall Brigade by old Jackson himself in March 1862 for ordering a retreat in the face of heavy enemy pressure at the battle of Kernstown. Both men had something to prove this day.[44]

Several hundred yards north of Pickett's division, the men of Pettigrew's and Trimble's six brigades waited in similar solemn contemplation of what lay ahead. Their ranks had been shredded two days before, and now they were preparing to face battle again. "We were aroused to a sense of our situation," recalled a North Carolina officer, "and no man who viewed that ground but felt that when the charge was made that all thought *would* be, blood must flow and gallant spirits must take their final flight."[45]

Lee and Longstreet rode the lines of the various assault divisions during this time. The men had been warned not to make any noise that would attract Yankee notice to their massed presence, so when the commanding general approached they did not cheer but instead rose to their feet and lifted their hats in silent salute.[46]

Along the Union line on Cemetery Ridge, infantrymen napped, read, or chatted. Soldiers of the ethnically Irish Sixty-ninth Pennsylvania, part of Brigadier General Alexander Webb's Philadelphia Brigade, entertained themselves by picking up rifles and cartridge boxes abandoned on the field when last evening's Confederate

assault crested just to the left of their position. Some of the cartridges they found were "buck and ball," containing one round
musket ball and two buckshot each. The Philadelphians took apart
the surplus ammunition and then loaded their extra rifles with a
dozen buckshot each. After a time, they came to have "a large pile
of guns." One never knew when they might come in handy. Other
regiments took similar steps.[47]

The Sixty-ninth's line ran for about eighty yards along a low
stone fence on the forward (that is, western) slope of Cemetery
Ridge. Just behind the regiment's left wing was a thick copse of
small trees—oak, chestnut, and sassafras, none of their trunks more
than a few inches thick—that stood out prominently on this otherwise treeless stretch of ridge. On either side of the Sixty-ninth, the
stone fence was unoccupied, providing firing lanes for two of the
many Union batteries that lined the ridge. On the Sixty-ninth's right
and about fifty yards back was Lieutenant Alonzo H. Cushing's
Battery A, Fourth U.S. Artillery. To the left and about the same distance behind were the guns of Lieutenant T. Fred Brown's Battery
B, First Rhode Island. The rest of the Philadelphia Brigade was more
or less in line with the guns. Farther to the left, beyond Brown's
battery, the rest of Gibbon's division held a line about even with
the Sixty-ninth's, though without a stone fence. To the right, beyond Cushing's battery, the Sixty-ninth's stone fence made a right
angle east and ran backward for about eighty yards before making
another right angle and running once again parallel (and now quite
close) to the crest of Cemetery Ridge. The first, or westernmost, of
those angles would come to be known as "the Angle." The stretch
of fence north of the two angles was occupied by more batteries
and by the troops of Brigadier General Alexander Hays's division
of the Second Corps. Those two Union center divisions, Gibbon's
and Hays's, were veteran units but small in size due to much attrition. Together they totaled just over 4,200 men.[48]

A few score yards behind Gibbon's line sat the little band of
officers who had dined on the tough old rooster that noon. It was
now just 1:07 P.M., and Gibbon, Hancock, and some of the others
were still sitting around their empty mess-chest table. Hancock was
dictating to one of his staff officers an order about meat rations.
Others dozed on the ground nearby. Their repose was interrupted
by the report of a single Confederate cannon followed a few seconds later by a second. Then a whole cascade of blasts tumbled
over each other as 164 Rebel cannon opened fire on the Union lines.

The officers jumped up, eager to get to their commands, even as shells began bursting all around them, wreaking havoc on horses and men. Terrified horses broke away from orderlies or plunged and shied so that their would-be riders could scarcely mount. Grabbing up his sword, Gibbon hurried toward the front on foot.[49]

NOTES

1. Jeffry D. Wert, *Gettysburg: Day Three* (New York: Simon & Schuster, 2001), 31.

2. Quoted in Daniel N. Rolph, *My Brother's Keeper: Union and Confederate Soldiers' Acts of Mercy during the Civil War* (Mechanicsburg, PA: Stackpole Books, 2002), 38.

3. Charles Cummings to his wife, Elizabeth, July 6, 1863, in Jeffrey D. Marshall, ed., *A War of the People: Vermont Civil War Letters* (Hanover, NH: University Press of New England, 1999), 166–67.

4. Address given by Judge George Hillyer.

5. Simon Hubler Narrative, Simon Hubler Papers.

6. Address given by Judge George Hillyer.

7. Quoted in Coles, *From Huntsville to Appomattox*, 115.

8. Charles Cummings to his wife, Elizabeth, July 6, 1863, in Marshall, ed., *A War of the People*, 166–67; Jacob F. Slagle to "Dear Brother," September 13, 1863, Jacob F. Slagle Papers; Wert, *Gettysburg: Day Three*, 32.

9. Coddington, *The Gettysburg Campaign*, 450.

10. Franklin A. Haskell, *Haskell of Gettysburg: His Life and Civil War Papers*, ed. Frank L. Byrne and Andrew T. Weaver (Kent, OH: Kent State University Press, 1989), 132–35; Coddington, *The Gettysburg Campaign*, 449–51; Wert, *Gettysburg: Day Three*, 16–17; Earl J. Hess, *Pickett's Charge: The Last Attack at Gettysburg* (Chapel Hill: University of North Carolina Press, 2001), 34.

11. Wert, *Gettysburg: Day Three*, 17.

12. *OR*, vol. 27, pt. 2, p. 320; Richard Rollins, "Pickett's Charge and the Principles of War," *North & South* 4, no. 5 (June 2001): 13–24.

13. *OR*, vol. 27, pt. 2, p. 320; Coddington, *The Gettysburg Campaign*, 455–56; Hess, *Pickett's Charge*, 4–5; Bowden and Ward, *Last Chance for Victory*, 423–30.

14. *OR*, vol. 27, pt. 2, p. 359; William Garrett Piston, "Cross Purposes: Longstreet, Lee, and Confederate Attack Plans for July 3 at Gettysburg," in *The Third Day at Gettysburg and Beyond*, ed. Gary W. Gallagher (Chapel Hill: University of North Carolina Press, 1994), 31–55; Coddington, *The Gettysburg Campaign*, 456–57; Hess, *Pickett's Charge*, 4–5; Bowden and Ward, *Last Chance for Victory*, 431–33.

15. Pfanz, *Gettysburg: Culp's Hill and Cemetery Hill*, 287; Wert, *Gettysburg: Day Three*, 59.

16. *OR*, vol. 27, pt. 1, p. 761; pt. 2, p. 320; quotation from Wert, *Gettysburg: Day Three*, 54.

17. *OR*, vol. 27, pt. 1, pp. 774–75; Pfanz, *Gettysburg: Culp's Hill and Cemetery Hill*, 284–87; Wert, *Gettysburg: Day Three*, 54.

18. Pfanz, *Gettysburg: Culp's Hill and Cemetery Hill*, 291–92; Wert, *Gettysburg: Day Three*, 61.

19. Pfanz, *Gettysburg: Culp's Hill and Cemetery Hill*, 303–6.

20. Quotations from Wert, *Gettysburg: Day Three*, 61, 80.

21. *OR*, vol. 27, pt. 1, pp. 780–81, 812–14; first quotation from Pfanz, *Gettysburg: Culp's Hill and Cemetery Hill*, 341, second quotation 346; Coddington, *The Gettysburg Campaign*, 474; Wert, *Gettysburg: Day Three*, 70–73.

22. Pfanz, *Gettysburg: Culp's Hill and Cemetery Hill*, 328–29, 353; Wert, *Gettysburg: Day Three*, 90.

23. Wert, *Gettysburg: Day Three*, 85.

24. Pfanz, *Gettysburg: Culp's Hill and Cemetery Hill*, 307–8; quotations from Wert, *Gettysburg: Day Three*, 85–86.

25. *OR*, vol. 27, pt. 1, p. 808; Wert, *Gettysburg: Day Three*, 86; quotation from Pfanz, *Gettysburg: Culp's Hill and Cemetery Hill*, 321.

26. *OR*, vol. 27, pt. 2, pp. 504–5; Pfanz, *Gettysburg: Culp's Hill and Cemetery Hill*, 323–27; Wert, *Gettysburg: Day Three*, 88, 90; Coddington, *The Gettysburg Campaign*, 475–76.

27. Haskell, *Haskell of Gettysburg*, 113–14; Coddington, *The Gettysburg Campaign*, 482–84; Wert, *Gettysburg: Day Three*, 159–63; Hess, *Pickett's Charge*, 121–23; John Michael Priest, *Into the Fight: Pickett's Charge at Gettysburg* (Shippensburg, PA: White Mane Books, 1998), 8–9, 35–36, 40–43.

28. Hess, *Pickett's Charge*, 5–6; Wert, *Gettysburg: Day Three*, 99.

29. Richard Rollins, "Lee's Artillery Prepares for Pickett's Charge," *North & South* 2, no. 7 (September 1999): 42–43; Hess, *Pickett's Charge*, 6.

30. *OR*, vol. 27, pt. 2, p. 320; Wert, *Gettysburg: Day Three*, 100–103; Priest, *Into the Fight*, 14.

31. Edward Porter Alexander, *Fighting for the Confederacy: The Personal Recollections of General Edward Porter Alexander*, ed. Gary W. Gallagher (Chapel Hill: University of North Carolina Press, 1989), 255; Hess, *Pickett's Charge*, 9; Coddington, *The Gettysburg Campaign*, 458–59; quotation in Wert, *Gettysburg: Day Three*, 100.

32. Hess, *Pickett's Charge*, 13–14, 32; Wert, *Gettysburg: Day Three*, 104.

33. Hess, *Pickett's Charge*, 14–15, 20.

34. Ibid., 26.

35. Ibid., 35; Wert, *Gettysburg: Day Three*, 130, 163.

36. Wert, *Gettysburg: Day Three*, 154–57.

37. Ibid., 157–58.

38. Pfanz, *Gettysburg: Culp's Hill and Cemetery Hill*, 358; Wert, *Gettysburg: Day Three*, 159.

39. Wert, *Gettysburg: Day Three*, 92; Hess, *Pickett's Charge*, 85–86; Haskell, *Haskell of Gettysburg*, 144–47; Priest, *Into the Fight*, 43–45.

40. Quotations in Alexander, *Fighting for the Confederacy*, 254; Wert, *Gettysburg: Day Three*, 165; Hess, *Pickett's Charge*, 27; Coddington, *The Gettysburg Campaign*, 487–88; Priest, *Into the Fight*, 47.

41. Quotations in Wert, *Gettysburg: Day Three*, 165–66, and Alexander, *Fighting for the Confederacy*, 254–55; Hess, *Pickett's Charge*, 27–28; Coddington, *The Gettysburg Campaign*, 487–88; Priest, *Into the Fight*, 47.

42. Wert, *Gettysburg: Day Three*, 138–44; Hess, *Pickett's Charge*, 126.

43. Quotations from Hess, *Pickett's Charge*, 52, 54; Priest, *Into the Fight*, 31.

44. Steven E. Woodworth, *Davis and Lee at War* (Lawrence: University Press of Kansas, 1995), 234–37; Robert K. Krick, "Armistead and Garnett: The Parallel Lives of Two Virginia Soldiers," in *The Third Day at Gettysburg and Beyond*, ed. Gary W. Gallagher (Chapel Hill: University of North Carolina Press, 1994), 91–131; Hess, *Pickett's Charge*, 36–54; Wert, *Gettysburg: Day Three*, 108–14.

45. Gragg, *Covered with Glory*, 157.

46. Ibid., 158.

47. Wert, *Gettysburg: Day Three*, 150.

48. Hess, *Pickett's Charge*, 86 107.

49. Ibid., 117, 125, 127; Wert, *Gettysburg: Day Three*, 167; Coddington, *The Gettysburg Campaign*, 493; Priest, *Into the Fight*, 49–55; Richard Rollins, "The Failure of Confederate Artillery in Pickett's Charge," *North & South* 3, no. 4 (April 2000): 26–41.

CHAPTER NINE

THE APPALLING GRANDEUR
OF THE STORM

INFANTRYMEN CROUCHED or lay prone behind stone fences or low earthworks while shells rained down. Most of the soldiers on Cemetery Ridge were veterans of many battles and had heard thunderous cannonades before at Antietam, Fredericksburg, and Chancellorsville, but the most experienced men had never heard anything like this before. "This," one of them later recalled, "proved to be something far beyond all previous experience, or conception, and the scene was terrific beyond description."[1] Gazing across the valley toward the smoke-shrouded ranks of Confederate guns three-fourths of a mile away, a soldier of the First Minnesota could see only "banks of white vapor, from beneath which tongues of fire were incessantly darting."[2] Another in the First Delaware later remembered the scene as being "like some horrible night-mare where one was held spell-bound by the appalling grandeur of the storm."[3] This was no dream, however, but deadly reality. The shells plowed up the ground, smashed trees, wrecked cannon, blew up caissons and limber chests full of artillery ammunition, and dismembered horses and men.

In the Vermont Brigade, a bit south of the Angle and the clump of trees, an officer noted grimly that he could see at least some of the incoming shells in flight. So could soldiers of the Twelfth New Jersey, who were crouching behind the stone fence a few hundred yards north of the Angle. Everyone on the ridge could hear the projectiles "howling, shrieking" as they came in, then "striking, exploding, tearing."[4] A Minnesotan recalled, "We commended our soul to God, shut our teeth *hard* and lay flat on the ground, expecting every minute to be blown to atoms."[5]

Nearby, among the Bucktails of the 143d Pennsylvania, there was a bit of grotesque humor. As Sergeant Simon Hubler of Company L crouched on the ground, another soldier crawled up and stated "that a shell had struck a man in Company D of our Regiment, taking off his head just above the ears, and scattering his brain over seven other soldiers." As Hubler and his comrades digested this shocking report, one of their number spoke up to ask if the man had been killed. The others roared with laughter.[6]

While the Union troops on Cemetery Ridge took their pounding, Confederate shells hit Cemetery Hill as well. As a prime platform for Union artillery the hill was also a prime target for the Confederate guns, and since it was on the curve of the Union fishhook position, it could be hit from several directions at once. There, too, infantrymen flattened themselves against the ground, but not every shell could be dodged that way. One struck the fence behind which the Forty-fifth New York was sheltering, "sending hats, limbs & bodies flying through the air." On another part of the hilltop, six artillery horses were cut down by a single shell.[7]

One factor decreased somewhat the destructiveness of the Confederate bombardment. Numerous Union officers noticed that many of the incoming shells passed harmlessly over the ridge and hill to explode hundreds of yards to the rear. The Confederate gunners were less well trained than their Union counterparts, largely because the South could not provide enough ammunition for target practice. They were also inexperienced at long-range firing, because Southern batteries had usually reserved their scarce ammunition for use against Union infantry at short range. Finally, much of the artillery ammunition with which the underindustrialized South supplied its troops was defective. Specifically, the time fuses were defective. When the fuses should have detonated the shells in deadly air-bursts over the Union positions, instead they allowed them to sail harmlessly into the fields beyond.[8]

Harmless that might be for the Union troops who would do the fighting, but it was nothing short of terrifying to the assorted stragglers, teamsters, and other rear-area types who suddenly found themselves in the midst of the bombardment. They departed for safer regions with a speed that amused those combat soldiers who had the opportunity and inclination to glance that way. Also affected by the abundance of "overs" was Meade's own headquarters at the Widow Leister's house. Shells crashed into the house and yard with appalling frequency, slaughtering the staff officers' horses. Reluctantly, Meade gave the order to move his headquarters temporarily to Slocum's on Power's Hill, about a half-mile away.[9]

Meanwhile, the infantry on the front lines continued to hug the ground. Sergeant Major William B. Hincks of the Fourteenth Connecticut realized that in the extreme heat and the stress of the situation, he was sweating so much that a small mud puddle was developing on the ground beneath his face.[10] Enduring incoming fire when they could do nothing in reply was one of the war's most trying tests for soldiers' nerves. As minute by minute the intense bombardment dragged on, officers along Cemetery Ridge began to wonder how long their men could take it. Winfield Scott Hancock decided to do something about it. The Union artillerymen had not yet fired in reply, faithfully waiting out their fifteen-minute delay as per General Hunt's orders. Hancock had other ideas. He ordered the guns in his Second Corps sector to open up right away. The infantrymen needed to hear their own artillery giving it back to the Rebels.[11]

The Union gunners sprang to their pieces, and another thirty cannon added their roars to the general din. A few minutes later, the rest of the Union artillery joined in. Great banks of white smoke now billowed up from the blue-clad lines, shrouding them as similar clouds had already covered their foes. One Federal remembered that "the sun through the smoke looked like a great red ball."[12] To a Union staff officer on the ridge the guns seemed like "great infuriate demons, not of the earth, whose mouths blaze with smoky tongues of living fire, and whose murky breath, sulphur-laden, rolls around them and along the ground, the smoke of Hades."[13] Inside the cauldron of churning smoke belched out by their own guns, the artillerists worked methodically. Drill and teamwork took over, and there was "no flurry and no fuss."[14]

In one respect, however, the rushing adrenaline and fury of battle were making a difference in the way the guns were served. Whereas General Hunt wanted his gunners to fire slowly and methodically, no more than one round every two minutes, an experienced artillery officer on Cemetery Hill estimated that his and the other Union guns were firing at a rate of from two to four rounds per minute.[15] The result was a continuous roar in which no single discharge was distinguishable. Many soldiers were deaf or nearly so for several days afterward. The concussions of the guns shook the ground where the infantrymen lay, and the muzzle blasts sprayed some of them with dirt and gravel, even as the explosions of incoming shells were doing the same.[16]

In the heart of the flame and smoke and noise that rolled up and out from the Union position, between the Angle and the clump of trees, was Battery A, Fourth U.S. Artillery, commanded by Lieutenant Alonzo Cushing. Battery A was taking a beating. Incoming fire detonated two of its six ammunition-filled limber chests, side by side and at almost the same moment, creating a terrific blast. Another Rebel shell smashed the wheel of the No. 3 gun, and the crew started to bolt for the rear. Cushing headed them off with drawn revolver, threatening to shoot down any man who fled. They turned around and, under his direction, fetched a spare wheel from the caisson, replaced the broken one, and got the gun back into action.[17]

As the bombardment went on, much the same thing happened to two other guns of the battery, and Cushing had them repaired as well. "He was as cool and calm as I ever saw him," recalled a member of the battery. Yet the continued pounding took its toll. Guns were smashed too badly for repair. Men and horses were smashed as well. Casualties among the cannoneers became so severe that Cushing had to call on nearby infantry for volunteers to serve the remaining guns. Fifty soldiers of the Philadelphia Brigade responded. Cushing, grievously wounded, refused to leave the field and continued to direct his guns.[18]

While Cushing's battery and several others nearby were being wrecked, the artillery duel was coming out much differently in other sectors. The superior ammunition, superior positions, and superbly trained crews of the Union artillery began to tell on the Confederate batteries. As the Federal gunners warmed to their work and got the range on their counterparts across the way, they were soon dismounting Confederate pieces, exploding their caissons and limber chests, and mangling the gray-coated gunners. Two guns of the Palmetto Light Artillery were left without a single man to work them or a horse to pull them—all had become casualties. Loss of personnel silenced three guns of the Washington Artillery. Southern artillery officers, like their Union counterparts, strove heroically to hold their men to the work. Major James Dearing, commanding the artillery battalion attached to Pickett's division, rode back and forth behind his gunners, waving a flag and shouting encouragement. Nonetheless, Confederate fire gradually became somewhat wild and scattered under the impact of the Union return fire, and the effectiveness of the bombardment decreased.[19]

Inevitably, the infantrymen of Pickett's and Pettigrew's divisions suffered along with the Confederate gunners, as Union shells aimed in the general direction of the smoke-shrouded Rebel artillery sailed over the guns and into the hollows where the Confederate assault troops were waiting. To one member of Pickett's division it seemed "as if we were placed where we were for target practice for the Union batteries." Brigadier General James Kemper recalled how the Union shells "pelted them and ploughed through them, and sometimes the fragments of a dozen mangled men were thrown in and about the trench left by a single missile." A soldier of the Seventh Virginia later described how "in any direction might be seen guns, swords, haversacks, heads, limbs, flesh and bones in confusion or dangling in the air or bounding on the earth." The ground shook, he added, as if in an earthquake.[20]

In the midst of the carnage came Longstreet, calmly walking his horse along the line. Whatever his faults in other respects, Longstreet's best qualities gleamed brightly in this sort of situation where his presence and demeanor infused strength into the very spirits of his men. His unshakable calmness and physical courage were contagious, and Kemper thought his steadiness in this trying circumstance "the grandest moral spectacle of the war."[21]

That sort of performance was expected of Civil War generals. Even as Longstreet rode his lines near Seminary Ridge, several Union officers were doing much the same on Cemetery Ridge. Hancock sat serenely on the back of his slowly walking horse while all around him men hugged the ground to escape the exploding shells. When subordinates remonstrated at the risk he was taking, he replied simply, "There are times when a corps commander's life does not count." Brigadier General Alexander Hays was also mounted. "Most of the time he was riding up and down the lines in front of us," wrote a soldier, "exhorting the 'boys' to stand fast and fight like men." Hays also gave the practical advice that the men should gather up and load all the discarded rifles within reach. They might come in handy.[22]

As the bombardment entered its second half-hour, Gibbon decided that he, too, should see his men and be seen by them. On foot he strode along a few yards in front of his line of prone infantrymen who were suffering relatively little as the bulk of the Confederate fire passed over their heads toward the Union batteries or the rear areas beyond them. "What do you think of this?" Gibbon called to his men. "O, this is bully," "We are getting to like it," came the replies. "O, we don't mind this."[23] The soldiers also cheered Gibbon, impressed with his courage under fire. "See there," some shouted, "see Gen. Gibbon."[24]

About the time Gibbon was walking his lines, the Army of the Potomac's chief of artillery, Henry Hunt, was inspecting his hard-working gunners on Cemetery Hill. Things were going much better there now than they had earlier, though the hill was still a dangerous place. The Eleventh Corps artillery had just succeeded in silencing Rebel Second Corps guns on Benner's Hill. Hunt stopped to talk with Eleventh Corps artillery chief Major Thomas W. Osborn, and Eleventh Corps commander Oliver Howard joined them. The three men agreed that after the bombardment ended, the Confederates would probably launch an infantry assault. Osborn suggested that the Union guns should cease fire so as to give the Rebels the impression that they had been silenced. Then the gray-clad infantry would advance while the Union guns still had some long-range ammunition left. Hunt at once saw the genius of this idea and rode off to implement it, ordering battery after battery to cease firing. He also ordered some of the hardest-hit batteries to pull out of line while he moved up fresh batteries from the artillery reserve, thus bringing the firepower on Cemetery Ridge back up to pre-bombardment levels.[25]

Hunt could not be everywhere, however, and some half-wrecked batteries remained in line. In the hundred-yard space between the Angle and the clump of trees, Battery A, Fourth U.S. Artillery, fought on. Only two cannon remained usable, and one of those was manned by infantrymen. When Brigadier General Alexander Webb, commanding the Philadelphia Brigade, told Cushing that he expected the Rebels to charge, the badly wounded lieutenant replied, "Then I had better run my guns right up to the stone fence and bring up all the canister alongside of each piece." Then, leaning on his faithful first sergeant, he hobbled forward while his men wheeled up the two remaining serviceable guns by hand. The Seventy-first Pennsylvania moved up and took position at the wall just to the right of Cushing's guns.[26]

Three-quarters of a mile away, Confederate Colonel Edward Porter Alexander was facing the most difficult decision of his military career, and one that should rightly have belonged to his superior, James Longstreet. Alexander had originally intended to continue the bombardment only about fifteen minutes, twenty at the most, in order to make sure that his guns had enough ammunition left to support the infantry attack. At that point in the bombardment, however, the whole of the Union artillery had just opened up with a roar from Cemetery Hill all the way to Little Round Top. Alexander could not bring himself to send infantry forward into that maelstrom, so he kept the guns firing, minute after minute, while ammunition supplies dwindled alarmingly. At 1:25 P.M., Alexander could still see no reduction in Union return fire, but with caissons and limber chests nearing critical states of emptiness, he wrote a dispatch to Pickett. "If you are able to advance at all, you must come at once," he wrote, "or we will not be able to support you as we ought." Alexander added honestly that the enemy's fire had not diminished, with several batteries firing from the central section of Cemetery Ridge toward which the assault would be directed.[27]

An eager George Pickett took Alexander's note from the courier who brought it. At thirty-eight, Pickett was almost a caricature of a Virginia cavalier, complete with long hair that he wore in perfumed ringlets. After graduating dead last in the West Point class of 1846, he became an Old Army friend of Longstreet, who had racked up a record almost as dismal four years earlier. They served together in the Mexican War, and when Captain Longstreet fell wounded while carrying the flag in the assault on Chapultepec, his friend Lieutenant Pickett had picked up the colors and charged on. In the current war, Pickett had advanced in rank chiefly through Longstreet's patronage. Wounded in June 1862 while leading a brigade, Pickett had returned to duty late in September of that year and taken over the command of a newly organized division. The component brigades had all seen combat before, but Pickett and his men had not yet had a chance to show what they could do together as a division. Pickett read Alexander's note and believed that chance had come. "Boys," he said to his waiting staff officers, "let us give them a trial." General and staff mounted up and galloped off to get the division formed and ready to advance.[28]

Meanwhile, Alexander was still anxiously watching the Union lines for some sign that his bombardment was taking effect. Then, about ten minutes after sending his note to Pickett, he thought he saw what he had been looking for. The guns in the Union center slackened their fire, then ceased altogether. Peering through his field glasses through occasional rifts in the banks of smoke, Alexander caught glimpses of Union batteries limbering up and galloping to the rear. Then all along the line from Cemetery Hill to Little Round Top, the Federal guns began to fall silent. This was it, Alexander thought. For the first time in a major battle during this war, Confederate artillery had beaten down its Union counterpart. "I was a good deal elated by the sight," he later admitted. It was 1:40 P.M., and Alexander dashed off another note to Pickett to relay the exciting news that the artillery in the Union center was pulling out. "For God's sake come on quick," the artillery officer added, "or we cannot support you. Ammunition nearly out."[29]

Pickett had not been wasting time. After giving orders to ready his division, he had ridden to Longstreet, who by this time had seated himself on a rail fence, and showed him Alexander's first note. "General," Pickett asked eagerly, "shall I advance?" Longstreet could not bring himself to speak the order and merely nodded assent. Pickett, by contrast, was full of zest. "I shall lead my division forward, sir," he announced and rode off toward his troops. Galloping to where the men of Kemper's brigade were still lying on the ground, he shouted, "Up, men, and to your posts! Don't forget today that you are from old Virginia!" Hastily the men scrambled to their feet and formed their battle lines.[30]

These Confederates were shaken by the losses they had sustained during the bombardment, and they were also suffering from the heat. It was 87 degrees now and humid, and a slight south breeze was very slowly drifting the dense banks of powder smoke away from the battlefield. There were a number of cases of heatstroke in Confederate ranks. Among the casualties from the Union shelling was Colonel Birkett Fry, commanding what was left of the Tennessee Brigade in place of James J. Archer, who had been captured when the brigade was savaged by the Iron Brigade two days before. Fry took a shell fragment in the shoulder but refused to leave his command. His brigade, on the right of Pettigrew's line, was the unit of direction. All the other units in the assault were to align themselves on it.[31]

Many of those Confederates who had escaped the ravages of bursting shells and blazing sun were suffering intense anxiety about what lay before them. "*Oh*, if I could just come out of this charge safely," thought Virginian John Dooley, "how thankful *would I be*!" Large numbers of the infantrymen preparing to advance had very little expectation of coming out safely. So far, at least, the men were prepared to march to their deaths, but some accounts suggest that morale was shaky. A lieutenant in the First Virginia heard several comments in the ranks to the effect "that Pickett's Division had been condemned to be shot and was marching up to execution."[32]

Pickett's brigade commanders did their best to inspire the men. Garnett, resplendent in full-dress uniform, waving his hat and cheering his men, took his place in front of his brigade. Contrary to Pickett's orders that all officers should advance on foot, Garnett was mounted. Kicked by a horse a couple of days before, Garnett was still somewhat lame and probably could not have made the advance on foot. After the aspersions that Stonewall Jackson had cast on his behavior at Kernstown, there was no way Richard B. Garnett was going to stay behind in this charge. He was not the only mounted man to go forward. Kemper was on horseback, and so were a dozen or so other officers for various reasons.[33]

Louis Armistead approached Leander Blackburn, color bearer of the Fifty-third Virginia. "Sergeant, I want you and your men to plant your colors on those works," the brigadier admonished. "Do you think you can do it?" Blackburn said he would try. Armistead gave the sergeant a drink from his flask. Then, drawing his sword with a flourish, he shouted to the troops around him, "Men, remember what you are fighting for! Your homes, your firesides, and your sweethearts! Follow me!" Walking twenty paces in front of his brigade's line, he placed his black slouch hat on the point of his sword, lifted it above him, and strode forward. The infantry advance had begun.[34]

Longstreet, apparently still sensing a chance to call off the attack, mounted and rode too, straight to Colonel Alexander, whom he asked for a report of the situation. The artillery officer explained that the Confederate artillery had silenced the enemy's guns but had so little ammunition left it could not give the infantry any further help. Even now some of the Confederate batteries were beginning to fall silent for lack of shells. Longstreet jumped at this. "Go and halt Pickett right where he is," he ordered, "and replenish your ammunition."

"General, we can't do that," Alexander explained. It would take two hours for the caissons to go all the way to the Confederate supply train and back, and even then the guns would have enough ammunition for only another fifteen minutes of firing. That was all the artillery ammunition the Confederates had in Pennsylvania. Besides, by that time the Yankees would have recovered from whatever damage they had suffered in the bombardment. "Our only chance is to follow up now."

Longstreet responded slowly, with frequent pauses, while gazing at the Union lines. "I don't want to make this attack—I believe
it will fail—I do not see how it can succeed—I would not make it
even now, but that General Lee has ordered and expects it."
Alexander had the impression that the general was looking for some
word from him that might even yet enable him to cancel the advance, but it was not an artillery colonel's place to make such a
decision, and Alexander said nothing.[35]

Within a few minutes, the advancing infantry lines of Pickett
and Pettigrew had passed through Alexander's batteries. The
artillerists standing near their red-hot but now-silent guns waved
their hats and cheered the foot soldiers on. Although a few guns
out on the flanks still had ammunition and kept firing, the great
artillery bombardment was effectively over. It had wrecked several batteries in the Union center and inflicted perhaps 5 percent
casualties on the Union infantry there. On the other hand, Union
return fire had inflicted a slightly higher casualty rate on Pickett's
and Pettigrew's waiting infantry, and the Confederate artillery had
exhausted its ammunition to such an extent that it would no longer
be a factor in the coming attack. If the Yankee line was to be broken, the job would have to be done by the surviving infantrymen
of Pickett, Pettigrew, and Trimble.[36]

The ground was open and very gently rolling, and most of the
advancing formations marched with parade-ground precision.
Pickett's brigades had started from a point well south of Pettigrew's.
By the time they had advanced several hundred yards, Pickett and
his officers recognized the need to march by left oblique, as soldiers called it, moving crabwise forward and to the left so as to
close up on Fry's Tennesseeans on the right of Pettigrew's line.[37]

Pettigrew had problems of his own. Neither Pickett nor
Longstreet had sent him notice that the attack was about to begin.
When he saw Pickett's men stand up, he ordered his own division
to rise as well. Not until he saw Pickett's line moving forward did
he realize that the order to advance had been given, and by that
time Pickett had a lead of perhaps as much as 300 or 400 yards.
Riding to the front of his old brigade, Pettigrew called to its new
commander, James K. Marshall, "Now Colonel, for the honor of
the good Old North State. Forward!" Even then, Joseph Davis, finding that service as military aide to his uncle, the Confederate president, had not quite prepared him for field service, missed the start

of the division's advance and had to hurry his brigade along to catch up. On the far left of Pettigrew's advance, Brockenbrough's tiny Virginia brigade, plagued by poor leadership, seemed lost. Following behind Pettigrew as planned, Trimble's two brigades moved forward in good order.[38]

As the gray-clad ranks advanced a hundred yards or so beyond their own Confederate gun lines, Union long-range artillery fire began hitting them and continued to dog them as they marched on. Federal guns on Little Round Top and the southern end of Cemetery Ridge still had plenty of long-range ammunition left and were using it to good advantage. Other guns on Cemetery Hill joined in as well. A single shell could slaughter a dozen men or more, tearing huge gaps in the advancing line. The survivors moved left or right as needed to plug the holes even as they kept on marching forward. A soldier of the Seventh Virginia recalled how the line swayed and became unsteady "because at every step a gap must be closed."[39] Among the early casualties was Pettigrew himself, wounded in the hand by a fragment of a shell that also killed his horse. He kept going. Another early casualty was Sergeant Blackburn, who had promised Armistead he would try to plant his colors on the Union breastworks. Blackburn was killed by a direct hit. Another member of the color guard picked up the blood-spattered flag and marched on.[40]

As the advance neared its halfway point, Union skirmishers opened fire. Several hundred yards in front of Cemetery Ridge, the thin line of skirmishers was intended to provide warning of enemy advance, but these Federals were determined to get their licks in before they went scampering back to the main defensive line. They scored a number of hits, and the handful of mounted officers were particular targets. Among them were Colonel Lewis B. Williams of the First Virginia and Colonel Eppa Hunton of the Eighth. Both men were sick and unable to make the charge on foot and had gotten special permission to ride horses in the attack. Hunton was severely wounded, Williams mortally, by Union skirmishers' bullets.[41]

With each yard the attackers advanced, some of the men in the formation found that their courage failed them, and they dropped out of ranks, fleeing to the rear or taking cover as best they could. Typically during the Civil War, a hotly engaged line of battle would lose a steady trickle of men who were either habitual shirkers or who, on this one occasion at least, could not summon the emotional resources to face the enemy any longer. Their comrades ignored them for the most part, closed up their shrinking ranks, and kept marching.[42]

Back on Cemetery Ridge, the soldiers along the main Union battle line had no need of skirmishers to tell them that the Rebels were coming and in massive force. As the thick banks of powder smoke drifted slowly northward, revealing the broad, shallow valley between the ridges, the Federals saw Pettigrew's line move out of the woods on Seminary Ridge and Pickett's advance up out of a swale. Rarely did Civil War battlefields offer this sort of wide-open view of 12,000 troops in line of battle, nor could the enemy usually be seen approaching over such a long distance. Reactions on Cemetery Ridge ranged from awe to nervousness to relief that the bombardment was over and now at last the blue-clad infantry would have someone to shoot back at. The Yankees could not help but admire the fine formations and the steady, silent advance, as majestic and inexorable as a mighty river. "It was magnificent," recalled an officer of the Fourteenth Connecticut. "Onward they came," wrote a captain of the Sixty-ninth Pennsylvania, "and it would seem as if no power could hold them in check."[43]

The Federals made their preparations. Artillery commander Henry Hunt galloped this way and that shouting orders, ensuring that his batteries got into the most advantageous positions. Meade dispatched orders to units in other sectors, drawing reinforcements to the threatened center of the Union line. Gibbon and Hays rode along their lines speaking to the troops. "Let them come up close before you fire, and then aim low, and steadily," Gibbon told his men. "We must hold this Line to the Last Man." Hays exhorted, "They are coming, boys; we must whip them." Lieutenant Frank Haskell, a member of Gibbon's staff, remembered individual soldiers arranging their cartridge and cap boxes for handy access and officers opening their pistol holsters. Some of the artillerymen were rolling their guns a few feet closer to the stone fence, and here and there along the line a color sergeant waved the Stars and Stripes defiantly at the advancing enemy.[44]

After the skirmishers had fired their scattering shots, the first Union troops to engage the attackers were those of the Eighth Ohio, who had spent the day in the ditches along the Emmitsburg Road supporting the skirmishers in front of Hays's division, not far from the smoldering ruins of the Bliss barn. This put them opposite the far northern end of the advancing Confederate line. Smoke was

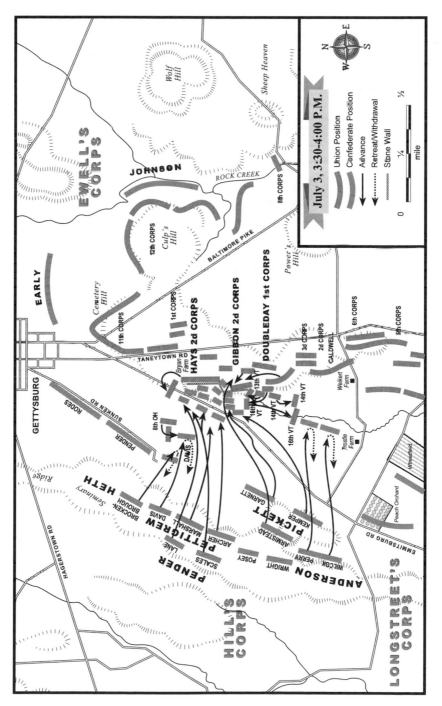

still thick on this end of the field, but Lieutenant Colonel Frank Sawyer, commanding the Eighth, knew a major force was approaching when his skirmishers fired and began to fall back across the cornfield in front. Sawyer was not ready to fall back yet, so he ordered his 150 men forward across the cornfield to join the skirmishers at the rail fence on the other side. No sooner had they all taken their places at the fence than Brockenbrough's hapless Virginia brigade emerged from the smoke 100 yards ahead. Outnumbered more than two to one, the Ohioans nevertheless stood their ground and opened fire. It was too much for Brockenbrough's already demoralized troops. Their hearts had never been in this charge, and now their legs carried them pell-mell to the rear.[45]

As the other eight attacking brigades continued their silent, steady advance, Pickett, riding just behind his troops, dispatched a staff officer to Longstreet. He believed his division could reach the crest of Cemetery Ridge, but he feared they could not hold on there without strong support, which the staff officer, Captain Robert A. Bright, was to request from Longstreet. Arriving where Longstreet had resumed his seat on a rail fence on Seminary Ridge, Bright delivered his message. Longstreet asked where the troops were who had been ordered to cover Pickett's flank, and Bright showed him Brockenbrough's panicked brigade, now fleeing frantically toward them across the open fields in front.

Just then, visiting British officer Arthur Fremantle, colonel of Her Majesty's Coldstream Guards, approached Longstreet, exclaiming, "General, I would not have missed this for anything in the world." "The devil you wouldn't!" Longstreet retorted, "I would like to have missed it very much; we've attacked and been repulsed: look there!" The general pointed to Brockenbrough's fugitives. Turning to Bright, Longstreet said, "Bright, ride to General Pickett and tell him what you have heard me say to Colonel Fremantle." As Bright turned to go, Longstreet added, "Tell General Pickett that Wilcox's Brigade is in the peach orchard; and he can order him to his assistance." Notified by Bright, Pickett sent orders to Wilcox to advance and cover his southern flank, and he sent another staff officer with a renewed plea to Longstreet for reinforcements. Wilcox moved forward in obedience to the order, but the staff officer sent to Longstreet could not find him during the attack. That was all the help Pickett, Pettigrew, and Trimble were going to get.[46]

Over on Cemetery Ridge, the troops in the main Union line of battle waited and watched while their artillery ripped into the Confederate ranks from left and right. Captain Henry L. Abbott of the Twentieth Massachusetts saw shells "tumble over squads in the rebel lines." The Union guns directly in front of the Confederate advance, however, remained silent. In the sector around the clump of trees and the Angle, the Federal artillery had already expended all of its long-range ammunition and was loaded with deadly but short-range canister, waiting for the Rebels to come within its 300- to 400-yard reach.[47]

The Confederates strode onward through the bursting shells. Angling across their front was the Emmitsburg Road. Kemper's men, on the right wing of Pickett's line, reached and crossed it first. Then came Garnett's troops, on the left side of Pickett's formation, with Armistead's brigade following behind, midway between the other two. Pickett's men had relatively little trouble at the road. Where they crossed it was still outside of prime rifle range from the Yankee lines, and the fences on either side of the road had been largely destroyed by the previous day's fighting and so posed little obstacle. On the north side of the road, about the middle of Pickett's front, stood the Codori farm about a quarter-mile from the Union line. Pickett stopped there, making the farm his command post while his men strode steadily onward. Things were different for Pettigrew's men, still farther to the Confederate left. They hit the road even closer to the Yankee line and in a sector where sturdy post-and-rail fences still lined both sides of the roadbed.

The Confederate formation was tightly closed up now with no gap between Pickett and Pettigrew. The range to the Union line was less than 200 yards, and the blue-clad soldiers were leveling their rifles over the top of the stone fence. Garnett's brigade had just cleared the Emmitsburg Road and was pushing up the final gentle slope toward the stone fence. Directly ahead of them was the clump of trees. Just in front of the trees waved the Stars and Stripes and the green regimental flag of the Sixty-ninth Pennsylvania. Other flags dotted the Union line in both directions. To the left of Garnett's men, forming a continuation of their line, Fry's Tennesseeans, the extreme right of Pettigrew's division, prepared to negotiate the rail fences.

The Union volley flashed along the slope of Cemetery Ridge not in a single cataclysmic crash but rather in a long, rolling crescendo of thousands of rifle shots within the space of a few dozen seconds, as regiment after regiment triggered its fire into the solid Rebel ranks. Before the last regiment had volleyed, the first had reloaded and was firing again. Many of the Union regiments were firing off the stockpiles of loaded rifles they had laid by. To one Union officer "the incessant rattle of musketry sounded like the grinding of some huge mill."[48]

Fry's Tennesseeans were just climbing the fence when the volley struck them, and one of them later remembered that the bullets against the fence rails "rattled with the distinctness of large raindrops pattering on a roof." Not all the bullets struck wood. A Union soldier watching from behind the stone fence noted how his foes "dropped from the fence as if swept by a gigantic sickle." Fry never made it to the fence, falling just short of it with a bullet in the thigh. His men plunged ahead, tumbling over the first fence, dashing across the road, and clambering over the second fence while bullets cut down dozens of men at every step. Others, unable to make themselves go any farther, dropped prone and availed themselves of the scant cover of the road's slightly cut grade.[49]

Just to the Tennesseeans' left, the story was much the same in the North Carolina brigade that had been Pettigrew's before he inherited the division. Colonel Marshall had led it out today. He was twenty-four and had graduated from the Virginia Military Institute one day short of three years before. That anniversary, however, was one Marshall would not reach. Like Colonel Fry, he fell before reaching the Emmitsburg Road, two rifle bullets striking his forehead at almost the same moment. His men were falling fast, too.[50]

The Union artillery in front was firing now, all along the stretch of stone fence from Ziegler's Grove and the small barn of a free black farmer named Abram Bryan (or Brian) down to the clump of trees and beyond—the whole front of Pettigrew's and Pickett's line. The Federal gunners were using their deadly short-range canister ammunition, each round of which was a bucket of balls that transformed a half-ton field piece into a gigantic sawed-off shotgun. It could be loaded double, and many of the Union batteries were firing it that way, sweeping down whole sections of the Confederate line at every blast.

In moments that seemed like ages, Pettigrew's survivors moved beyond the Emmitsburg Road and its fences. Fry's and Marshall's brigades tried to keep their parade-ground lines, but gaps opened constantly as Union rifle bullets peppered their ranks and double loads of canister plowed broad lanes. To the right of Fry's and Marshall's men, a tiny remnant of Davis's Mississippi brigade pressed on toward the Bryan barn. The Mississippians' alignment was gone now, but their courage was not. In all, perhaps 1,000 of the 4,500 men of Pettigrew's division advanced beyond the Emmitsburg Road.[51]

On the opposite, southern end of the attacking Confederate line, Kemper's brigade was taking especially heavy punishment from a large concentration of Union guns several hundred yards south of the clump of trees. The brigade lost formation and swerved hard to the north, fleeing the pounding they were taking but still moving toward Union lines. Now, however, Kemper's left flank largely overlapped Garnett's right. Garnett's brigade, in the center, was faring little better. Formation disintegrated, and the survivors moved forward in a loose swarm dotted with battle flags.[52]

Twelve thousand Confederates had set out from Seminary Ridge twenty minutes before, their numbers almost three times those of the Union defenders of this stretch of Cemetery Ridge. They were not so numerous now. As Pickett's division gathered itself for the final rush, it probably had somewhat over 4,000 men left in its ranks. Pickett's numbers, along with those that Pettigrew and Trimble carried forward across the Emmitsburg Road, would be somewhat superior to those of the defenders, including immediate reinforcements, whom they would actually meet and engage on Cemetery Ridge.[53]

With the Yankee line now in plain view, Kemper rode his horse back to where Armistead was still walking ahead of his brigade. "General, I am going to storm those works," Kemper announced, "and I want you to support me." Armistead agreed. Kemper spurred back to his troops while Armistead shouted to his brigade, "Forward, double quick!"[54]

The Confederate attackers raised the Rebel Yell and plunged forward up the final hundred yards of gentle slope, loading and firing as they came. In the Union lines, General Gibbon went down, badly wounded. Amid the remains of Battery A, Fourth U.S. Artillery, Lieutenant Alonzo Cushing took a bullet in the mouth and toppled over dead. His gunners still struggled to load triple canister in the battery's two remaining guns. The Rebels were less than seventy yards away, coming fast. Right behind them rode Garnett astride his big bay horse, shouting, "Faster men, faster, we're almost there!" The canister was rammed home, rammer staffs pulled out, primers set, and gunners took hold of the firing lanyards. Out in front the charging Rebels "pulled their caps down over their eyes and bowed their heads as men do in a hail storm." The range was down to twenty yards now. With a turn of the shoulder and yank of the forearm, each gunner ripped the lanyard out of its primer and the two guns roared. Scores of Confederates went down, but the rest came on, still shrieking their Rebel Yells.[55]

The surviving gunners of Cushing's battery broke for the rear, and so did the men of the Philadelphia Brigade around them. In front of the clump of trees, the Sixty-ninth Pennsylvania formed a knot of resistance, stabbing with bayonets, clubbing with rifle butts, and shooting point-blank across the stone fence with the men of Pickett's division. General Webb, commander of the Philadelphia Brigade, frantically tried to rally the rest of his men to retake their position, as did Gibbon's aide Lieutenant Haskell, flailing at skulkers with the flat of his sword. For the moment, however, a dynamic equilibrium had been reached. The blue-clad soldiers could not retake the wall, but the gray-clad ones could not get over it, so they stood some eighty yards apart and slaughtered each other as fast as they could load and fire. The outcome depended on which side could get the most reinforcements the fastest. Haskell, noting that "those red flags were accumulating at the wall every minute," galloped off to look for help.[56]

Garnett's, Kemper's, and some of Fry's men clustered along the front of the fence. Garnett lay dead a few feet away. Fry had gone down back by the Emmitsburg Road, and Kemper was directing the portion of his brigade farther to the south. Then Armistead emerged from the battle smoke, running twenty yards in front of his brigade with his hat rammed down to the hilt of his uplifted sword. "Now give 'em the cold steel, boys," cried Armistead, and he led the surging mass of Confederates from all four brigades over the stone fence and past Cushing's silent guns.[57]

Fierce fighting raged inside the Angle, around the clump of trees, and along the stone fence in both directions, but the Confederates could not expand their breakthrough. Armistead strode to one of Cushing's guns and placed his hand on it. "The day is ours, men," he shouted, "come turn this artillery upon them!" Then another blast of Union rifle fire caught him. He doubled over "like a person with cramp," observed a Union soldier a few yards away, "pressed his left hand on his stomach, his sword and hat . . . fell to the ground. He then made two or three staggering steps, reached out his hands trying to grasp the muzzle of what was then the 1st piece of Cushing's battery, and fell." Stubbornly, his men still clung to their position inside the Angle. They hoped other Confederate troops might move up to support them and anxiously asked one another, "Why don't they come?"[58]

Instead, Union reinforcements were moving up from various directions to support the defenders. On the north end of the Confederate front the Eighth Ohio, having dispatched Brockenbrough's hapless brigade, swung 90 degrees to the left and fired into the flank of Davis's. Seeing the effect this was producing, General Hays swung several more Union regiments forward and to their left into a position between the Ohioans and the rest of the Union line, whence they poured a deadly fire directly into the flank of Pettigrew's and Trimble's troops. This was the end of the road for Pettigrew's brave men, who had come so far at such terrible cost. Because of the offset produced by the Angle, Pettigrew's men had eighty yards farther to go before reaching the stone fence, and that proved to be a few yards too far. The determined color bearer of the Twenty-sixth North Carolina, accompanied by one man of the color guard, actually made it all the way to the fence, but they got there alone and had to surrender. Other survivors, scattered across the field between the stone fence and the Emmitsburg Road, had to make their choice between surrender and turning to run the gauntlet of fire back toward Confederate lines. Trimble's troops, who had suffered much the same punishment as Pettigrew's, now crumbled as well. When staff officer Charles Grogan asked Trimble, who by then was lying on the ground with a severe leg wound, if he should try to rally them, the crusty old fighter replied, "No, Charley, the best these brave fellows can do, is to get out of this."[59]

At the opposite end of the Confederate front, just south of the sector held by the Union Second Corps, Brigadier General George Stannard swung his Vermont Brigade out into a flanking position similar to the one Hays's men had assumed. The Vermonters blasted the flank of Kemper's brigade, most of whose members had not crossed the stone fence. For many of Kemper's soldiers this was too much. All but trapped and faced with what seemed to be certain death or surrender, scores of them chose the latter. Stannard's Vermonters were exultant. Unlike most Union troops at Gettysburg, Stannard's men were short-term nine-month volunteers whose enlistments were nearly up. This, their first and last battle, was turning out to be not only a cataclysmic struggle but also a huge success.[60] "I would not have missed it for any consideration," wrote the Sixteenth Vermont's Lieutenant Colonel Charles Cummings three days later. "I never before was so proud of being a Vermonter," exulted Private Royal D. King of the Fourteenth Vermont the following week.[61]

There would be time for exultation later. For now, the Rebel return fire was still dangerous, and numbers of the Vermonters went down. As General Hancock sat his horse watching approvingly the advance of Stannard's brigade, he, too, was hit, a nasty wound in the thigh. Helped to dismount by staff officers, Hancock refused to be carried from the field until the outcome of the attack was decided.

That would not take long. Another wave of Union reinforcements surged toward the dwindling band of Confederates at the Angle. Lieutenant Haskell had gone first to the neighboring brigade commanded by Colonel Norman Hall, just south of Webb's contested position around the clump of trees. Hall's men had been hit, too, and temporarily pushed back from the stone fence in some places. Things had stabilized now, however, and even before Haskell's arrival, Hall had already dispatched three of his five regiments to aid Webb's hard-pressed Philadelphians. They closed in on the Rebels near the clump of trees and exchanged volleys at murderously short range.[62]

Meanwhile, Haskell had ridden on to the southernmost brigade of Gibbon's division, Brigadier General William Harrow's. With no threat in front, Haskell took all four of Harrow's regiments, including the remnant of the heroic First Minnesota. They came on at a dead run, Haskell riding in the lead, waving them on with his sword. "It was impossible to get there in order," recalled the Nineteenth Maine's Colonel Francis Heath. "Everyone wanted to be first and the men of the various commands were all mixed up. We went up more like a mob than a disciplined force."[63]

Haskell noticed that some of the Confederates seemed to be wavering under the fire of Hall's troops. "See!" he shouted. "See the 'chivalry.' See the gray-backs run!"[64] No one could hear him amid the din of battle, but the men had seen it too. With a deep-throated roar the mass of Union soldiers charged directly into the Confederate ranks. The fight became, in the words of one participant, "a perfect melee, and every man fought for himself." A Minnesota soldier later explained, "We knew very well what we were there for and proceeded to business without ceremony." Hall's men and the Philadelphia Brigade piled in. Furiously, men shot, stabbed, hacked, clubbed, and punched their enemies. Captain Alexander McCuen of the Seventy-first Pennsylvania swung his sword at a

Rebel color bearer, took off the man's head with a single stroke, and found himself holding the flag of the Third Virginia. All around him other men fought for other flags or just fought. Outside the stone fence, many Confederates who had not crossed it stood firing into the Federals in support of their comrades around the clump of trees.[65]

Inexorably, however, the Union troops gained the upper hand. Rebel resistance crumbled within minutes. "It was almost as bad going back as it was coming forward," wrote a soldier of the Fourteenth Virginia. "They continued to shoot at us." Hundreds of Pickett's men chose surrender instead, just as many of Pettigrew's men were doing farther north at about the same time. The rest set out on the long and dangerous hike back to Seminary Ridge.[66]

Even as Pickett's, Pettigrew's, and Trimble's divisions were coming to grief on Cemetery Ridge, a bizarre anticlimax began back on Seminary Ridge. The five brigades of Anderson's division that were slated as support for the attack were belatedly getting under way. It had been Longstreet's duty to order their advance, and why he waited so long to start them has never been explained. Lee had expected them to go in right behind the main assault. By the time they were ready to advance, observers on Seminary Ridge could tell that the assault was failing. Longstreet promptly countermanded his order to the three brigades earmarked to support Pettigrew's left, and they never went forward at all. For some reason, however, also never explained, Longstreet allowed the two brigades on Pickett's right to go forward. Union artillery pounded these brave but hapless Confederates, and then Stannard's Vermonters paused from the business of rounding up Pickett's prisoners to turn and charge the new advancing force. The result was that Stannard's men greatly added to their already impressive bag of prisoners and sent the remnant of Anderson's two brigades fleeing back toward Seminary Ridge.[67]

On Cemetery Ridge the fight was over. Here and there a Yankee took a potshot at the scattered fugitives fleeing back toward Seminary Ridge. Other bluecoats herded their vast crowds of prisoners to the rear. A handful of Confederate artillerists who still had a little ammunition left continued lobbing shells onto the ridge, inching the casualty count upward. For most of the Union troops, however, this was a time to deal with the dawning realization that they not only had soundly repulsed the attack but also had thereby finally defeated Robert E. Lee in a major battle. Cheers resounded from one end of the ridge to the other, while a brass band stood near the Leister house and belted out "Hail, Columbia."[68]

General Hays, along with two members of his staff, rode their horses all around his division while each officer dragged in the dust behind him several of the twenty or twenty-one Confederate battle flags the division had captured. Hays's men loved it. They cheered wildly and tossed their caps in the air as the trio rode by. One of the staff officers called it "the grandest ride men ever took." Gibbon's division had taken more than a dozen additional Confederate flags for a grand total of thirty-eight.[69]

Meade arrived on the scene in the midst of the festivities, having missed the attack and repulse, and could not believe the fight was over. Just what Meade thought Hays was doing riding around his division—if the fight were still in progress—or how he thought Hays in that case might have come by his ample supply of Rebel flags is hard to say. To an officer who pointed out the flags in response to his query about the outcome of the fight, Meade barked that he did not care about flags. Finding Lieutenant Haskell near the clump of trees, Meade demanded, "How is it going here?" Haskell reported the Union victory, but Meade was still incredulous. "What? Is the assault entirely repulsed?" Haskell assured him that it was. Meade gave orders to prepare in case the Rebels should renew the attack.[70]

Elsewhere along the Union line, the troops of Caldwell's division of the Second Corps had been mostly spectators in the fight. Having suffered high casualties near the Wheatfield the day before, they had had only shelling to endure this day. Still they felt the excitement and relief at seeing the seemingly unstoppable Confederate assaulting column crushed and turned back. The battlefield was still far from quiet—"rebels and our men . . . could be seen running and firing" and at least one Rebel battle flag was still in view—when Major Leman Bradley, commanding the Sixty-fourth New York, asked Chaplain John H. W. Stuckenberg of the neighboring 145th Pennsylvania to hold a service of thanksgiving for the troops. The men remained behind their low breastworks and removed their caps while Stuckenberg stepped several paces to the front to address them and lead them in prayer. "I thanked God that we had been spared," Stuckenberg wrote in his diary that night, "prayed for the many wounded and remembered the relatives and friends of the killed. The soldiers felt deeply and many were moved to tears."[71]

Tears came for different reasons three-quarters of a mile away on Seminary Ridge, where the remnants of the once-proud Confederate attacking column came straggling back from their bloody errand to Cemetery Ridge. The assault had cost the attackers dearly. Pickett's division had lost more than 2,600 men killed, wounded, and captured—not quite half of its pre-battle strength of 5,800 men. Incredibly, Pettigrew's and Trimble's divisions, which had already suffered severely on the first day of the battle, took even higher casualty rates than Pickett's men did on July 3. Some North Carolina, Mississippi, and Tennessee companies simply ceased to exist. The proud Twenty-sixth North Carolina, which had taken some 800 men into action against the Iron Brigade in Herbst's Woods two days before, could now muster scarcely seventy men in its ranks. Overall the assault had cost the Army of Northern Virginia more than 6,500 men—55 percent of the total force engaged. Union losses were about 1,500 men.[72]

Lee rode among the returning Confederate survivors, striving to restore their spirits and encouraging them to form ranks again and prepare to repel the Union assault he expected must surely follow. As he walked his horse, Lee talked to the men. "Fall back to the rear and reform your lines as well as you can," he told them. "It was not your fault this time. It was all mine." Meeting a distraught Cadmus Wilcox, who complained that he could not rally his brigade, one of the two supporting brigades that advanced last and was roughly handled, Lee replied, "Never mind, General, never mind. It is all my fault, and you young men must help me out the best you can." The important thing now was to prepare for the coming Yankee attack, and so Lee continued riding through the returning fugitives and repeating the same message: "All this will come right in the end; we'll talk it over afterwards; but, in the meantime, all good men must rally. We want all good and true men just now."[73]

Pickett, meanwhile, was providing little help in rallying his troops. Unable to control his emotions or his men, the weeping Pickett moaned to staff officers, "Great God, where, oh! where is my division?" To Longstreet, who tried to buck up his old friend, the blubbering cavalier blurted, "General, I am ruined. My division is gone; it is destroyed."[74]

The attack that Lee feared never came. Hancock, finally being carried to the rear for treatment, took time to dictate a dispatch to Meade, reporting the extent of his corps's victory that afternoon and urging, "If the Sixth and Fifth Corps have pressed up, the enemy will be destroyed."[75] During the attack, Meade had ordered reinforcements to the center of his line from throughout the army. By the time the attackers streamed back toward Seminary Ridge, Meade had available in that sector eighteen brigades from four different corps. He could have thrown those troops at Seminary Ridge or he could have launched the Fifth and Sixth Corps at Hood's and McLaws's divisions in the area of the Round Tops. Neither option looked appealing to Meade. The Confederate positions were strong; the ground in front of them was either rough and broken or else open and exposed. Meade did not know, though perhaps he should have guessed, the state of the ammunition chests of the Confederate artillery, and no one could be sure at that moment how much fight was left in the Rebel infantry, especially the troops that had just been repulsed in their own charge. Meade decided not to risk it. Later historians would praise him for the wisdom and prudence of this decision, but some general was going to have to win the war someday. Meade's choice meant it would be another day and another man.[76]

The armies remained in place the rest of that day and into the next with no significant combat between major units. A Union cavalry commander made an ill-conceived foray against the Confederate right flank on the afternoon of July 3. Like a similar Confederate cavalry foray around the Union right flank and rear earlier in the day—indeed, more or less simultaneous with the great Confederate assault—this one featured dramatic cavalry charges, thundering hooves, and flashing sabers but accomplished little beyond emptying a few saddles. What the cavalry actions lacked in significance, they almost made up in dramatic flair. In the action behind the Confederate right flank, twenty-six-year-old Elon J. Farnsworth of Illinois, who had jumped from captain to brigadier general just five days before, led a desperate Union saber charge, was repulsed, and fell dead with five bullets in him. In the action behind the Union right flank, twenty-four-year-old George A. Custer of Michigan, who had also jumped from captain to brigadier general five days since, likewise led a desperate Union saber charge. Reckless of personal safety, Custer galloped madly ahead of his charging formation but miraculously escaped injury. The charge succeeded and helped drive back Jeb Stuart's foray toward the Union flank and rear. Custer had a rendezvous to keep in the sagebrush-clad hills of Montana eleven years hence.

Late on the afternoon of July 3, Lee pulled Hood's and McLaws's divisions back to Seminary Ridge from the advanced positions they had won at such cost twenty-four hours before. When a regiment of Georgians was slow in going, the Yankees gave them a brisk prod. A brigade of the Pennsylvania Reserves probed forward into Rose's Woods, precipitating a sharp skirmish. The Pennsylvanians had things pretty much their own way, winning a number of prisoners and, though no one could know it yet, the right to claim in years to come that they had fired the last shots of the battle of Gettysburg.

NOTES

1. Hess, *Pickett's Charge*, 127.
2. Wert, *Gettysburg: Day Three*, 168.
3. Hess, *Pickett's Charge*, 128.
4. Ibid.; quotation from Wert, *Gettysburg: Day Three*, 168.
5. Wert, *Gettysburg: Day Three*, 168.
6. Simon Hubler Narrative, Simon Hubler Papers.
7. Pfanz, *Gettysburg: Culp's Hill and Cemetery Hill*, 360–62; Wert, *Gettysburg: Day Three*, 172; Priest, *Into the Fight*, 64.
8. Rollins, "The Failure of Confederate Artillery in Pickett's Charge," 26–41.
9. Priest, *Into the Fight*, 61; Hess, *Pickett's Charge*, 132–36.
10. Hess, *Pickett's Charge*, 128; Priest, *Into the Fight*, 61.
11. Wert, *Gettysburg: Day Three*, 175.
12. Hess, *Pickett's Charge*, 142.
13. Haskell, *Haskell of Gettysburg*, 150.
14. Priest, *Into the Fight*, 62; quotation from Wert, *Gettysburg: Day Three*, 175.
15. Hess, *Pickett's Charge*, 129.
16. Ibid.
17. Kent Masterson Brown, *Cushing of Gettysburg: The Story of a Union Artillery Commander* (Lexington: University Press of Kentucky, 1993), 234–35; Hess, *Pickett's Charge*, 142–43; Priest, *Into the Fight*, 67.
18. Brown, *Cushing of Gettysburg*, 234–35; quotation from Hess, *Pickett's Charge*, 142–43.
19. Priest, *Into the Fight*, 70; Wert, *Gettysburg: Day Three*, 178–79.
20. Hess, *Pickett's Charge*, 154; Priest, *Into the Fight*, 69.
21. Hess, *Pickett's Charge*, 154–55.
22. First quotation from Hess, *Pickett's Charge*, 146; second quotation from Wert, *Gettysburg: Day Three*, 169.
23. Haskell, *Haskell of Gettysburg*, 153.
24. Hess, *Pickett's Charge*, 139; Priest, *Into the Fight*, 80–81.
25. Pfanz, *Gettysburg: Culp's Hill and Cemetery Hill*, 362–63; Hess, *Pickett's Charge*, 145, 150.
26. Brown, *Cushing of Gettysburg*, 241–42; Hess, *Pickett's Charge*, 143, 196–97.

27. Quotation from Hess, *Pickett's Charge*, 159–60; Alexander, *Fighting for the Confederacy*, 255–58; Wert, *Gettysburg: Day Three*, 185.

28. Sifakis, *Who Was Who in the Civil War*, 506; quotation from Hess, *Pickett's Charge*, 160.

29. Quotation from Hess, *Pickett's Charge*, 160; Wert, *Gettysburg: Day Three*, 186; Priest, *Into the Fight*, 77–78.

30. Quotations from Hess, *Pickett's Charge*, 161, 166; Wert, *Gettysburg: Day Three*, 187; Priest, *Into the Fight*, 77.

31. Wert, *Gettysburg: Day Three*, 180; Hess, *Pickett's Charge*, 156.

32. Hess, *Pickett's Charge*, 166–68, 171, quotation from 167; Priest, *Into the Fight*, 84–85.

33. Hess, *Pickett's Charge*, 169.

34. Quotation from Hess, *Pickett's Charge*, 168–69; Wert, *Gettysburg: Day Three*, 191.

35. Wert, *Gettysburg: Day Three*, 187–88.

36. Hess, *Pickett's Charge*, 163–65, 169.

37. Ibid., 175–77.

38. Ibid., 182–84; quotation from Gragg, *Covered with Glory*, 177.

39. Priest, *Into the Fight*, 91; quotation from Wert, *Gettysburg: Day Three*, 198–99.

40. Hess, *Pickett's Charge*, 171–72, 185, 188.

41. *OR*, vol. 27, pt. 1, p. 417; Hess, *Pickett's Charge*, 172–73; Wert, *Gettysburg: Day Three*, 199, 210.

42. Priest, *Into the Fight*, 99–103.

43. *OR*, vol. 27, pt. 1, p. 417; first quotation from Priest, *Into the Fight*, 90; Wert, *Gettysburg: Day Three*, 194–95, second quotation, 195.

44. Haskell, *Haskell of Gettysburg*, 158–59, first quotation, 159; second and third quotations from Hess, *Pickett's Charge*, 198–99.

45. Hess, *Pickett's Charge*, 189–90.

46. Priest, *Into the Fight*, 103–5.

47. Hess, *Pickett's Charge*, 196.

48. Ibid., 210; quotation from Wert, *Gettysburg: Day Three*, 207.

49. Wert, *Gettysburg: Day Three*, 204–5, second quotation, 204; first quotation from Hess, *Pickett's Charge*, 201.

50. Hess, *Pickett's Charge*, 202; Gragg, *Covered with Glory*, 175, 192.

51. Hess, *Pickett's Charge*, 203–9.

52. Ibid.

53. Ibid., 233.

54. Ibid., 220.

55. *OR*, vol. 27, pt. 1, p. 417; Wert, *Gettysburg: Day Three*, 211–12; Brown, *Cushing of Gettysburg*, 250–52; Hess, *Pickett's Charge*, 228–29, 245–46.

56. Wert, *Gettysburg: Day Three*, 212–24; Haskell, *Haskell of Gettysburg*, 162–65; Hess, *Pickett's Charge*, 246–47, 262; Priest, *Into the Fight*, 140–41.

57. Wert, *Gettysburg: Day Three*, 223.

58. Hess, *Pickett's Charge*, 262–69, quotations from 262, 263, and 269, respectively.

59. Ibid., 215–18, 248–57, quotation from 257; Gragg, *Covered with Glory*, 197–200; Wert, *Gettysburg: Day Three*, 235.

60. Wert, *Gettysburg: Day Three*, 226–28; Hess, *Pickett's Charge*, 226–27; Howard Coffin, *Nine Months to Gettysburg: Stannard's Vermonters and the*

Repulse of Pickett's Charge (Woodstock, VT: Countryman Press, 1997), 222–44.

61. Jeffrey D. Marshall, ed. *A War of the People: Vermont Civil War Letters* (Hanover, NH: University Press of New England, 1999), 169, 171.

62. Haskell, *Haskell of Gettysburg*, 165–67.

63. *OR*, vol. 27, pt. 1, p. 420; quotation from Wert, *Gettysburg: Day Three*, 229; Priest, *Into the Fight*, 148–50.

64. Haskell, *Haskell of Gettysburg*, 167.

65. Hess, *Pickett's Charge*, 289–95; Wert, *Gettysburg: Day Three*, 230–31, quotation from 230.

66. Hess, *Pickett's Charge*, 307–15; quotation from Wert, *Gettysburg: Day Three*, 231.

67. Wert, *Gettysburg: Day Three*, 239–45; Hess, *Pickett's Charge*, 296–306.

68. Wert, *Gettysburg: Day Three*, 245–50.

69. Ibid., 235, 245, quotation from 245; Hess, *Pickett's Charge*, 317–19.

70. Haskell, *Haskell of Gettysburg*, 173–74.

71. Stuckenberg, *I'm Surrounded by Methodists*, 83.

72. Wert, *Gettysburg: Day Three*, 291; Hess, *Pickett's Charge*, 333–35.

73. Wert, *Gettysburg: Day Three*, 251.

74. Ibid., 252; Hess, *Pickett's Charge*, 326.

75. Quoted in Wert, *Gettysburg: Day Three*, 247.

76. Wert, *Gettysburg: Day Three*, 253–54; Hess, *Pickett's Charge*, 323–24.

CHAPTER TEN

I HOPE I MAY LIVE TO SEE THE END OF THE WAR

THE BATTLE OF GETTYSBURG was over. Confederate casualties on the third day came to well over 8,000 men; Union casualties, scarcely 3,000. That lopsided ratio more than evened out the totals for the whole three-day battle. Meade's overall casualties came to just over 23,000. The numbers of Lee's losses are hard to fix, but they are estimated to have been at least equal to Meade's and possibly as high as 28,000—out of an army that had been somewhat smaller at the outset of the battle.

More important than the appalling butcher's bill was the fact that the hitherto seemingly invincible Lee had been defeated. His latter-day admirers would maintain staunchly that such was not the case, that Lee had performed well enough to win the battle but had somehow been let down by nearly all of his major subordinates. If only Hill, Ewell, Longstreet, Stuart, and Rodes had performed up to their previous standards, they lament; if only Stonewall Jackson had lived to take part, if only William Dorsey Pender had not died midway through the battle or John Bell Hood not been wounded, all would have been different. Yet such explanations really do little to defend Lee. Instead, they only shift to other fields the problem of upholding his reputation. If Lee's victories were dependent on splendid performances by his subordinates, they were not really his. If it was not Lee who was defeated at Gettysburg, then it was not Lee who was victorious at Second Bull Run, Fredericksburg, and Chancellorsville.

The fact that it was Lee who was defeated at Gettysburg does not exonerate his generals for their roles in the Army of Northern Virginia's failure. Ewell and Rodes had been below par. Stuart took counsel of his ego, stretched his orders, and failed to do his part toward victory. Longstreet had been the worst offender. Disagreeing with his commander's plan was all very well—and looks even better in hindsight—but Longstreet's stubbornness, conceit, and self-will made him a detriment to Lee's efforts rather than the strong help he should have been. Lee may once have called him his "old war horse," but at Gettysburg he behaved more like a mule.

Bad generals, or good ones having bad days, are part of what every commander must overcome, and not everyone in the Army of Northern Virginia performed poorly at Gettysburg. Numerous officers, including brigade commanders John B. Gordon, William Barksdale, Joseph Kershaw, Abner Perrin, and Lewis Armistead, had been splendid, and the rank and file of the Army of Northern Virginia had, as always, fought magnificently. This time, Lee had simply failed to parlay that mix of factors into victory.

If Lee's defeat was not entirely the fault of his own generals—though some of them undeniably did their part—neither was it wholly the doing of George G. Meade. His performance was adequate, if unspectacular. Meade made small mistakes but avoided fatal ones, and he succeeded in overcoming the results of mistakes by some of his own subordinates. Given that he had been in command only three days when the battle started, he did a very respectable job. Still the fact remains that neither with three days nor with nine months to prepare for a clash would Meade ever be the equal of Lee as a general.

The real victors of Gettysburg were the hard-marching, hard-fighting, long-suffering soldiers of the Army of the Potomac—the Iron Brigade, the Bucktails, the Ploughboys, and other First Corps troops selling their lives as dearly as possible on the ridges west of town on July 1; Amos Humiston and his comrades of the 154th New York fighting for the brickyard, the Orange Blossoms vying for the pile of rocks called Devil's Den, the lumberjacks and prairie farmers of the First Minnesota hurling themselves into the face of overwhelming numbers on July 2; the Green Mountain Boys of Vermont and the city boys from Philadelphia combining to hurl back Pickett's Charge; and all the others. They had not enjoyed much success thus far in the war. They had followed a collection of the most inept army commanders America would ever produce and fought against one of the best. Yet they proved at Gettysburg that when even adequate generalship gave them a fighting chance for victory, they could meet the best the South had to throw at them. They knew that now, and they exulted in it. Lieutenant Augustus Van Dyke was a member of the Fourteenth Indiana, part of Samuel Carroll's brigade that had charged to the rescue of the guns on Cemetery Hill on the night of July 2. In a letter to his father two days later, he wrote, "The result of the three days of battle at this point has given an additional stimulus to celebrate this anniversary of our independence. The Army of the Potomac has nobly redeemed itself and taught the insolent Rebels what it is to fight on one's own soil."[1]

Many Confederate soldiers believed that their leaders had not done well at Gettysburg. "There was nothing in it to brag about, except the heroic gallantry of the men," recalled the Sixteenth Mississippi's David Holt many years later. "As far as the general officers were concerned, they could not have bungled up things more nor shown less military skill." Holt remembered much grousing among his fellows about the blunders of their corps and division commanders, but, at least in Holt's memory of his Mississippi comrades, Lee's own reputation survived intact. Other Confederates were less generous. Infantryman William D. Lyon wrote in a letter home only a few days after the battle, "Gen. Lee made a great mistake in storming the heights."[2]

As for their defeat at the hands of the despised Northern soldiery, Lee's men were sullen and unwilling to admit the drubbing they had taken. "They no doubt think we have been badly whiped," complained the Forty-fourth Virginia's Thomas Boatright. "So have they if we have." Tellingly, however, Boatright had to admit that it bothered him that "we had to leave our wounded in their hands."[3] Frustrated that the advantages of terrain that had always before belonged to the Army of Northern Virginia had this time been held by the Army of the Potomac, Virginia artillerist William W. Parker maintained, "We can whip the Yankees any day on a *fair field*." Revenge and hatred were major themes in the Rebels' post-battle writings. A survivor of Pickett's Charge seethed with animosity toward those who had defeated him. "Before this campaign I imagined I hated the Yankee race with a perfect hatred," the soldier wrote. "I find I was mistaken, they are too mean spirited, too low and cringing to hate. I despise them thoroughly, my contempt for them knows no bounds." Men like him would be ready to fight on for a very long time.[4]

On the evening of July 3, Lee made his plans for retreat. The army's extensive wagon train would have to go first. The miles-long column of ambulances and other wagons was loaded down

with both the plunder taken in Pennsylvania and thousands of the
less seriously wounded. It was slow and vulnerable and would need
a head start. Late on the night of July 3, Lee ordered Brigadier General
John D. Imboden, commander of one of the army's less efficient
cavalry brigades, to escort the column, starting out late in the afternoon of July 4 for Hagerstown, Maryland, and then for
Williamsport on the Potomac. Independence Day dawned overcast
and drizzly, and by noon, rain was falling in sheets, marking the
beginning of a rainy spell lasting several days. Through the roaring downpour, Imboden set out with his long, creaking caravan of
misery right on schedule. Meanwhile, Lee pulled Ewell's Second
Corps back to the west side of Gettysburg so that the Army of Northern Virginia formed a long, straight line along Seminary Ridge and
Oak Ridge. Meade, concerned about the need to rest and to resup-
ply his army, waited. After nightfall, Lee issued orders for his army
to take up the march back toward the Potomac, and by the evening
of July 5 the only Confederates left near Gettysburg were the nearly
7,000 who were too badly wounded to travel.[5]

The retreating Confederates took their booty with them, including kidnapped Pennsylvania citizens of African descent. Some of
these people were able to escape. Others were freed by sympathetic
white Pennsylvanians who actually attacked a small detachment
of Confederates near Greencastle, forcing them to release the thirty
to forty black women and children in their possession. No such
opportunities presented themselves where the main columns of
Lee's army were present. Not far from the Potomac, one young black
man resisted so stoutly his captors' intentions of carrying him south
into slavery that the Rebels became enraged. They stripped him,
hacked him with knives, disemboweled and mutilated him, and
then doused him with turpentine and set him on fire. Pursuing
Union troops found him lying in a barn, dying in extreme agony,
"grinding his teeth & foaming at the mouth."[6]

Perceiving Lee's retreat, Meade on July 5 directed his chief of
staff to prepare orders for the Army of the Potomac to follow, but
the only operations he actually initiated that day and the next were
cautious probes after the retreating Confederates. On the morning
of July 7, feeling certain at last of what Lee was doing, Meade
finally put his army in motion over muddy roads and through occasional downpours. By that time, Lee's army was already in
Hagerstown.[7]

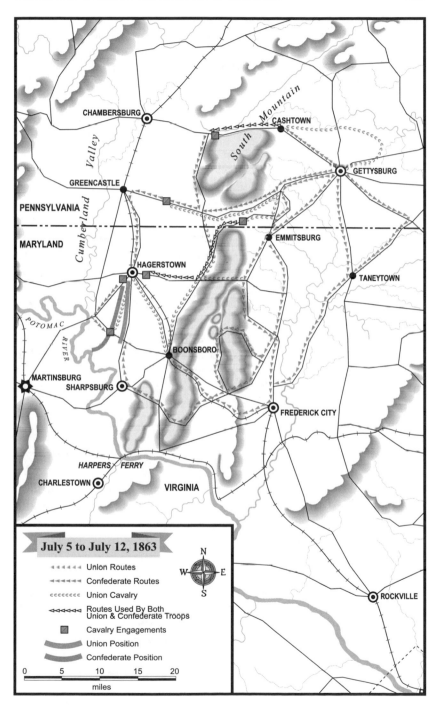

CHAMBERSBURG

CASHTOWN

South Mountain

Valley

GETTYSBURG

GREENCASTLE

PENNSYLVANIA

Cumberland

MARYLAND

EMMITSBURG

HAGERSTOWN

TANEYTOWN

POTOMAC

RIVER

BOONSBORO

MARTINSBURG

SHARPSBURG

FREDERICK CITY

HARPERS FERRY

CHARLESTOWN

VIRGINIA

July 5 to July 12, 1863

◀◀◀◀◀◀ Union Routes

◀◀◀◀◀◀ Confederate Routes

ccccccc Union Cavalry

◀◀◀◀◀◀ Routes Used By Both
Union & Confederate Troops

▇ Cavalry Engagements

Union Position

Confederate Position

N

W   E

S

0   5   10   15   20

miles

ROCKVILLE

Over the course of the next week, Meade pursued cautiously while Abraham Lincoln, in Washington, and many soldiers in the ranks of the Army of the Potomac fervently hoped they would corner Lee and destroy his army before it could reach Virginia. President Lincoln expressed his anxious concern in numerous prodding dispatches, mostly using General Halleck as an intermediary. The soldiers could express their hopes only in diaries and letters. In the 136th New York, Private John T. McMahon noted in his diary, "I suppose we shall follow them as fast as we can go."[8] "I think that Ole Lee will get caught if he don't look out before he gets out of Pennsylvania," wrote the Eleventh New York's Thomas Dadswell to his father on July 5.[9] In a letter to his wife on July 7, Captain Royal N. Joy of the Ninety-fourth New York wrote that although it would mean "another hard battle," he hoped "we shall succeed in gobbling up Lee and his whole army. . . . If we destroy Lee's army and Grant takes Vicksburg, I think it will about wind up the concern."[10]

Meade also hoped to catch and trap Lee's army, but he was wary lest somehow the wily Confederate gain an advantage over him. His cavalry harassed Lee's retreating columns, and Providence handed him an additional opportunity when the heavy rains of the past week raised the Potomac far above ford stage. Union cavalry had already dashed in behind Lee and destroyed his pontoon bridge, so the Army of Northern Virginia found itself trapped on the north bank and unable, for the time at least, to return to its namesake state.

Meade closed in cautiously. By July 12 he was confronting Lee near Williamsport. The Confederate army had its back to the river but was heavily entrenched in a strong defensive position. The men of the Army of the Potomac expected action. From the camp of the Fourteenth Indiana, Augustus Van Dyke wrote his father, "The spirit of the army is such that they will do most desperate fighting. . . . The men know now that Lee's Army is not invincible and that the Army of the Potomac can win a victory if it is allowed to. Our army . . . ought to drive the Rebels into the Potomac."[11] Meade, who by this time had received moderate reinforcements, wired Halleck in Washington that he would attack the following day "unless something intervenes to prevent it." What intervened was another of Meade's councils of war. The spirit of George McClellan lived on in the brass of the Army of the Potomac, even if the "Young Napoleon" himself had for nine months now been "awaiting orders" at his home in New Jersey. The majority of corps commanders, with the same abundance of scientific reasons that always prevented their idol and former commander from getting things done, advised against making an assault. Meade postponed the operation in order to study the situation further.

After another day of examining the ground, Meade determined to carry out a plan very similar to the one he had deferred. He ordered an attack for the morning of July 14, but when the blue-clad troops advanced that morning, they found that Lee had escaped. The Confederates had put together another pontoon bridge, and the river level had fallen somewhat. Partially by fording and partially on the new bridge, they had crossed the river between nightfall on July 12 and daylight on July 14. Once again, aggressive cavalrymen were the only Union troops to make contact, sweeping up a number of Confederate stragglers and skirmishing with the Confederate rear guard just before it crossed the river. Only two Confederates were killed in that fight. One of them was James J. Pettigrew, who had survived the carnage of July 1 and 3 at Gettysburg with a minor wound, only to be felled by one of the final shots of the campaign.[12]

Back at Gettysburg, meanwhile, the work of cleaning up the destruction and debris of battle was only beginning. "My pen cant decribe the seen," wrote a Wisconsin soldier. "The dead dying and the wounded begers all decription. They lay in Piles about the Brest Works and for miles they lay lyke Wheat Bundells in a good hearvest feald—Men, horsis, Mules, Broken Canan, Canan Caridges, Bugles, Drummes, Swords, and Muskettes lay strewd all over the fealds— grain feelds all Stompt in the Earth. The most horabel Sight man ever saw."[13] Most observers found the human remains to be the most disturbing. The Twentieth Indiana's Dennis Tuttle wrote his wife that he could have walked between a quarter- and a half-mile on the bodies of the slain without ever stepping on the ground. He told her that he could write no more about it: "It makes me heartsick to think of it."[14]

All public and many private buildings were filled to overflowing with the wounded. Among them was twenty-six-year-old Strong Vincent, who had fallen, badly wounded, at the height of his brigade's heroic stand on the slopes of Little Round Top. General Meade wired Washington to recommend his promotion to brigadier general and granted Vincent's request for permission to go home to recuperate. The surgeon, however, had to break the news that the young colonel was not strong enough to travel. "Then," Vincent told his aide, "I want you to send for my wife as soon as possible." The lieutenant rode hard for the nearest telegraph office, but his efforts were in vain. On July 7, long before his wife could reach Gettysburg, Vincent died while feebly reciting the Lord's Prayer.[15]

In a macabre way, the problem of the dead was just as pressing as that of the wounded. The bodies of thousands of dead men and horses lay decaying in the fields in the hot July sun, and the stench on the steamy, humid air was overpowering. The work of burial had to go on apace. Small details of troops left behind by the army, occasionally aided by civilians, did the sexton's work for the battle's multitudes of slain. The Union dead usually got individual graves. The Confederates, unless recognized as important officers, were thrown into long trenches. The body of Richard Garnett, one of Pickett's brigade commanders who had fallen twenty-five feet from the stone fence, went unrecognized and was laid in a mass grave along with his men.

As they worked through the north side of Gettysburg, the burial parties found the body of Amos Humiston, still in the sheltered nook into which he had crawled, mortally wounded, during his flight from the brickyard on July 1. In his hand he still clutched the picture of Frank, Alice, and Fred, on which he had gazed in his last moments. Thus far, sadly, his case was not unique. Thousands of Civil War dead, at this battle and in all the others, were never identified. Soldiers wore no dog tags in this war. If comrades from their company or perhaps regiment did not find them, their anonymity in death was complete despite the fact that burial parties on the Gettysburg battlefield, as elsewhere, found a number of letters, photos, and Bibles or Testaments in the hands of dead soldiers. The overworked burial details, racing against the rapid advance of natural processes, had no time for lengthy investigations of identity.

Someone, however, was moved by the sight of the photo of three children in Humiston's hands. It was widely reproduced and became the subject of a nationwide campaign to find the family of this unknown soldier. The situation touched the sympathies of the North and eventually led to fundraising efforts on behalf of the children of deceased Union soldiers. It also inspired James Gowdy Clark's ballad, "The Children of the Battlefield":

Upon the field of Gettysburg
The summer sun was high,
When Freedom met her haughty foes
Beneath a Northern sky.
Among the heroes of the North,
Who swelled her grand array,
And rushed like mountain eagles forth
From happy homes away,
There stood a man of humble mien,
A sire of children three,
And gazed into a little frame,
Their pictured forms to see. . . .

Several months after the battle the effort succeeded in bringing the sad news to Philinda Humiston back in Portsville, New York, thus ending the suspense and growing apprehension she had felt since Amos's letters had stopped coming after Gettysburg. Thousands of soldiers' families all over the country would never receive that sort of closure for the loss of their loved ones.[16]

And the war went on.

Lincoln felt anguish at what he perceived as Meade's loss of a golden opportunity to crush Lee and end the war. "We had them within our grasp," he said to his secretary, John Hay. "We had only to stretch forth our hands and they were ours. And nothing I could say or do could make the Army move. . . . Our Army held the war in the hollow of their hand and they would not close it."[17]

Many soldiers of the Army of the Potomac expressed dismay at Lee's escape, sensing that with the departure of the Confederate army from Northern soil had gone their own best hopes for a speedy termination of the war. In the Sixth Corps's crack Vermont brigade (a different unit from Stannard's short-term Vermont brigade), Cornelius Chapin wrote to his brother, "To make an attack upon them would have involved great loss, but I think the result would have offered great compensation, for our troops would have fought as they never fought before and Lee again defeated would not have had an army worth the name."[18] The Fourteenth Indiana's Augustus Van Dyke opined that Meade was not to blame and that his comrades also absolved the commanding general, but Charles H. Roundy of the Thirteenth Massachusetts believed the opposite. "My growl about allowing Lee to escape after Gettysburg was felt by

every soldier in the army," he recalled. "If Lee or any of his generals could have taken command [of the Army of the Potomac], he
would have pushed the invading army into the river, and ended
the war."[19]

The Third Maine's Charles N. Maxwell may have summed up
best the feelings of the long-suffering soldiers of the Army of the
Potomac as they saw stretching out before them a war few of them
seemed likely to outlive. "All were chagrined at the escape of Lee,"
he wrote. "All were anxious to make an attack, preferring to fight
him here to Virginia." Maxwell still hoped that Gettysburg, along
with recent Union victories in other theaters of the war, had broken the back of the rebellion and that peace would come soon. "I
hope this war will give the death-blow to slavery, and that I may
live to see the end of the war." Yet, if he did not, he had confidence
in the nation's future. "This is the great object of my life—to aid in
crushing this monstrous rebellion. I believe it matters little when a
man dies, but how and where, that is all-important; and in no way
can a man die so gloriously as when he dies for his country. . . . I
have full confidence that the all-wise Dispenser of human events
will not let this country, the beacon-light of the struggling millions,
go down in darkness and despair."[20]

NOTES

1. Augustus M. Van Dyke to "Dear Father," July 4, 1863, Augustus M.
Van Dyke Papers, Indiana Historical Society.

2. First quotation from Holt, *A Mississippi Rebel*, 195; second quotation from William D. Lyon to his brother George, July 18, 1863, William D.
Lyon Papers.

3. Thomas F. Boatright to "My Darling Wife," July 18, 1863, Boatright
Papers, SHC.

4. Quoted in Peter Carmichael, " 'We Will Make Them Howl Worse
than They Are Now Laughing: Lee's Soldiers React to Gettysburg," *Civil
War* 60 (February 1997): 46–51.

5. *OR*, vol. 27, pt. 2, pp. 299, 322, 360; Coddington, *The Gettysburg
Campaign*, 537–39.

6. Ted Alexander, " 'A Regular Slave Hunt,' " 86–87.

7. *OR*, vol. 27, pt. 2, pp. 322, 361; Coddington, *The Gettysburg Campaign*, 545–55.

8. John T. McMahon, *John T. McMahon's Diary of the 136th New York,
1861–1864*, ed. John Michael Priest (Shippensburg, PA: White Mane, 1993),
54.

9. Dadswell Letter, July 5, 1863, Thomas Dadswell Papers, Pearce Civil
War Collection, Navarro College, Corsicana, Texas.

10. Royal N. Joy to "Dear Wife," July 7, 1863, Royal N. Joy Papers, Civil War Miscellaneous Collection, U.S. Army Military History Institute, Carlisle, Pennsylvania.

11. Augustus M. Van Dyke to "Dear Father," July 12, 1863, Augustus M. Van Dyke Papers.

12. *OR*, vol. 27, pt. 2, pp. 361, 609; Coddington, *The Gettysburg Campaign*, 566–72.

13. Robert B. V. Bird to "Frend Rosey," August 21, 1863, Bird Family Papers.

14. Dennis Tuttle to "My Dear Wife," July 5, 1863, Dennis Tuttle Papers, Pearce Civil War Collection, Navarro College, Corsicana, Texas.

15. Judson, *History of the Eighty-third*, 67.

16. Dunkelman, *Gettysburg's Unknown Soldier*, 128–248.

17. Quoted in Coddington, *The Gettysburg Campaign*, 572.

18. Marshall, ed., *A War of the People*, 175.

19. Charles H. Roundy Memoirs, Civil War Miscellaneous Collection, U.S. Army Military History Institute, Carlisle, Pennsylvania.

20. Post, ed., *Soldiers' Letters from Camp*, 260–63.

BIBLIOGRAPHICAL ESSAY

With countless books existing on the battle of Gettysburg, I can hardly undertake a comprehensive discussion of Gettysburg literature. Rather, I will mention only a classic or two and a handful of the newest and most interesting books. There are many other good ones, and students of the battle should seek them out. Much of the best cutting-edge research on the Gettysburg campaign has been published in the various issues of *North & South* magazine, from 1998 to the present.

The classic lengthy study is Edwin B. Coddington's *The Gettysburg Campaign: A Study in Command* (New York: Simon & Schuster, 1968). Though somewhat dated and highly sympathetic to Meade, Coddington's work remains the standard treatment of the campaign. To counterbalance, after a fashion, Coddington's admiration of Meade comes a recent book, *Last Chance for Victory: Robert E. Lee and the Gettysburg Campaign*, by Scott Bowden and Bill Ward (Cambridge, MA: Da Capo Press, 2001), a highly argumentative and controversial defense of Lee's actions. In many ways this book is the epitome and, one would think, culmination of the school of thought, popular among Southern adherents of the Lost Cause, that holds that in truth and in essence Lee really won the battle—it just did not turn out that way in actual events because all his subordinates let him down. This view, in turn, may be counterbalanced by an even more recent book, A. M. Gambone's *Lee at Gettysburg: Commentary on Defeat* (Baltimore: Butternut & Blue, 2002). So eager is Gambone to combat the exaggerated defenses of Lee's role that he goes to the opposite extreme, leaving the reader with the impression that Lee was the only Confederate general who turned in a less-than-sterling performance in Pennsylvania. By all odds the clearest and most thoughtful examination of the Confederate high command at Gettysburg is Brooks D. Simpson's " 'If Properly Led': Command Relationships at Gettysburg," in *Civil War Generals in Defeat*, ed. Steven E. Woodworth (Lawrence: University Press of Kansas, 1999).

Over the past decade and a half, Harry W. Pfanz has set the pace in Gettysburg studies with his three in-depth looks at different phases and sectors of the battle. His first book, *Gettysburg: The*

Second Day (Chapel Hill: University of North Carolina Press, 1987), investigates in painstaking detail every facet of the July 2, 1863, struggle for Little Round Top, Devil's Den, Houck Ridge, the Wheatfield, the Peach Orchard, and Cemetery Ridge. Pfanz followed this magisterial work with *Gettysburg: Culp's Hill and Cemetery Hill* (Chapel Hill: University of North Carolina Press, 1993), in which he deals in similar depth with operations on the less-studied end of the battlefield—from the decision of Union Major General Oliver O. Howard to establish a position on Cemetery Hill and that of Confederate Lieutenant General Richard S. Ewell not to attack that position on the evening of July 1 through the fighting on Culp's Hill and Cemetery Hill on the evening of July 2 and the morning of July 3. Pfanz's most recent product is *Gettysburg—The First Day* (Chapel Hill: University of North Carolina Press, 2001). Slightly shorter and less detailed than his previous books, this one is nevertheless satisfyingly thorough and surpasses Pfanz's already high standard of skillful writing. All three works are characterized by exhaustive research and judicious analysis.

Other recent scholars have also addressed the various sectors and phases of the battle. David G. Martin's *Gettysburg, July 1* (Conshohocken, PA: Combined Books, 1995) is a comprehensive account of the fighting on the first day and by far the most detailed account of that portion of the engagement. Richard S. Shue's *Morning at Willoughby Run: July 1, 1863* (Gettysburg, PA: Thomas Publications, 1995) is another recent book on the first day's fighting. Gary W. Gallagher's edited sequence of essay collections deals with various aspects of the three days in succession: *The First Day at Gettysburg: Essays on Confederate and Union Leadership* (Kent, OH: Kent State University Press, 1992); *The Second Day at Gettysburg: Essays on Confederate and Union Leadership* (Kent, OH: Kent State University Press, 1993); and *The Third Day at Gettysburg and Beyond* (Chapel Hill: University of North Carolina Press, 1994).

The third day's fighting, and especially Pickett's Charge, has become the subject of much recent scholarship, some of which demonstrates that excellent and careful historians can disagree about matters of detail in a story as complicated as that of Gettysburg. Three recent and excellent books are John Michael Priest's *Into the Fight: Pickett's Charge at Gettysburg* (Shippensburg, PA: White Mane Books, 1998); Jeffry D. Wert's *Gettysburg: Day Three* (New York: Simon & Schuster, 2001); and Earl J. Hess's *Pickett's Charge: The Last Attack at Gettysburg* (Chapel Hill: University of North Carolina

Press, 2001). Another excellent but very different study is *Pickett's Charge in History and Memory* by Carol Reardon (Chapel Hill: University of North Carolina Press, 1997), an examination of how that dramatic event has lived on (and evolved) in song and story over the century since the battle.

Another type of Gettysburg book deals with a single unit. William Thomas Venner's *The 19th Indiana Infantry at Gettysburg: Hoosiers' Courage* (Shippensburg, PA: Burd Street Press, 1998) is a detailed and dramatic account of a regiment in the hard-hit Iron Brigade. Warren Wilkinson and Steven E. Woodworth's *A Scythe of Fire: The Civil War Story of the Eighth Georgia Regiment* (New York: HarperCollins, 2002) devotes a long chapter to that unit's participation in the Gettysburg campaign, including its bloody fight in Rose's Woods, along the west branch of Plum Run, and in the Wheatfield. Rod Gragg's *Covered with Glory: The 26th North Carolina Infantry at Gettysburg* (New York: HarperCollins, 2000) tells the story of that hard-hit regiment. Howard Coffin's *Nine Months to Gettysburg: Stannard's Vermonters and the Repulse of Pickett's Charge* (Woodstock, VT: Countryman Press, 1997) recounts the tale of Stannard's Vermont brigade. *The Last Full Measure: The Life and Death of the First Minnesota Volunteers*, by Richard Moe (New York: Henry Holt, 1993), relates the deeds of that heroic regiment both at Gettysburg and before.

A couple of the recent and notable books on individuals are Kent Masterson Brown's *Cushing of Gettysburg: The Story of a Union Artillery Commander* (Lexington: University Press of Kentucky, 1993) and Mark H. Dunkelman's *Gettysburg's Unknown Soldier: The Life, Death, and Celebrity of Amos Humiston* (Westport, CT: Praeger, 1999). Biographies exist for all of the high-ranking generals.

Finally, those visiting the Gettysburg battlefield may benefit from the use of a guidebook. While many good ones exist, my favorite is Mark Grimsley and Brooks D. Simpson's *Gettysburg: A Battlefield Guide* (Lincoln: University of Nebraska Press, 1999).

INDEX

[As is true in many military histories, a person's name in the index may signify troops commanded by him as well as the person himself. Italic page numbers indicate illustrations.]

Abbott, Henry L., 195
Adams County (Pennsylvania), 41
Alexander, Edward Porter:
    confers with Longstreet about calling off attack on Cemetery Ridge, 189–190; on confidence in Lee, 10; given responsibility for ordering Pickett to charge, 173–174; orders Pickett to charge Cemetery Ridge, 186–188; told getting to Cemetery Ridge not as hard as it looks, 170
Anderson, George T. "Tige": at Devil's Den, 122; at Emmitsburg Road, 114; plundering by his troops, 110; retreats to Plum Run, 151; at Rose's Woods, 135, 142–143, 145; at Wheatfield, 136–137, 138, 142, 145
Anderson, Richard H., 99, 112, 145, 169–170, 201
Anderson, "Rocky Mountain," 62
Angle, the, 176, 198, 200
Antietam, Battle of, 6, 11, 141
Aquia Creek (Virginia), 14
Archer, James J.: deployed south of Cashtown Road, 51–52; at Herbst's Woods, 60, 62; reaches Willoughby Run, 55; taken prisoner, 58–59, 188; warned that Union troops are nearby, 42–43
Aristocracy, North's lack of bemoaned, 29
Armistead, Lewis: in assault on Cemetery Ridge, 189, 197, 198–199; at Malvern Hill, 175; performance as commander, 210
Army, Confederate: artillery shells, supply and usage, 182; morale of, 3, 4, 9–10; pillaging and plundering by, 21–28; size, in Virginia, 2; total victory as goal, 2. *See also* Army of Northern Virginia; Army of Northern Virginia, units of
Army, Union: call issued for 300,000 enlistees, 65; First U.S. Artillery, 58; Harpers Ferry garrison, 36–37; highest casualty rate during war, 148; morale of, 3–4, 6; pillaging and plundering by, 24, 26, 27; size, in Virginia, 2; size, prewar, 1; total victory as goal, 2. *See also* Army of the Potomac; Army of the Potomac, units of
Army of Northern Virginia: advance into Cumberland Valley, 16, 21–22, 28; advance into Shenandoah Valley, 11–16; artillery, quality of, 182; capturing free blacks, 22, 27–28; casualties at Gettysburg, 76, 84, 167, 190, 191, 196, 209; cavalry, effectiveness of, 12; compared to Army of the Potomac, 6, 70; confidence in Lee, 9–10; defeated, 201, 209–210; destruction of Shenandoah Valley, 16; escapes after Gettysburg, 215; General Orders Number 72, 25–26, 27; gunners, training of, 182;

Army of Northern Virginia
    (*continued*)
  hatred for opponents, 211;
  largest division, 73; Lee's
  command of, 4; prisoners of
  war captured by, 60, 84, 88, 91,
  94, 98; prisoners of war surrendered by, 58–59, 61, 62, 76, 127,
  137, 148, 162, 188, 201; reorganization, 10–11; retreats from
  Gettysburg, 212–215; size, 9;
  strategy behind Gettysburg
  campaign, 7–9; subsistence
  requirements, 25; Winchester
  victory, 14–15
Army of Northern Virginia, units
    of: Palmetto Light Artillery,
  184; Washington Artillery of
  New Orleans, 173–174, 184;
  Stonewall Brigade, 165, 175;
  Tennessee Brigade, 52, 188;
  Texas Brigade, 5, 114, 116, 118,
  120–121, 135, 136; First Corps,
  10, 11, 15, 16, 17, 39–40, 164,
  173; First Maryland Battalion,
  167; First Texas, 116, 118, 120,
  122; First Virginia, 174, 191;
  Second Corps, 10, 11, 14, 16, 17,
  39, 106, 156, 186, 212; Second
  Mississippi, 61; Second Virginia, 167; Third Arkansas, 120,
  122, 127, 136, 138; Third Corps,
  10–12, 16, 26, 39–40, 107, 168,
  169; Third South Carolina, 26,
  139; Third Virginia, 201; Fourth
  Alabama, 22–23, 24, 107, 116,
  125, 162; Fourth Texas, 118, 125,
  126, 131; Fifth Texas, 116, 125;
  Seventh Virginia, 185, 191;
  Eighth Georgia, 135, 137;
  Eighth Virginia, 174, 191; Ninth
  Georgia, 135, 137, 138, 150, 161;
  Eleventh Georgia, 137, 150;
  Eleventh North Carolina, 80,
  81; Thirteenth Alabama, 52;
  Fourteenth South Carolina, 90;
  Fourteenth Tennessee, 57;
  Fourteenth Virginia, 201;
  Fifteenth Alabama, 124–125,
  126; Sixteenth Mississippi, 23;
  Twenty-third North Carolina,

76; Twenty-sixth North Carolina, 80, 83–84, 199, 203; Thirty-
  seventh Virginia, 167–168;
  Forty-fourth Virginia, 24; Forty-
  seventh Alabama, 124–125, 126;
  Forty-eighth Alabama, 127;
  Fifty-third Virginia, 189; Fifty-
  ninth Georgia, 136
Army of the Potomac: advances
  to confront Lee's army, 37–39;
  artillery, superiority in, 184–
  185; artillery chief, 112, 186;
  attitude of troops toward
  generals, 37; casualties at
  Gettysburg, *81,* 83, 148, 181–
  182, 184, 190, 209; cavalry,
  effectiveness of, 12–13; combat
  readiness, 6; compared to Army
  of Northern Virginia, 6, 70;
  conflicting orders given by
  generals, 47–48, 97–98; defeats
  Lee, 201, 209–210; Germans in,
  86–87; gunners, training of, 182;
  lack of aggressiveness, 6; Lee
  discovers its whereabouts, 32,
  40–41; McClellan's command
  of, 4, 6; Meade's command of,
  37; officer corps, 6, 210; performance of soldiers, 210–211;
  Pope's command of, 6; positioned between Lee's army and
  Washington, 14–15; prisoners of
  war captured by, 58–59, 61, 62,
  76, 127, 137, 148, 162, 188, 201;
  prisoners of war surrendered
  by, 60, 84, 88, 91, 94, 98; Provost
  General, 13; reception upon
  arrival in Gettysburg, 43;
  soldiers' dismay at Lee's
  escape, 217–218; soldiers' joy at
  being out of Virginia, 39;
  soldiers' view of their leaders,
  211; suspicions of Lincoln, 6;
  uniforms, 60; Winchester
  defeat, 14–15
Army of the Potomac, units of:
  Bucktails regiments, 78, 79–80,
  90, 162; Irish Brigade, 141–142;
  Iron Brigade (Black Hat
  Brigade), 50, 54, 57, 58–59, 61–
  62, 78, 80–81, 84, 90, 188, 203;

Maine Light Artillery, Battery B, 57; Pennsylvania Reserves, 36, 37, 150, 205; Philadelphia Brigade, 175–176, 184, 198, 200; Vermont Brigade, 181, 199; First Corps, 17, 35, 47–48, 74, 79, 90–91, 110, 166; First Delaware, 181; First Maryland, Eastern Shore, 167–168; First Minnesota, 147–148, 152, 181, 200, 210; First Pennsylvania Light Artillery, 156, First Rhode Island, Battery B, 176; First U.S. Sharpshooter Regiment, 112; Second Corps, 48, 100, 110, 152, 154, 163, 168, 176, 183, 199, 202; Second Massachusetts, 166; Second U.S. Artillery, Battery B, 51; Second Wisconsin, 54, 57, 58–59, 84, 89; Third Corps, 35, 47–48, 68, 96, 100, 112–113, 120, 144; Third Maine, 112, 144, 218; Third Michigan, 39; Third Wisconsin, 166; Fourth Maine, 120, 121–122; Fourth U.S. Artillery, Battery A, 176, 184, 186, 197; Fifth Corps, 35, 48, 100, 111, 112, 119, 124, 128, 139, 141, 143, 150, 152; Fifth Michigan, 141; Fifth U.S. Artillery, Battery B, 130; Sixth Corps, 11, 48, 69, 100–101, 111, 150, 152, 217; Sixth Wisconsin, 39, 54–55, 60–61, 93–94; Seventh Wisconsin, 54, 84, 89, 94; Eighth Illinois Cavalry, 43, 50, 79; Eighth New York Cavalry, 57; Eighth Ohio, 192–194, 199; Ninth Massachusetts Battery, 161; Eleventh Corps, 35, 47–48, 53, 64, 65–66, 74, 86–89, 94, 96, 110, 154, 186; Twelfth Corps, 18, 35, 36, 48, 68, 96–97, 100, 110, 112, 152, 154–155, 165, 172; Twelfth New Jersey, 181; Thirteenth Massachusetts, 217; Thirteenth Pennsylvania Reserves, 78; Fourteenth Brooklyn, 60, 93; Fourteenth Connecticut, 183, 192; Fourteenth Indiana, 210, 214, 217;

Fourteenth Vermont, 200; Sixteenth Michigan, 123, 127, 129–130; Sixteenth Vermont, 199; Seventeenth Maine, 120, 136–137, 138, 139, 140–141; Nineteenth Indiana, 54, 57, 78–79, 80, 81, 90; Nineteenth Maine, 200; Nineteenth Pennsylvania, 64; Twentieth Indiana, 215; Twentieth Maine, 123, 126; Twentieth Massachusetts, 195; Twenty-fourth Michigan, 50, 54, 80, 81–83, 83–84; Twenty-fifth Ohio, 95; Twenty-sixth Pennsylvania Militia, 31; Twenty-seventh Indiana, 166; Fortieth New York, 122; Forty-fourth New York, 35, 123, 125, 130; Fifty-sixth Pennsylvania, 59, 60; Sixty-first New York, 86; Sixty-fourth New York, 86; Sixty-ninth Pennsylvania, 175–176, 195, 198; Seventy-first Pennsylvania, 186, 200; Seventy-sixth New York, 59, 60, 94; Eighty-third Pennsylvania, 122–124, 125; Eighty-fourth New York ("the Red-legged Devils"), 60, 61; Ninety-fourth New York, 214; Ninety-fifth New York, 60, 61; Ninety-ninth Pennsylvania, 122; 121st Pennsylvania, 95; 124th New York ("the Orange Blossoms"), 120–121, 210; 136th New York, 214; 140th New York, 129–130; 143d Pennsylvania, 64, 78, 80, 84, 89, 93, 181; 145th Pennsylvania, 142; 147th New York ("the Ploughboys"), 59–60, 166; 149th Pennsylvania, 78, 80, 84; 150th Pennsylvania, 78; 154th New York, 65, 66, 91, 210; 157th New York, 88

Artillery: Confederates bombard Cemetery Hill, 182; Confederates bombard Cemetery Ridge, 181–184; Confederates run out of shells at Cemetery Ridge, 189–190; deafness caused by, 183; Hunt orders waiting before returning fire, 174, 183; at

Artillery (*continued*)
McPherson's Ridge, 57, 59, 62;
Osborn recommends ceasing
fire to suggest Union guns out
of action at Cemetery Ridge,
186; at Peach Orchard, 135, 174;
at Seminary Ridge, 174;
training of gunners, 182; Union
artillery chief, 112, 186; Union
rate of fire, 183; Union superiority, 184–185
Avery, Isaac E., 155, 156
Ayres, Romeyn, 128

Baltimore & Ohio Railroad, 16
Baltimore Pike, 48, 68, 69, 112, 164
Barksdale, William, 114, 144–145,
162, 210
Barlow, Francis Channing, 86–88
Barnes, James, 119, 140
Baxter, Henry, 74–76, 86
Benner's Hill, 151, 186
Benning, Henry "Rock": at
Devil's Den, 135, 151; at
Emmitsburg Road, 114; at
Slaughter Pen, 121–122; at
Wheatfield, 142, 145
Berden, Hiram, 112
Beverly's Ford (Rappahannock
River), 13
Biddle, Chapman, 79, 80–81
Biesecker's Woods, 114
Birney, David B., 140
Blackburn, Leander, 189, 191
Blackford, Charles Minor, 28–29
Blacks: Confederate commitment
to slavery, 29; free black farmer
of Gettysburg, 196;
kidnappings of free blacks, 22,
27–28, 212
Blanchard, Asa, 80, 81–83
Bliss, Fred, 162
Bliss, William, 168
Blue Ridge Mountains (Virginia),
16, 18, 30
Boatright, Thomas F., 24, 25, 28,
211
Boynton, Jonathan, 88
Bradley, Leman, 202
Brandy Station, Battle of, 12–13
Brewer, Sam, 9

Bridgeport (Maryland), 97
Bright, Robert A., 194
Brockenbrough, John: in assault
on Cemetery Ridge, 191, 194; at
Herr Ridge, 52; at McPherson's
Ridge, 77; on need to fight, 50
Brockway, Charles B., 156
Brooks, E. P., 61
Brooks, John R., 142–143
Brown, Hiram L., 142
Brown, John, 77
Brown, Lizinka, 10
Brown, T. Fred, 176
Bryan (or Brian), Abram, 196
Buckles, Abe, 80
Buford, John, 44; career, 43–44;
effectiveness, 73; at
McPherson's Ridge, 51, 53;
recognizes strategic importance
of Gettysburg, 45; skirmishes
with Heth's men, 50–53
Bull Run, First Battle of, 4, 147
Bull Run, Second Battle of, 6, 10,
11, 44, 209
Bullock, George B., 76
Burgwyn, Henry K., 77, 83
Burns, John L., 78, 79, 91
Burnside, Ambrose, 6
Butterfield, Daniel, 163

Caldwell, John C., 141–143, 145,
202
Caledonia Ironworks, 30
Calef, John H., 51, 52
"The Campbells Are Coming," 55
Carlisle (Pennsylvania), 21, 32
Carlisle Road, 63, 73
Carroll, Samuel S., 156, 210–211
Cashtown (Pennsylvania), 32, 39
Casualties: Army of Northern
Virginia suffers, 76, 84, 167, 190,
196, 209; Army of the Potomac
suffers, *81*, 83, 148, 181–182,
184, 190, 209; first day, 76, *81*,
83, 84; only civilian death, 172;
second day, 148, 161, 162–163;
third day, 167, 181–182, 184,
190, 191, 196, 209; totals, 209
Cavalry: at Brandy Station, 12–13;
cavalry actions after Cemetery
Ridge victory, 204; in destruc-

tion of Shenandoah Valley, 16; effectiveness of Confederate, 12; effectiveness of Union, 12–13; rifles used by, 51; versus infantry, 44

Cedarville (Virginia), 14

Cemetery Hill: Confederates bombard, 182; doubts about wisdom of attacking, 99; Early at, 155; Ewell launches diversionary attack against, 151, 155, 157; fighting at, 151–152, 155–157; Hancock before attacking, 172–173; Howard at, 186; Humiston at, 66; Hunt at, 174, 183, 186, 192; Kemper announces pending assault on, 174; Lee fails to attack, 99–100; Lee reviews preparation for assault on, 174; location, 66, 108, 154; Meade before attacking, 172–173; in Meade's fishhook formation, 110; Rodes advances slowly to, 156; Union retreats to, 89, 92–95, 98

Cemetery Ridge: Armistead in assault on, 189, 197, 198–199; Brockenbrough in assault on, 191, 194; Confederates bombard, 181–184; Confederates run out of shells, 189–190; Davis in assault on, 190–191, 196–197, 199; fighting at, 146–148, 176–177, 181–201; Garnett in assault on, 189, 195, 197, 198; Hancock at, 146–147, 176, 200; Kemper in assault on, 195, 197, 198, 199; Law in Lee's plan for attacking, 169; Lee reviews preparations for attack on, 175; Longstreet, Alexander confer about calling off assault on, 189–190; Longstreet briefs Pickett about attack, 170–171; Longstreet countermands his order to reinforce, 201; Longstreet objects to attacking, 164, 169–171, 173, 190, 209; Longstreet reviews preparations for attack on, 175; McLaws in Lee's plan for

attacking, 169; Pender in Lee's plan for attacking, 170; Pettigrew in assault on, 171, 175, 199, 201, 203; Pickett before assault, 174, 175; Pickett briefed about, 170–171; Pickett charges, 186–189, 194, 201; Rodes in Lee's plan for attacking, 170; Sickles's dissatisfaction with assigned position at, 111–112; Trimble before assaulting, 171, 175; Trimble in assault on, 191, 199, 203; Wright reaches crest, 170

Centerville (Virginia), 17

Chamberlain, Joshua Lawrence, 126–127, 128

Chamberlayne, John Hampden, 25–26

Chambersburg (Pennsylvania): Confederate troops at, 16, 17, 39; Confederates demand supplies, 21; destruction in, 22; search for blacks in, 28

Chambersburg Pike: condition, 45; fighting along, 50, 59–62, 74, 78; movements along, 57

Chancellorsville, Battle of: German-American Eleventh Corps at, 87; Hooker at, 6; Howard at, 65–66; Jackson at, 10, 65–66, 87, 108; Lee at, 6–7, 107–108, 169, 209; Sickles at, 48, 111

Chapin, Cornelius, 217

Charleston (South Carolina), 1

Chesapeake & Ohio Canal, 16

Chester Gap (Virginia), 14

"The Children of the Battlefield" (Clark), 216–217

Civil War: Eastern theater, 2, 3, 13, 15; highest Union casualty rate, 148; newspaper coverage, 2; origins, 1, 58; total victory as goal, 2; troops drifting out of ranks, treatment of, 191–192

Civilian death, only, 172

Clark, James Gowdy, 216–217

Clark, John M., 125

Codori farm, 113, 145, 195

Coey, James, 59

Coles, Robert, 24
Columbia Bridge (Wrightsville), 32
Colvill, William, 147–148
Confederate armies. *See* Army,
  Confederate; Army of Northern
  Virginia; Army of Northern
  Virginia, units of
Confederate States of America:
  cabinet approves Gettysburg
  campaign, 8–9; capital, 1, 2;
  founding, 1; member states,
  number of, 1; money of, 25;
  postmaster general, 9; presi-
  dent, 1; secretary of war, 8;
  Virginia's importance to, 1–2
Copeland, Jeff, 135
Corby, William, 142
Cormany, Rachel, 28
Coster, Charles R., 91–92
Crawford, Samuel W., 150
Cree, Jemima, 28
Cromwell, James, 120–121
Crosby, Alanson, 92
Crotty, Daniel, 39
Culp, John Wesley, 167
Culp's Hill: Army of the Potomac
  takes control of, 168; Early at,
  165; Ewell launches diversionary attack against, 151, 155, 157;
  Ewell prepares to assault, 164–
  165; fighting at, 152–155, 157,
  165–168; Johnson at, 152, 155,
  165, 168; location, 89; Meade
  allows Slocum to leave troops
  at, 152; in Meade's fishhook
  formation, 110; Rodes at, 165;
  saddle-shaped, 154; Slocum
  leaves troops on, 152; strategic
  importance, 96, 154; Union
  occupies, 96, 98; Union takes
  control of, 168
Culpeper Court House, 12
Cumberland Valley, Confederate
  advance into, 16, 21–22, 28
Cumberland Valley Railroad, 32
Cummings, Charles, 199–200
Cunningham, Burl, 78–79, 80
Currier, Horace, 94
Cushing, Alonzo H., 176, 184,
  197–198
Custer, George A., 204

Cutler, Lyman: encounters
  refugees, 54; at Oak Ridge, 75;
  at Seminary Ridge, 74; suffers
  losses, 62; supports Hall at
  McPherson's Ridge, 57, 59

Dadswell, Thomas, 214
Davis, Jefferson: approves
  Gettysburg campaign, 8;
  character of, 7; chosen president of Confederacy, 1; compared to Lee, 7–8; gives Lee
  command of Army of Northern
  Virginia, 4; holds back Pickett's
  divisions, 175; plantation near
  target, 8
Davis, Joseph: advances in rank
  through nepotism, 51–52; in
  assault on Cemetery Ridge,
  190–191, 196–197, 199; north of
  Chambersburg Pike, 59, 60, 62;
  at Willoughby Run, 55
Dawes, Rufus, 39, 55, 60–61, 94
De Trobriand, Philippe Régis: at
  Slaughter Pen, 122; at Stony
  Hill, 137, 140; at Wheatfield,
  120, 136, 141
Dearing, James, 184
Death, anonymity in, 216
Deep Run (Virginia), 11–12, 14
Devil's Den: Anderson at, 122;
  Benning at, 135, 151; Caldwell
  wins back, 142–143; fighting at,
  120–122, 135, 151; Hood at, 122;
  Law at, 120; location, 108, 114;
  Robertson at, 135, 151; Sickles
  positions troops at, 113; Union
  troops at, 118
Devin, Thomas C., 45
Doles, George P., 88
Dooley, John, 188
Doubleday, Abner: extends front
  along Oak Ridge, 74; fires
  answering shot at Fort Sumter,
  58; First Corps commander, 50,
  53; orders pause on Seminary
  Ridge, 89; reinforces Baxter, 79;
  superseded by Howard, 65

Early, Jubal A.: advances toward
  Susquehanna, 30–31; ap-

proaches from northeast, 86; attacks Barlow's forces, 87–88; attacks brickyard, 91–92; at Cemetery Hill, 155; at Culp's Hill, 165; doubts wisdom of attacking Cemetery Hill, 99; turns forces toward Gettysburg, 63; at Winchester, 14–15, 16

Eastern theater: Lincoln's strategy for, 13, 15; as sideshow, 3; as source of recruits, 2

Eggleston, Corporal, 61–62

Ellis, A. Van Horne, 120–121

Emmitsburg (Pennsylvania), 48, 98

Emmitsburg Road: Anderson at, 114; Benning at, 114; Confederates cross in attacking Cemetery Ridge, 195, 197; fighting along, 114; Hood at, 114; Kershaw at, 114; Law at, 114; in Lee's plan of attack for second day, 108–109; McLaws at, 114; movements along, 43, 52; Robertson at, 114; troops positioned along, 112–114, 192

Ewell, Richard S.: advances into Shenandoah Valley, 14–16; defeats Milroy at Winchester, 14–15; demands supplies from towns, 21; doubts wisdom of attacking Cemetery Hill, 99; given command of the Second Corps of the Army of Northern Virginia, 10; at Groveton, 10; launches diversionary attacks against Culp's Hill and Cemetery Hill, 151, 155, 157; marriage, 10; opposes becoming second day's primary attacker, 106; performance as commander, 209; prepares for assault on Culp's Hill, 164–165; pulled back from Gettysburg, 212; turns toward Gettysburg, 63

Farnsworth, Elon J., 204

Flags: as bunting, 39; capturing enemy, 61–62, 76, 202; pinned to dresses, 29

Fort Sumter, 1, 58

Frederick (Maryland), 36

Fredericksburg, Battle of, 6, 37, 141, 209

Fremantle, Arthur, 10, 194

Friendly-fire incidents, 154

Front Royal (Virginia), 14

Fry, Birkett, 188, 195–196, 198

Garnett, Richard B.: in assault on Cemetery Ridge, 189, 195, 197, 198; brigade commanded by, 174; buried in mass grave, 216; disparaged by Jackson, 189; relieved of command of Stonewall Brigade, 175

Geary, John W., 165

General Orders Number 72 (Army of Northern Virginia), 25–26, 27

Germans, in Army of the Potomac, 86–87

Gettysburg (Pennsylvania): citizens of, 78, 94, 155, 172, 182, 196; Confederates in, 172; disposing of dead and wounded after battle, 215–216; Lutheran Theological Seminary, 52; only civilian death, 172; plundering in, 31; reception given Army of the Potomac, 43; refugees from, 54, 64; strategic importance recognized by Buford, 45; topography, 66

Gettysburg, Battle of: heavy fighting unexpected, 45; Meade's uncertainty about fighting at Gettysburg, 53, 69; preliminary skirmishes, 31; strategy behind Lee's campaign, 7–9; total casualties, 209; unknown soldier, 216–217

Gettysburg, Battle of, first day (July 1, 1863), 47–70, 73–101; Archer taken prisoner, 58–59; casualties, 76, 81, 83, 84; Confederate victory, reasons for, 98; Confederates advance to Gettysburg, 63; fighting along Mummasburg Road, 86; fighting at brickyard in town,

Gettysburg, Battle of, first day
(*continued*)
91–92; fighting at Herbst's
Woods, 55–62, 60, 80–83;
fighting at McPherson's Ridge,
77–84; fighting at Oak Ridge,
73–76; fighting at Seminary
Ridge, 89–91; fighting between
Heth's and Buford's men, 50–
53, 55; fighting north of
Chambersburg Pike, 59–62;
fighting north of town, 86–89;
Heth spots Union horsemen,
42–43; Hill orders renewal of
fighting after losses at Herbst's
Woods, 62–63; Howard com-
mits to holding Gettysburg, 66;
Howard orders fallback from
north and west of town, 88–89,
95; Howard relieved of command, 95–96; Lee decides to
attack on next day, 101; Lee
fails to attack Cemetery Hill,
99–100; Lee's first notice of
fighting, 63; Lee's presence on
battlefield, 98, 100; Meade
decides to go to Gettysburg,
100; Meade fails to enunciate
clear plan of operations, 68, 97;
Meade gives Hancock com-
mand, 69, 95–96, 97; Meade
misinterprets Reynolds's
commitment to hold
Gettysburg, 53; Meade reserves
reinforcements, 100; Meade's
marching orders, 48–49;
Reynolds commits to holding
Gettysburg, 53, 96; Reynolds
dispatches "hurry" orders for
reinforcements, 64; Reynolds
killed, 57–58; Sickles arrives,
97; Slocum fails to reinforce
Howard, 68–70, 88; Slocum
finally goes to Howard's aid,
96–97; Slocum given command,
97; Union advances to
Gettysburg, 50, 52–55, 57–58;
Union collapse south of town,
threat of, 140; Union occupies
Culp's Hill, 96, 98; Union
retreats to Cemetery Hill and

Culp's Hill, 89, 92–95, 98;
Union takes position on north
side of town, 67–68
Gettysburg, Battle of, second day
(July 2, 1863), 105–131, 135–157,
161–164; Barksdale's Peach
Orchard breakthrough, 144–
145; Berden encounters Confederates along Seminary Ridge,
112; Caldwell wins back area
from Devil's Den to Stony Hill,
142–143; casualties, 148, 161,
162–163; Confederate successes,
crest of, 149; Confederates
retreat to Seminary Ridge, 148–
149; Ewell launches diversionary attacks against Culp's Hill
and Cemetery Hill, 151, 155,
157; fighting along Emmitsburg
Road, 114; fighting at Cemetery
Hill, 151–152, 155–157; fighting
at Cemetery Ridge, 146–148;
fighting at Culp's Hill, 152–155;
fighting at Devil's Den, 120–
122, 135, 151; fighting at Houck
Ridge, 136, 138; fighting at
Little Round Top, 118, 122–131,
150; fighting at Peach Orchard,
114–116, 139, 144–145; fighting
at Plum Run (Valley of Death),
136–138, 139, 149–150; fighting
at Rose's Woods, 122, 135–136,
139, 143, 145; fighting at
Seminary Ridge, 114–118;
fighting at Slaughter Pen, 121–
122, *123*; fighting at Stony Hill,
139–140, 142; fighting at
Wheatfield, 140–144, 145;
friendly-fire incidents, 154;
Hood entangles his troops with
Longstreet's, 110; Johnston
reports scouting to Little Round
Top, 108; Lee decides on plan of
attack, 105–109; Lee decides to
renew attacks next day, 163–
164; Lee gives order for attack,
109; Lee's plan of attack, 108–
109; Longstreet launches main
attack against Union's left, 144,
151; Longstreet retraces steps
after being sighted, 109–110;

Meade assesses continuing or falling back, 163; Meade focuses on left wing, 152, 157; Meade orders fishhook formation, 110–111; Meade predicts Lee will attack Union's center tomorrow, 163; prayers before battle, 142; Sickles puts Third Corps out of position on high ground along Emmitsburg Road, 112–114; troops available for battle, number of, 101; Union line collapses from Peach Orchard to Houck Ridge, 145; Union retreats from Houck Ridge, 122; Warren establishes defense at Little Round Top, 118–120; Warren organizes reinforcement of Little Round Top, 128–129; weather, 105; Wright reaches crest of Cemetery Ridge, 170

Gettysburg, Battle of, third day (July 3, 1863), 164–177, 181–205; Alexander orders Pickett to charge, 186–188; casualties, 167, 181–182, 184, 190, 191, 196, 209; cavalry actions after Cemetery Ridge victory, 204; Confederate morale drops, 188–189; Confederates bombard Cemetery Hill, Ridge, 181–184; Confederates deploy artillery on Seminary Ridge, Peach Orchard, 174; Confederates run out of artillery shells, 189–190; deafness caused by artillery fire, 183; displays of courage by generals, 185–186; Ewell prepares for assault on Culp's Hill, 164–165; fighting at Bliss's barn, 168; fighting at Cemetery Ridge, 176–177, 181–201; fighting at Culp's Hill, 165–168; fighting between Maryland neighbors, 167–168; Hancock returns fire without waiting, 183; Hunt orders waiting before returning artillery fire, 174, 183; last shots fired, 205; Lee defeated by North, 201, 209– 210; Lee plans retreats from Gettysburg, 211–212; Lee revises plan of attack, 168–170; Lee takes responsibility for defeat, 203; Longstreet countermands his order to reinforce assault on Cemetery Ridge, 201; Longstreet gives Alexander responsibility to order Pickett to charge, 173–174; Longstreet objects to attacking Cemetery Ridge, 164, 169–171, 173, 190, 209; Meade fails to launch assault after victory at Cemetery Ridge, 203–204; Meade incredulous about victory, 202; Osborn recommends ceasing artillery fire to suggest Union guns are out of action, 186; Pickett charges Cemetery Ridge, 186–189, 194; prayers after victory, 202; preparations for attack on Cemetery Ridge, 171–177; skirmishes at Rose's Woods, 205; troops available for battle, number of, 163; Union artillery's rate of fire, 183; Union artillery's superiority, 184–185; Union celebrates victory, 201–202; Union takes exclusive control of Culp's Hill, 168; weather, 188

Gibbon, John: at Cemetery Ridge, 146, 148, 163, 172, 176–177, 192, 197; displays courage, 185–186; flags captured by, 202; uniforms worn by his men, 54

Gibbons, James Sloan, 65

Giles, Val C., 126, 131

Gordon, John B., 87, 88, 155, 209

Grant, Ulysses S., 7

Greencastle (Pennsylvania), 22, 212

Greene, George S., 152–155, 165

Greenwood (Pennsylvania), 30

Grogan, Charles, 199

Groveton, Battle of, 10

Hagerstown (Maryland), 16, 18, 212

Hall, James A., 57, 59, 62

Hall, Norman, 200

Halleck, Henry W.: acts as intermediary between Lincoln and Meade, 214; feuds with Hooker, 17–18, 36–37; fumes at ease of Lee's march through Pennsylvania, 15; orders Meade to cover Washington, 37

Hancock, Winfield S., 70; before Cemetery Hill attack, 172–173; at Cemetery Ridge, 146–147, 176, 200; displays courage, 185; given command by Meade, 69, 95–96, 97; returns fire without waiting, 183; at Seven Days' battles, 4; urges fighting at Gettysburg, 100; at Wheatfield, 142

Hanover (Pennsylvania), 48, 69

Harpers Ferry (West Virginia), 16, 36–37

Harris, Avery, 64

Harrisburg (Pennsylvania), 16

Harrisburg Road, 63, 86

Harrison, Henry T., 32, 41

Harrow, William, 200

Haskell, Frank, 192, 200, 202

Hay, John, 217

Hays, Harry T., 155, 156, 176, 185, 202

Hazlett, Charles E., 130, 131

Heath, Francis, 200

Heidlersburg (Pennsylvania), 63, 86

Heidlersburg Road, 86

Herbst's Woods, fighting at, 55–62, 80–83

Herr Ridge, 51, 52, 59, 62

Heth, Henry: advances toward Gettysburg, 47; authorized to chase horsemen at Gettysburg, 42; incapacitated, 171; losses suffered by, 107; at McPherson's Ridge, 77, 79, 89; seeks shoes in Gettysburg, 41–42, 50; skirmishes with Buford's men, 50–53

Hill, Ambrose Powell: authorizes Heth to chase horsemen at Gettysburg, 42; character of, 41; compared to McClellan, 10–11; crosses Potomac, 16; at Deep Run, 11–12, 14; given command of Third Corps of Army of Northern Virginia, 10–11; losses suffered by, 106–107; orders renewal of July 1 fighting after losses at Herbst's Woods, 62–63; at Seven Days' battles, 5; suffers from gonorrhea, 63, 109

Hillyer, George, 150, 161

Hincks, William B., 183

Holt, David, 9, 211

Honeycutt, Frank, 83

Hood, John Bell: at Devil's Den, 122; at Emmitsburg Road, 114; entangles his troops with Longstreet's, 110; ignores plundering, 26–27; at Seminary Ridge, 116, 205; at Seven Days' battles, 5

Hooker, Joseph: at Brandy Station, 12–13; at Chancellorsville, 6; closeness to Sickles, 48; demands Harpers Ferry garrison be released to him, 36–37; demands to be relieved of command, 37; feuds with Halleck, 17–18, 36–37; Lincoln's dissatisfaction with, 15, 17–18; positions Army of the Potomac between Lee's army and Washington, 14–15; recommends attacking Lee's rear flank, 11–12; recommends attacking Richmond, 13; reluctance to fight, 13, 15, 35, 36; reports Confederate movement away from Fredericksburg, 11; uncertainty about Lee's motives, 18

Horses: hidden in houses, 32; slaughtered by cannon fire, 182

Hospitals, field, 162

Houck Ridge, 108, 114, 136; 124th New York retreats to, 121; fighting at, 136, 138; Sickles positions troops at, 113; Union collapse at, 145; Union retreat from, 122

Howard, Oliver O., 67; career, 65; at Cemetery Ridge, 186; at Chancellorsville, 65–66;

commits to holding Gettysburg,
66; mutual distrust of Eleventh
Corps, 86; ordered to hurry up,
53, 64; orders fallback from
north and west of town, 88–89,
95; positions army on north
side of town, 67–68, 74; relieved
of command, 95–96; sends
Slocum telegram about fighting, 69, 96; supersedes
Doubleday's command, 65
Hubler, Simon: flees through
town, 93; gives water to dying
Confederate soldier, 161–162;
hears joke, 181–182; ordered to
close up ranks after comrade
falls, 78; retreats from
McPherson's Ridge, 84;
scrounges while regiment
moves, 64; shot at McPherson's
farm, 80
Humiston, Amos: becomes
unknown soldier, 216; at the
brickyard, 91; at Cemetery Hill,
66, 92; representative Union
soldier, 64–65, 210
Humiston, Philinda, 217
Hummelbaugh, Jacob, 162
Humor, 181–182
Humphreys, Andrew A., 140, 145,
146
Hunt, Henry J.: artillery chief,
112, 186; at Cemetery Hill, 186;
at Cemetery Ridge, 174, 183,
192; reviews Sickles's assigned
position, 112
Hunton, Eppa, 174, 191
Husted, Albert N., 130

Imboden, John D., 16, 212
Infantry: typical rifles, 51; vs.
cavalry, 44
Iverson, Alfred, 75–76

Jackson, Joseph, 155
Jackson, Thomas J. "Stonewall":
at Chancellorsville, 10, 66, 87,
108; disparages Garnett, 189
Jenkins, Albert G., 15–16, 21, 28
Johnson, Edward: at
Chambersburg, 39; at Culp's

Hill, 152, 155, 165, 168; in
Cumberland Valley, 21; at
Hagerstown, 16; sends battery
to Brenner's Hill, 151; at
Winchester, 15
Johnston, Samuel R., reports
scouting to Little Round Top,
108
Joy, Royal N., 214
Judson, Amos, 124–125

Kelly, Patrick, 142
Kelly, William, 83
Kelly's Ford (Rappahannock
River), 13
Kemper, James L.: announces
pending assault on Cemetery
Ridge, 174; in assault on
Cemetery Ridge, 195, 197, 198,
199; recalls Union shells, 185
Kernstown, Battle of, 175, 189
Kershaw, Joseph B.: at
Emmitsburg Road, 114; perfor-
mance as commander, 210;
retreats to Stony Hill, 151; at
Stony Hill, 139–140; west of
Rose's Woods, 138
Key, Philip Barton, 48
King, Felix, 137
King, Royal D., 200

Lamb, William, 139
Lancaster County (Pennsylvania),
30, 32
Lane, John R., 83
Lang, David, 145
Latimer, Joseph W., 151
Law, Evander McIvor: advances
to Gettysburg, 107, 109; at
Devil's Den, 120; at
Emmitsburg Road, 114; in Lee's
plan for attacking Cemetery
Ridge, 169; at Seminary Ridge,
116–118
Lee, Fitzhugh, 9
Lee, Robert E., 3; at Antietam, 6,
11; authorizes attack on
McPherson's Ridge, 77; at Bull
Run (Second Battle), 6, 11; at
Chancellorsville, 6–7, 107–108,
169, 209; character of, 4, 7;

Lee, Robert E. (*continued*)
compared to Davis, 7–8; crosses
Potomac, 16; decides on second
day's plan of attack, 105–109;
decides to attack on second day,
101; decides to renew attacks
on third day, 163–164; defeated
by North, 201, 209–210; discovers whereabouts of Army of the
Potomac, 32, 40–41; escapes
after Gettysburg, 215; fails to
attack Cemetery Hill, 99–100;
first notice of fighting, 63;
given command of Army of
Northern Virginia, 4; gives
Ewell command of Second
Corps, 10; gives Hill command
of Third Corps, 10–11; gives
order for second day's attack,
109; headquarters, 101; his
confidence in his troops, 9–10;
his troops' confidence in him, 9;
ignores old lady's pleas, 27;
issues order against plundering, 25–26, 27; loses contact
with Stuart, 40–41, 98; Meade
fails to catch, crush him, 214–
215, 217–218; orders concentration of forces at Cashtown, 32,
40; performance at Gettysburg,
201, 209–210; presence on
battlefield, 98, 100; relationship
with Longstreet, 107; renown in
the North, 27, 29–30; retreats
from Gettysburg, 211–212;
reviews preparations for attack
on Cemetery Ridge, 175; revises
third day's plan of attack, 168–
170; at Seven Days' battles, 4;
strategy behind Gettysburg
campaign, 7–9; takes responsibility for defeat, 203
Leesburg (Virginia), 18, 35
Leister, Lydia, 163, 182
Lincoln, Abraham: anxious for
Meade to catch, crush Lee, 214;
dissatisfaction with Hooker, 15,
17–18; election of, effect on
South, 1; focus on defeating
Lee's army, 13, 15; gives
McClellan command of Army

of the Potomac, 4, 6; gives
Meade command of Army of
the Potomac, 37; gives Pope
command of Army of the
Potomac, 6; issues call for
300,000 enlistees, 65; rejects
Hooker's recommendation to
attack Lee's rear flank, 12;
rejects Hooker's recommendation to attack Richmond, 13;
relieves Hooker of command,
37; relieves McClellan of
command of Army of the
Potomac, 6; sacks Sigel, 66;
slavery, his position on, 1;
suspicions of in Army of the
Potomac, 6
Little Round Top, 108, *123*, *127*,
129; fighting at, 118, 122–131,
150; Johnston reports scouting
to, 108; Longstreet sighted
from, 109; in Meade's fishhook
formation, 110; Vincent at, 119–
120, 122–123, 124, 130; Warren
establishes defense at, 118–120;
Warren organizes reinforcement
of, 128–129
Longstreet, James, 5; advances to
Gettysburg, 99, 101; briefs
Pickett about attack on Cemetery Ridge, 170–171; confers
with Alexander about calling
off attack, 189–190; countermands his order to reinforce
assault on Cemetery Ridge, 201;
crosses Potomac, 16–17; delays
committing his troops, 109, 143,
144; displays courage, 185; as
First Corps commander, 10;
gives Alexander responsibility
to order Pickett to charge, 173–
174; launches second day's
main attack against Union's
left, 144, 151; misunderstands
Lee's plan of attack, 109; objects
to attacking Cemetery Ridge,
164, 169–171, 173, 190, 209;
opposes attacking on second
day, 101, 105–106, 107; ordered
to Shenandoah Valley, 14;
orders capturing of free blacks,

28; orders retreat from Plum Run, 150; at Pfitzer's and Biesecker's Woods, 114; relationship with Lee, 107; relationship with Pickett, 187; retraces steps after being sighted, 109–110; reviews preparations for attack on Cemetery Ridge, 175; at Second Battle of Bull Run, 44; at Seven Days' battles, 5; at Thoroughfare Gap, 44; waits at Seminary Ridge, 138

Lutheran Theological Seminary, 52

Lyon, William D., 31, 211

Mackenzie, Ranald S., 118–119

Maloney, Patrick, 59

Malvern Hill, Battle of, 77, 175

Manassas Junction (Virginia), 17

Manchester (Maryland), 48, 101, 111

Mansfield, John, 89

Marcy, Ellen, 10

Marshall, James K., 190, 196

Martinsburg (Virginia), 14

Maryland, slaveholders vs. loyalists in, 38

Maryland Heights (Maryland), 35

Maxey, Travis, 135

Maxwell, Charles N., 144–145, 218

McClellan, George B.: at Antietam, 6; character of, 4; command of Army of the Potomac, 4, 6; compared to Hill, 10–11; compliments Iron Brigade, 54; in New Jersey, 214–215; reluctance to fight, 4; at Seven Days' battles, 4; at West Point, 10

McClellan, Georgia Wade, 172

McConnellsburg (Pennsylvania), 21

McCreery, Westwood, 83

McCuen, Alexander, 200–201

McDermott, Daniel, 94

McLaws, Lafayette: delayed by Longstreet, 143–144; at Emmitsburg Road, 114; in Lee's plan for attacking Cemetery Ridge, 169; at Peach Orchard,

144; pulls back to Seminary Ridge, 205; waits at Seminary Ridge, 138; wants to scout assigned position, 109; west of Rose's Woods, 138

McMahon, John T., 214

McPherson's Ridge: artillery at, 57, 59, 62; Brockenbrough at, 77; Buford at, 51, 52; convergence with Seminary Ridge, 62; Cutler supports Hall at, 57, 59; fighting at, 77–84, 81; Iron Brigade at, 58; Ninety-fifth New York at, 62; Pender at, 89–90; Wadsworth at, 57

Meade, George G., 38; advised to fight at Gettysburg, 49; allows Slocum to leave troops on Culp's Hill, 152; assesses continuing or falling back, 163; career, 37; before Cemetery Hill attack, 172–173; decides to go to Gettysburg, 100; fails to catch, crush Lee, 214–215, 217–218; fails to enunciate clear plan of operations, 68, 97; fails to launch assault after victory at Cemetery Ridge, 203–204; focuses on left wing on second day, 152, 157; at Fredericksburg, 37; given command of Army of the Potomac, 37; gives Hancock command, 69, 95–96, 97; headquarters, third day, 182; incredulous about victory, 202; learns Sickles put Third Corps out of position, 113; marching orders given by, 48–49; misinterprets Reynolds's commitment to Gettysburg, 53; ordered to cover Washington, 37; orders fishhook formation, 110–111; performance as commander, 209; Pipe Creek contingency plan, 47, 49, 68–69, 100; ponders leading counterattack, 148; at Power's Hill, 182; predicts Lee will attack Union's center on third day, 163; pursues Lee in retreat, 212–215; reserves reinforcements, 100; self-

Meade, George G. (*continued*)
  confidence lacking, 96; at Seven
  Days' battles, 4; uncertainty
  about fighting at Gettysburg,
  53, 69
Meredith, Solomon "Long Sol,"
  54
Milroy, Robert H., 14–15
Montgomery (Alabama), 1
Moon, W. H., 52
Moore, John W., 122
Moore, P. M., 167
Morrow, Henry A., 80, 81–83
Mosely, John W., 162
Mounger, John C., 135
Mudge, Charles R., 166–167
Mummasburg Road, 74–75, 86
Musser, John D., 84

New Guilford (Pennsylvania), 109

Oak Hill, 66, 73
Oak Ridge, 66, 73–76
Oates, William C., 126
O'Neal, Edward A., 75
O'Rorke, Patrick, 129–130
Osborn, Thomas W., 186

Parker, William W., 211
Patrick, Marsena, 13
Paul, Gabriel, 86
Peach Orchard (Sherfy orchard):
  Barksdale breaks through at,
  144–145; Confederate artillery
  at, 174; fighting at, 114–116,
  139, 144–145; McLaws at, 144;
  Sickles positions troops at, 113;
  Union artillery at, 135; Union
  collapse at, 145
Pegram, William J., 47, 50, 51, 52
Pender, William Dorsey: backs up
  Heth in mission to drive off
  horsemen, 42; in Lee's plan for
  attacking Cemetery Ridge, 170;
  losses suffered by, 107; at
  McPherson's Ridge, 89–90;
  seeks revenge on Yankees, 26;
  wounded, 171
Pennsylvania: agriculture in, 28–
  29; loyalists in, 39; women in,
  29, 39

Perrin, Abner, 90, 209
Pettigrew, James J.: in assault on
  Cemetery Ridge, 171, 175, 199,
  201, 203; backs up Heth in
  mission to drive off horsemen,
  42–43, 52; career, 77; at Herbst's
  Woods, 81; killed, 215; at Seven
  Pines, 77; under fire, 185
Pfitzer's Woods, 114
Phipps, Bill, 23
Pickett, George E.: advances to
  Gettysburg, 107; arrives in
  Gettysburg, 164; before assault
  on Cemetery Ridge, 174, 175;
  briefed about attack on Cemetery Ridge, 170–171; charges
  Cemetery Ridge, 186–189, 194,
  201; crosses Potomac, 16–17; in
  Lee's plan for attacking Cemetery Ridge, 169; number of his
  troops killed, wounded,
  captured, 203; ordered to
  capture free blacks, 28; put
  under Lee's command, 8;
  relationship with Longstreet,
  187; under fire, 185; weeps after
  defeat, 203
Pillaging and plundering, 21–28
Pipe Creek (Pennsylvania), 47, 49,
  68, 69, 100
Planck farm, 162
Pleasanton, Alfred, 12–13, 45
Plum Run (Valley of Death,
  Rose's Run): Anderson retreats
  to, 151; fighting at, 120, 122,
  125, 136–138, 139, 149–150;
  Longstreet orders retreat from,
  150; Sickles at, 113; west fork
  of, 137
Plundering and pillaging, 21–28
Pope, John, 6
Potomac River, crossed by
  Confederate troops, 15–17
Power's Hill, 182
Prayer and prayers, 142, 202, 216
Prisoners of war: Confederate
  soldiers become, 58–59, 61, 62,
  76, 127, 137, 148, 162, 188, 201;
  Union soldiers become, 60, 84,
  88, 91, 94, 98
Pye, Edward, 61